Islam Through Western Eyes

ISLAM
THROUGH
WESTERN
EYES

FROM THE CRUSADES TO
THE WAR ON TERRORISM

JONATHAN LYONS

COLUMBIA UNIVERSITY PRESS—NEW YORK

Columbia University Press
Publishers Since 1893
New York   Chichester, West Sussex

Copyright © 2012 Columbia University Press
All rights reserved

Library of Congress Cataloging-in-Publication Data
Lyons, Jonathan.
Islam through Western eyes : from the crusades
to the war on terrorism / Jonathan Lyons.
p. cm.
Includes bibliographical references and index.
ISBN 978-0-231-15894-7 (cloth : alk. paper)
ISBN 978-0-231-52814-6 (ebook)
1. Islam—21st century. 2. Islam—Public opinion.
3. Islamophobia—Europe. 4. Islamic countries—Relations—Europe.
5. Europe—Relations—Islamic countries. 6. East and West. I. Title.
BP161.3.L.96   2012
303.48'2176701821—dc23   2011024499

Columbia University Press books are printed
on permanent and durable acid-free paper.
This book is printed on paper with recycled content.

Printed in the United States of America
c 10 9 8 7 6 5 4 3 2 1

References to Internet Web sites (URLs) were accurate at the
time of writing. Neither the author nor Columbia University Press
is responsible for URLs that may have expired or changed since
the manuscript was prepared.

To my mother, Evelyn Lyons,
who taught me respect for language

CONTENTS

ACKNOWLEDGMENTS

THE FORMAL AND theoretical aspects of this study took shape relatively recently, but many of the ideas and observations that provided its initial spark were gathered during the two decades I spent as a journalist, much of that in and around the Muslim world. As a result, the many debts incurred are largely impossible to recount and measure, much less repay. I would, however, like to thank Gary Bouma of Monash University for his insight and counsel throughout the lifetime of this manuscript. Greg Barton, director of the university's Centre for Islam in the Modern World, acted as an invaluable sounding board. Geneive Abdo first introduced me to a world of Islam at odds with most standard accounts, and I benefitted from her sharp eye and well-tuned ear.

A number of people read all or parts of the manuscript at various stages, to my great advantage. David L. Wank offered the kind of insightful commentary and encouragement that only an experienced colleague and lifelong friend could provide. Paul M. Cobb was more than generous with his time, expertise, and advice. Wael B. Hallaq directed my attention to the Western narrative of Islamic law. Bryan S. Turner and Abdullah Saeed provided useful commentary on an early version of the text. The anonymous referees made valuable suggestions. Deborah Lyons offered both erudition and sisterly support. My agent, Will Lippincott, helped me transform the dissertation into a published book as painlessly as possible. I owe thanks also to my editor, Anne Routon of Columbia University Press, for her enthusiasm for this project.

Finally, I offer special thanks to Michelle Johnson for her unflagging backing and sharp editorial sense over the years it took me to develop, research, and complete this work, a journey that often took me far from home. Needless to say, any errors of omission or commission in the book are my own.

Islam Through Western Eyes

I

WAR WITHOUT END?

This crusade, this war on terrorism, is going to take a while.

GEORGE W. BUSH

THE TERRORIST ATTACKS of September 11, 2001, and their aftermath are just the latest reminder of the West's complete and enduring failure to engage in any meaningful and productive way with the world of Islam. For almost ten centuries, attempts at understanding have been held hostage to a grand, totalizing Western narrative that shapes what can and, more important, what cannot be said and thought about Islam and the Muslims. This is no less true today, from the political arena to the counterterrorism think tanks, from the academy to the Internet "blogosphere," than it was in the medieval halls of the Roman Curia and the courts of the European Crusaders.

Further, this same narrative, which reflects what I call the anti-Islam discourse, exercises a profound and corrosive effect on a range of issues across the contemporary social sciences, including sociology, politics, the history of ideas, law, religion, international relations, human rights, and security studies. It casts a shadow over the way social scientists of various stripes think and write and speak about Islam and the Muslims. It shapes how social scientists listen to what Muslims say and interpret what they do. And it guides their research programs and publications, their private advice to governments, and their statements to the press and the public at large. These developments have, in turn, left Western societies both intellectually unprepared and politically unable to respond successfully to some of the most significant challenges of the early twenty-first century—the global rise of Islamist political power, the more narrow emergence of religious violence and terrorism, clashes between established social values and multicultural rights on the part of growing Muslim immigrant populations, and so on.

As a result of these failures, the notion of a looming "clash" of world civilizations, advanced first by Bernard Lewis (1990) and more comprehensively by Samuel Huntington (1993, 1996), is moving steadily from a theoretical exercise—one that the foreign-policy establishment and academics alike initially dismissed (e.g., Mottahedeh 1996; Gergez 1999; Abrahamian 2003)—toward a self-fulfilling prophecy.[1] To see how effectively this notion has captured Western imaginations, one has only to consider the successful Swiss referendum campaign in November 2009 to write into the Constitution a ban on the building of minarets or the decision by Oklahoma voters in November 2010 to bar the use of Islamic law in state courts. Tellingly, in the cases of both Switzerland and Oklahoma, no such "threats" ever existed. In such an atmosphere, it has been all too easy for the contemporary U.S. neoconservatives and their supporters worldwide, who have relied on this anti-Islam discourse to generate fear of the Muslim Other, to sell the "war on terrorism" as essential to Western security, and to lead the West into its greatest confrontation with Islam since the Middle Ages.

Properly unpacked, the anti-Islam discourse can be shown to provide more than just the context and imagery that surround the war on terrorism, the present wave of Islamophobia, or the broader cultural project advanced by adherents of Huntington's coming civilizational clash. Despite the interrogatory tone of the title to his original journal article—"The Clash of Civilizations?"—Huntington leaves little doubt that he expects a future conflict, driven not by ideology or economics but by culture: "The great divisions among humankind and the dominating source of conflict will be cultural" (1993:22). Perhaps more telling, the book-length version appeared three years later under virtually the same title, but without the question mark.

Although it is a relatively simple matter to "connect the dots" between this discourse and the present state of tensions between Islam and the West, to stop there would be to overlook the profound nature of a discourse that has silently shaped one thousand years of shared history and that seems destined to shape the future as well. Its powers extend well beyond the war on terrorism, and they explain a whole host of subtle but important derivative effects, without which the clash-of-civilizations thesis that underpins this war would quite literally be unthinkable.

Since September 11, 2001, the West has launched two major wars against Islamic countries; contributed directly through conflict to the deaths of tens of thousands of Muslims in Iraq and Afghanistan and indirectly to the loss of many tens of thousands more lives through disruptions to health and other basic services;[2] helped suppress popular religious and political aspirations across the Muslim world, from Palestine to Somalia to Southeast Asia; restricted civil liberties at home; and cracked down hard on its own Arab and Muslim populations in the name of counterterrorism.[3]

The Central Intelligence Agency, meanwhile, coordinated a clandestine campaign to kidnap suspected Muslim terrorists and shuffle them around the globe—often with the help of friendly security services—so they may be tortured in third countries or simply dumped into the juridical no-man's-land of the U.S. naval base at Guantánamo Bay without regard for the Constitution, the Geneva Convention, or many of the founding ideals of revolutionary-era America. The George W. Bush administration, armed with memoranda from like-minded legal scholars, went so far as to authorize the torture by U.S. forces of certain "high-value" prisoners as part of its self-declared war on terrorism. The resulting damage to the rule of law and other liberal values, not to mention to America's worldwide standing, has been significant.

Central to this anti-Islam discourse is a series of familiar ideas that echo across today's political arena, on the Internet, on "talk" radio, in the so-called quality press, and, all too frequently, in the academy. Such notions include the following: Islam is a religion of violence and is spread by the sword; its tenets are upheld by coercion and force; Islam's prophet, its teachings, and even its God are false; Muslims are irrational and backward, "medieval," and fearful of modernity; Islam is by nature fanatical; Muslims are sexually perverse, either lascivious polygamists or repressive misogynists or both; they are antidemocratic and despise Western notions of civic freedoms; and, finally, they are caught up in a jealous rage at the Western world's failure to value them or their beliefs.

This phenomenon is not, however, simply a matter of stereotypes— reassuring modes of thought and expression to castigate the Muslim as Other and simultaneously reinforce the value and values of the West; if it were, the well-defined boundaries of the discourse would have eroded or otherwise shifted significantly, at least in places, over more than one thousand years of increasing physical, intellectual, economic, and theological contact and contestation between East and West. Rather, we must recognize that fundamental to this discourse has been the creation in the Western consciousness—and thus in Western thought—of an impermeable conceptual barrier constructed from the very tissue of the discourse itself.

Rarely have the central themes of the anti-Islam discourse faced serious critical scrutiny or nuanced analysis. Rather, they are often asserted or simply left unstated and unacknowledged, so that they operate silently in the background as they shape our statements about Islam and the Muslims and define the disciplines that organize and classify such knowledge. In an observation as apt now as when it was first advanced nine hundred years ago, Guibert de Nogent, a chronicler of the First Crusade, noted that it was not important actually to know anything about Islam in order to attack it: "It is safe to speak evil of one whose malignity exceeds whatever ill can be spoken" (quoted in Rodinson 1987:11).

As a result, the West's "conversation" with Islam has always been a one-sided affair, essentially a dialogue with itself, revealing much about the subject but little or nothing about the object in question. In the vernacular of today, "It is all about us." This one-sidedness has meant a fatal decoupling of the Western idea of Islam from the meaning and content of Islam as a vital religious, social, and cultural institution in its own right. Incompatible with the West's interests or outside its conceptual understanding—or at times merely inconvenient—the belief system of the Muslims has been set aside in favor of a denatured Islam that better fits the established discourse.

Thus a Muslim woman cannot wear the veil simply because she believes that God has so ordained or to express her own religious feelings or identity; rather, her doing so must be the result of patriarchal repression by her husband, father, uncles, or brothers. Likewise, there is little incentive to trace the complex and at times contradictory record of traditional Islamic texts on violence, personal struggle, and resistance—signified in the Western mind under the emotive rubric of *jihad*.[4] Instead, a necessary, causal relationship between Islam and violence is posited, and countless examples are adduced to support it, the September 11 terrorist attacks being currently the most spectacular. Put another way, Islam qua Islam is allowed no independent existence but is effectively a creation of the Western mind. Unnoticed in the

Western world, this phenomenon has not gone by without comment among the Muslims: for decades, the religious revolutionaries of Iran have referred to this construct dismissively as "American Islam."

How, then, has the West's comprehensive idea of Islam persisted intact and essentially unchanged—thrived, even—over the course of one thousand years? What has so far retarded any real development or evolution—whether seen in terms of traditional Western notions of historical change, the "discontinuities" of Gaston Bachelard and the postmodern French philosophers, or Thomas Kuhn's "paradigm shift"—in the dominant narrative? As I argue in the pages that follow, the answer lies with the formation in the eleventh century of the anti-Islam discourse, which to the present day defines and explains Islam and regulates what it is that we hear and see of the Muslims. The same discourse determines the West's apprehension of any new observations or information about Islam by shaping them to fit its requirements and demands, by dismissing them as inaccurate or unimportant, or by ignoring them outright.

My central theoretical position is simple: the very idea of Islam reflects a Western discourse perpetuated by those social groups and institutions that stand to benefit from its survival. Three interrelated questions about the anti-Islam discourse provide the underlying structure of my analysis: How is this discourse formed? How does it operate? And, last, that classical problem in the social sciences: Cui bono? Who benefits? This approach moves away from a pure exercise in intellectual history and casts it instead as a matter for broader inquiry that cuts across a number of traditional disciplines. Herein also lies its explanatory power: When we open this particular window on Islam as discourse and take a look, what do we see that has not been seen before?

Here, I am largely following the work of Michel Foucault, particularly in the early phase of his career—roughly the period ending with his inaugural lecture at the Collège de France in 1970. Foucault has written widely on epistemological phenomena in strictly Western contexts, including studies of the discourses of madness (1961, 1988), clinical medicine (1994a), prison (1991, 1994c), and sexuality (1978). At one point, he proposed a study of what he called the "great division" between Occident and Orient, but he never carried out this project (1961:iv; see also Rosemann 1999:270). Foucault did, however, venture into the contentious issue of the 1979 Islamic Revolution in

Iran, supporting it much longer and more enthusiastically than most others among the European Left.[5]

Despite this lack of any specific focus on Islam, Foucault's methods—what he has referred to as his "toolbox"—can go a long way toward explaining why it is that certain things can be thought and said about Islam and the Muslims and certain other things cannot. This practical strand in Foucault's work is often obscured by the difficult, indirect, and at times maddeningly cryptic nature of much of his writings. Yet Foucault tells us clearly what he has in mind: "I would like my books to be a kind of 'toolbox' which others can rummage through to find a tool which they can use however they wish in their own area. . . . I don't write for an audience, *I write for users, not readers*" (1994c:523–524, emphasis added; quoted in O'Farrell 2005:50).

In an effort to build on Foucault's work and to address some of its limitations when applied to the West's anti-Islam discourse, I also take into account some classic studies in sociology—most notably the works of Max Weber, Karl Mannheim, and C. Wright Mills—as well as the cultural criticism of Edward Said. Whereas Foucault provides particularly effective tools for the excavation of evidence of the formation and operation of the West's anti-Islam discourse, the sociology of knowledge can help fashion a response to the final element of my analytical framework: Who benefits?

The philosopher and theologian Paul Ricoeur provides a useful definition of the last strand of my theoretical approach, even though that definition was originally presented amid a critique of sociology's limitations: "The sociology of knowledge rejects an immanent history of ideas which would be governed only by the structure of problems and their philosophical solutions. It attempts to replace the would-be history of ideas within the total dynamics of society" (1965:58). Yet a displacement of this "would-be history" and an examination of the social dynamic at work can best explain the unchanging and persistent nature of the anti-Islam discourse.

This latter approach, then, sets in relief several specific issues: Which social groups and institutions have benefited from excising the enormous Arab cultural contribution to the West from the history books? From the notion that Islam is inherently violent, or that it is fundamentally antipathetic toward women? Who benefits today from perpetuating these ideas? And how can I best account for the periodic ebbs and flows—the occasional ups as well as the predominant downs—in relations between Islam and the West as well as for the larger, more stable narrative arc that reaches from

Muhammad's revelation to the present day? Chapters 4, 5, and 6 address these underlying issues in a series of thematic explorations, which, when taken as a whole, make up this social history of the Western idea of Islam.

A few other prominent features of my approach also bear noting at this time. First and foremost, I have chosen to focus exclusively on the *West's* discourse of Islam—that is, the body of accepted and therefore *acceptable* Western knowledge about Islam and Muslims; any real exploration from the Muslim perspective is beyond the scope of this inquiry. This point cannot be overemphasized, for Western analysis and scholarship too often focus exclusively on what it is They say about Us and ignore the baseline assumptions, thoughts, texts, and symbols that make up Western-dominated Islamic studies and its associated disciplines.

Here, too, I want to avoid the fallacy scholars sometimes put forth that the Muslim world saw in the crusading Christians the same existential, civilizational threat that the latter clearly saw in it (e.g., von Grunenbaum 1961:31–63; echoed in Berger 1973:56). In fact, the caliphal court in Baghdad turned a blind eye to the fall of Jerusalem in 1099 despite pleas for help from local Muslims, and it took decades for the forces of Islam to set aside their internal squabbles and repel the invaders (C. Hillenbrand 1999:69–74). This fallacy is a critical error, for it presumes that whatever was going on in the West was mirrored or should have been mirrored in the East and that the two experiences can thus be understood and assessed in the same terms and in the same way. This assumption leads only to a dead end.

Second, it needs to be stressed that an analysis of the anti-Islam discourse can be carried out without direct reference to the West's claims to any truth-value in its statements about Islam; the truth—or lack thereof—of those statements produced is no defense against the underlying fact that the entire conversation takes place almost entirely within the very confines of the discourse. Many scholars have sought to refute, for example, statements linking violence, coercion, and authoritarianism to the very essence of the Muslim faith (e.g., Afsaruddin 2006a, 2008; Saeed 2006; Khatab and Bouma 2007). Others argue that the same link can be established for other faiths and belief systems, from Judaism to Scientology (Appelby 2000), or that violence lies at the heart of all religious experience (Girard 1977, 1996).

Although weighing in on this and other questions that the anti-Islam discourse has addressed may be instructive, it is not strictly necessary, for the argument of any individual scholar is dissipated in the face of the overwhelming power of the broader discourse at work. It need hardly be said that I do not mean to purvey some idealized universe free of all moral, political, or social values. Rather, I argue that we must first explore the way the anti-Islam discourse operates to produce such statements and to eliminate or bar other statements and why this discourse has remained intact across one thousand years. Only then can we begin to venture into the realm of assessment and evaluation.

Third, I have limited the scope of this inquiry by generally restricting myself to Islam as defined by the historical experience of the early Muslim empires, from Afghanistan, the subcontinent, and western China to North Africa and across to al-Andalus, or Muslim Spain. These areas were, after all, the "Muslim world" as apprehended by Christian Europe at the formation of the anti-Islam discourse, and in many ways they remain so today. The West's "discovery" of a wider Muslim *umma* (religious community) has done nothing notable to alter the discourse, except perhaps to strengthen its central foundation. When we are told, for example, that Indonesian Muslims practice a "softer" variant of the faith, this assertion is nothing but a reinforcement of the original narrative.

Throughout this study, I use the terms *Islam* and *Muslim* quite deliberately in both their religious and cultural meanings rather than fall back on the specific ethnic identities such as Arab, Persian, Kurd, and others that compose the diverse world of Islam. Marshall Hodgson's classic work *The Venture of Islam* (1974) proposes a calibrated set of distinctions among the terms *Islam*, meaning the faith itself; *Islamdom*, the counterpart to Christendom (that is, those areas where Islam predominates); and *Islamicate*, the civilizational complex as a whole. Bryan S. Turner (2003, 1:1–2) would add the terms *Islamist*, to encompass political Islam, and *Arabic*, as a subculture of Islamdom in which the Arabic language is dominant.

For my purposes, this terminology, although worth bearing in mind in other contexts, is subsumed in the broader anti-Islam discourse, which by its very nature does not make or require any such distinctions. At issue here is the West's discourse of Islam and Muslims, not a discourse of Arabs, Seljuk Turks, the Fatimids of Egypt, or whatever group may have predominated at a given historical moment. As far as Christendom was concerned, they all shared a single, overriding identity as Muslims, and it is this overarching religious identity that the anti-Islam discourse addresses. Today the West tends to think largely of Arabs when speaking of Islam, but in fact the object of the anti-Islam discursive formation has always been "Islam-ness," not "Arab-ness."

In short, the West's construction of Islam and Muslims has been essentialist, uniform, and not conducive to nuance and variation.

As we shall see in the course of this book, the discourse is always spelled out in terms of this Islam-ness, regardless of any ethnic, national, or even scriptural identifier applied to the Muslims at a given moment. Such ethnic complexities were particularly opaque to European Christendom, which had only the vaguest notion of the distant Muslim peoples. Pope Urban II's original call to crusade, for example, was directed against the Persians—"an accursed race, a race wholly alienated from God," in one version of the pope's declaration of war—rather than against the socially and politically ascendant Arabs. Others equally damned the Arabs or the Turks or simply lumped them all together as "Saracens"—that is, the children of Abraham's wife, Sarah—or as "Ishmaelites," named for Abraham's eldest son. Finally, "the West" is taken here to encompass the lands of medieval Christendom and the modern states and societies—including their associated discursive practices—that have emerged from them and that dominate the world today.

The continuity of such broad categories as "Islam" and "the West" as well as their utility within the established narrative came into sharp relief with the terrorist attacks of September 11, 2001. Five days later, President George W. Bush (2001b) wrapped himself and the nation securely in the mantle of Christian holy war, first declared in the eleventh century: "This is a new kind of—a new kind of evil. And we understand. And the American people are beginning to understand. This crusade, this war on terrorism, is going to take a while."

The White House immediately expressed the president's regret over use of the word *crusade*, acknowledging that it might have "upset" the Muslim world (Fleischer 2001). Nonetheless, Bush repeated the term five months later when he made it clear that this military campaign, like its medieval forerunners, would extend beyond a single nation or a single people to represent a civilizational alliance of like-minded forces. Thanking the Canadian military for joining the effort, Bush (2002b) said: "They stand with us in this incredibly important crusade to defend freedom, this campaign to do what is right for our children and our grandchildren."

President Bush later guarded his public use of language more carefully, but powerful figures in his administration clearly felt no such compunction, and they spoke out without sanction or rebuke from the White House. John Ashcroft, then attorney general with responsibility for enforcement of America's beefed-up security laws, told a conservative radio interviewer: "Christianity is a faith in which God sends his son to die for you," whereas Islam is "a religion in which God requires you to send your son to die for him" (quoted in Sheer 2002). The top intelligence officer then in charge of the Pentagon's pursuit of Osama bin Laden, Lieutenant-General William G. Boykin, assured the Christian Right that the U.S.-led war on terrorism was a struggle between the beneficent God of the Christians and the false "idol" worshipped by Muslims. Boykin asked members of the Good Shepherd Community Church in Sandy, Oregon: "Why do they hate us? The answer to that is because we're a Christian nation. We are hated because we are a nation of believers" (quoted in Arkin 2003).[6]

Accompanying this rhetoric from U.S. officials has been a groundswell of popular Islamophobia, running from North America through Europe and on to Australia, that has dented the very idea of liberal democratic society. Since 2001, the incidence of hate crimes in America against Muslims and Arabs in general—or those presumed to be Arabs—has also risen sharply, although data available from the Council on American–Islamic Relations (2008), a Muslim advocacy group, report some significant improvement between 2006 and 2007. One study by the Pew Forum on Religion and Public Life (2004) found that 46 percent of Americans surveyed said that Islam was more likely than other religions to encourage violence, a substantial increase from the previous year. That number has since fluctuated between a high of 45 percent and a low of 35 percent as of August 2010 (Pew Forum 2010).

According to data collected by the Pew Forum (2007) in 2006, the number of American respondents saying that Islam had nothing in common with their own religious faith increased from 59 percent to 70 percent since an earlier survey in 2005. Asked to give one-word impressions of Islam, those surveyed offered negative attributes twice as often as positive ones; *fanatic* was the second most frequent response (after *devout*), but the terms *radical* and *terror* were also popular. Fifty-eight percent of these same respondents said they knew "little or nothing" of Islam (Pew Forum 2007). A follow-up study in 2009 found that 65 percent of those interviewed felt Islam differed "very much" or "somewhat" from their own beliefs and values—the highest figure for any faith in the survey—although the number of respondents linking Islam to violence declined somewhat, to 38 percent.

A separate survey of religious attitudes in America by Robert Wuthnow found that 23 percent of respondents said that it should be illegal for Muslim groups to meet and practice their faith, and 47 percent and 40 percent, respectively, said that the words *fanatical* and *violent* applied to Muslims. By contrast, 25 percent regarded Hindus as "fanatical," and 23 percent applied the word to Buddhists (Wuthnow [2003] 2004:164). The Gallup Organization found that a majority of Americans see "little" or "nothing" to admire in Islam or the Muslim world (Abdo 2006a).

Australia's Muslim and Arab community has likewise faced a sharp increase in incidents of racial and ethnic hatred in the aftermath of the September 11 attacks on New York and Washington, D.C., aggravated by the 2002 and 2005 Bali bombings, which targeted Australians and other foreigners (Poynting and Mason 2006:367). A 2003 study for Australia's Human Rights and Equal Opportunity Commission reported that 87 percent of Muslims surveyed had experienced racist abuse or violence since the September 11 attacks (Poynting and Noble 2004). A survey of European attitudes showed rising antagonism toward Muslims in 2008 over previous years, with 52 percent in Spain, 50 percent in Germany, 46 percent in Poland, and 38 percent in France now displaying negative attitudes (Pew Forum 2008).

Anti-Muslim sentiment is particularly virulent on the Internet, from which it easily spills over into the cultural mainstream and into the old-line media world of television, radio, newspapers, and books (Tirman 2010). Prominent supporters of the Bush administration, in particular members of the Christian Right, have been regular features of old and new media alike, routinely condemning Islam and its prophet. The late Reverend Jerry Falwell, whose Christian Right lobby wields enormous influence within the Republican Party, called Muhammad "a terrorist . . . a violent man, a man of war" ("Falwell Brands" 2002). America's premier televangelist, Pat Robertson (2002), labeled the Prophet "an absolute wild-eyed fanatic" and "a killer." And the Reverend Jerry Vines, past president of the Southern Baptist Convention, the largest Protestant denomination in America, with an estimated 16 million members, said that Muhammad was a "demon-possessed pedophile," asserting that he had twelve wives, the youngest of whom was nine years old (quoted in Sachs 2002).[7] As of this writing (October 2010), the number of hits generated by an Internet search of Muhammad and "pedophile" has increased tenfold in the three years that I have been tracking this informal index. It is important to note that this number has been swollen recently by a vigorous online defense of Muhammad mounted by Muslim believers. When I first started tracking the figures in 2007, the field was almost exclusively in the hands of anti-Islam polemicists. Yet the number of hits easily exceeded 100,000 all the same.

Public attitudes reflect the public discourse. The 2007 Pew survey, for example, found that the media was the single biggest influence on Americans' attitudes toward Islam, especially among those with negative opinions toward Muslims. The Western media have displayed virtual unanimity that the terrorist attacks represent an existential threat to America, to its core values, and, in fact, to Western civilization as a whole—all framed as part of a declaration of cultural war by the angry, antimodern, and alien forces of Islam. Historian Ervand Abrahamian (2003:530), in a review of the coverage of September 11 and its aftermath in what he calls the "quality" media aimed at "the American literati and intelligentsia"—defined in the study as the newspapers the *New York Times*, *Washington Post*, and *Wall Street Journal* and the news magazines *Time*, *Newsweek*, *New Republic*, and *Atlantic Monthly*—found a remarkably consistent message in the headlines and content of news stories.

In a note introducing a special section that would run for four months, the flagship *New York Times* promised its readers "complete worldwide coverage of the roots and consequences of September 11." This daily feature, bannered "A Nation Challenged," and the newspaper's other pages proffered such headlines as "This *Is* a Religious War," "Jihad 101," "Barbarians at the Gate," "The Force of Islam," "Divine Inspiration," "Defusing the Holy Bomb," "The Core of Muslim Rage," "Dreams of Holy War," "The Deep Intellectual Roots of Islamic Rage," and "A Head-on Collision of Alien Cultures" (Abrahamian 2003:531).

The contemporary reverberations of Islamophobia have spread around the globe, as the clamor in late 2005 and early 2006 over the publication of a series of Danish cartoons of Muhammad made all too clear. Around 140 people were killed, mostly in the Muslim world, during public protests against the cartoons, which were originally created for Denmark's biggest newspaper and then reprinted widely in the name of free speech. Danish embassies were set on fire, and some Muslim countries announced boycotts of Denmark's exports. The moral outrage of Muslims at lampoons of the Prophet was met by equal outrage among Westerners at the notion of restraint on freedom of expression and at the notion that Muslims could be so outraged (Lyons 2010).

The affair began with the publication in September 2005 of twelve editorial cartoons of Muhammad in the daily *Jyllands-Posten*. One of the images portrays the Prophet with a bomb-shaped turban. In another image, Muhammad is pleading with a queue of would-be suicide bombers outside heaven's gate: "Stop. Stop. We ran out of virgins." This latter is a reference to the assertion, popular in some Western circles, that suicide attacks are motivated by promises of sexual reward in the afterlife and cannot possibly be rational or deliberate acts of military, political, or personal resistance (Lyons 2010).

Major dailies in Germany, France, Italy, Belgium, the Netherlands, and many other countries around the world published some or all of the cartoons. France's influential *Le Monde*, for example, reprinted two of the original cartoons, created one of its own for the front page, and made all twelve of the Danish images available online. Virtually all other French newspapers also carried examples in support of *Jyllands-Posten* (Berkowitz and Eko 2007:780).

In Australia, the controversy fed seamlessly into the "values debate"— essentially a running proxy war over multiculturalism, national identity, and, by extension, national security in a rapidly changing world. For the most part, it served as fuel for those who felt that the country's official policy of multiculturalism was pandering to demands by Australia's Muslims that, by virtue of their religious and cultural practices, they be treated differently from the non-Muslim majority. Concerns over national security were not far beneath the surface. Marking the fifth anniversary of the attacks of September 11, Prime Minister John Howard warned his audience: "There is a section of the Islamic population which will not integrate . . . [and has] values and attitudes which are hostile to Australia's interests" (quoted in "Those Who Don't Share Our Values" 2006).

Pope Benedict XVI has also firmly planted the banner of Christian particularism in the post–September 11 landscape. In an address on September 12, 2006, at the University of Regensburg, where he had taught in the 1970s, the pontiff (2006) quoted what the late-fourteenth-century Byzantine emperor Manuel II Paleologus said in a religious debate with a "learned [Muslim] Persian" on the subject of holy war: "Show me just what Muhammad brought that was new, and there you will find things only evil and inhuman, such as his command to spread by the sword the faith he preached." The pope did acknowledge a well-known injunction in the Qur'an against "compulsion in religion" (2:256)[8] but assured his listeners that "experts" had dated it to the early years of Muhammad's prophethood, when the Muslim community was still too weak to compel obedience among nonbelievers.

Benedict (2006) then went on to argue that the use of force in religion offends Christian rationality but is in keeping with the Muslim conception of a

God whose omnipotence transcends any such category—that is, one who can literally defy reason: "The decisive statement in this argument against violent conversion is this: not to act in accordance with reason is contrary to God's nature." Many Muslims were outraged by these claims. In their eyes, the pope had explicitly passed over a chance to repudiate the emperor's charges that Islam offered nothing but violence, a move they considered a Vatican endorsement of those charges; he had also failed to acknowledge the Catholic Church's own sponsorship of the anti-Muslim Crusades or other acts of inhumanity in the name of God, such as the Inquisition, the brutal suppression of the Cathar heresy in southern France, and the expulsion of Jews and Muslims from the Iberian Peninsula; and he had repeated the charge that Islam and by extension its conception of God were not rational, unlike his own Christian faith.

Evangelical Christians, meanwhile, have been even more explicit than Pope Benedict in casting doubt on the theological teaching that the God of the three major monotheist faiths is one and the same. In fact, after September 11 the relative few among American evangelical preachers and commentators who had been willing even to countenance such a view hardened their attitudes significantly. Recent years have seen an outpouring of anti-Islam polemical works by leading evangelical figures disputing the "one God" thesis and locating the September 11 attacks and other acts of terrorism specifically within the Islamic holy texts (Cimino 2005:165–166).

Of course, the anti-Islam discourse hardly stands alone. The Western experience can be defined by a number of such fundamental discourses, each of long standing and great power. They include the discourse on gender, the discourse on race, the discourse on the Enlightenment and the idea of "progress" in general, and the discourse on science—to name a few of the most prominent. The anti-Semitic discourse, perhaps, deserves specific mention, for it might appear at first glance to resemble that of the Western narrative of Islam. Any such comparison, however, is misleading. Although Jews were regular targets of persecution, discrimination, and organized violence across medieval Europe, they retained a necessary place in Christian theology and exegesis and thus retained a legitimate, if problematic, place in Western thought and society. Augustine taught that the existence of the Jews bore witness to the validity of Christian scripture's claims to roots in the Old Testament, and Christian eschatology held that some Jews were destined to convert as an immediate prelude to the End of Time.

Unlike the Cathar heretics and later the Muslims, the Jews could never fully be cast as Others; as such, they could never become the explicit targets of Christian holy war, although "collateral damage" has often been heavy. In a letter exhorting the people of England to join the Second Crusade, Bernard of Clairvaux, one of the leading voices of the twelfth-century Latin church, cautioned would-be holy warriors that the Jews, widely blamed in the popular imagination for the death of Jesus, must not be harmed amid this revival of religious zeal: "The Jews are for us the living words of Scripture, for they remind us always of what our Lord suffered. They are dispersed all over the world so that by expiating their crime they may be everywhere the living witnesses of redemption" (1953:462). Nor did the Jews ever present, despite anti-Semites' favored tropes, anything like the economic, political, intellectual, and religious challenges to Western Christendom that were posed by Islam.[9]

I have chosen to examine the anti-Islam discourse for a number of reasons. First of all, it has not previously been properly recognized or studied. In fact, little attention has been paid in general to Western historical narratives of Islam beyond the classic works of Norman Daniel (1960, 1966, 1975) and Richard Southern (1962) and the more recent studies by John V. Tolan (2002, 2008). By contrast, the literature on the treatment of Jews and heretics has been considerable. For example, Robert Moore's *Formation of a Persecuting Society: Power and Deviance in Western Europe, 950-1250* (1987) explores the persecution of "deviants"—that is, Jews, heretics, lepers, homosexuals—but makes no mention of the Muslims (cited in Tolan 2002:xvi). Second, the anti-Islam discourse interacts or overlaps to varying degrees with each of those prominent discourses listed earlier, making it central to our understanding of Western civilization as a whole. Third, I believe that it can shed light on a whole range of intellectual, social, and political problems facing the social sciences and, more broadly, contemporary Western societies.

The anti-Islam discourse, for example, pervades Western histories of ideas. Scholars have known since the late 1950s of almost certain links between Copernicus's "revolutionary" planetary theory and the work of Muslim astronomers two hundred to three hundred years earlier—that is, from the fourteenth and thirteenth centuries, respectively. Yet the West largely clings to the notion that whatever intellectual glories once existed in the Muslim world—if it acknowledges them at all—were extinguished for good by the masterful antiscience polemics of the Muslim theologian Abu Hamid al-Ghazali, who died in 1111.[10] As a result, the full import of this information about Muslim astronomers and subsequent discoveries about the longevity of Arab science well past the "end date" assigned by the West's traditional historical narrative remain largely unexamined.

However, to explore these discoveries would mean to step outside the anti-Islam discourse, which assures us that Islamic science fell victim early on to Islamic obscurantism in the formidable person of al-Ghazali. Given such a turn in Muslim intellectual life, what use could there be to speak of, say, late medieval Islamic science? Or what need to probe Copernicus's connections to the Muslim world? Such silence is indeed deafening. A more cogent explanation for the decline of Islamic science would avoid the "Ghazali trap" and might take into account the role of geopolitical, economic, and social factors.

There is also considerable evidence that Muslim intellectual and cultural traditions played an important role in the rise of the European university, an event trumpeted by the predominant historical narrative as a defining moment in the emergence of Western civilization. Classic exemplars of this latter tendency include Charles Homer Haskins (1957) and Edward Grant (1996), who calls the rise of the universities a "peculiarly Western phenomenon" (34). Yet Muslim traditions dating to before the advent of universities in the West included the grouping of foreign students into associations, or "nations," similar to the medieval practice at the University of Paris and elsewhere; the wearing of distinctive dress or gowns by the teaching masters; the awarding of a chair as a seat of honor and comfort for a distinguished teacher; the granting of a recognized degree, in this case the teaching license—in Arabic, the *ijaza*—to permit students deemed ready to take on pupils of their own; and a number of specific concepts familiar to advanced Western education, such as the *studium generale* and, quite possibly, the *artium baccalareus*, or bachelor of arts degree (Makdisi 1981b).

The presence of the anti-Islam discourse has again all but precluded serious investigation into any links between the Arabs' educational institutions and practices and the development of that treasured Western cultural accomplishment, the university. Despite reasonable evidence and a sophisticated analysis, George Makdisi's work on the subject has been effectively rejected outright (see the discussion of this rejection in Hallaq 2002–2003:5–6).

Turning back to Foucault, this time invoking his principle of "reversal" in an attempt to peek behind the established discourse, we can ask what the effects might be if the dominant anti-Islam discourse as it applies to the history of Western ideas were rejected—or at the very least set aside. Many enormously exciting possibilities suddenly begin to suggest themselves. Miscellaneous facts that have been merely floating around, with no theoretical home to call their own, suddenly start to fall into place.

These facts include the "mystery" of the Muslim provenance of Copernicus's mathematical work and of our university system; the Arabic origins of much of the Western scientific lexicon; the unmistakable strains of the Muslim philosophers Avicenna and Averroës throughout the works of Thomas Aquinas and other seminal Western thinkers; the links between medieval Arabic poetry and that of the troubadours; the powerful Arabic literary influences on such quintessentially "Western" figures as Dante and Cervantes; and the undoubted genius and creativity of the great Muslim legal minds. Once the veil of the anti-Islam discourse is pulled back, these orphaned bits of information, small enough to ignore as curiosities or aberrations on their own, begin to provide a new coherence and a new meaning to the broader picture of the relationship between East and West.

If we cast an eye back over the past millennium of relations between Islam and the West, it is certainly possible to identify an alternative narrative that removes their undoubted contestation from the accepted framework of East versus West and places it within a single cultural arena (as has been done, for example, in Makdisi 1990; Voll 1994; Esposito 1999; Turner 2001, 2003; Bulliet 2004; and Lyons 2009a). Yet the prevailing discourse is so powerful and authoritative that such an approach has failed to make any serious inroads into Western thought. The result is an unnatural and clearly unhelpful separation of two rich and powerful cultural traditions that share far more than we are generally prepared to acknowledge. This separation, in turn, distorts Western understanding of the Muslim world and its culture and all but guarantees that any attempt at East–West communication will result in what the Turks call "a dialogue of the deaf."

Islam Through Western Eyes, then, seeks to create a framework that takes into account not only the discursive formation that one might call "Islam," but also the interconnected relations and activities of those I term "Islam experts"— that is, those responsible for statements that make up "serious speech" on the topic of Islam and the Muslims. Such statements lead a rarefied existence and are privileged by claims to truth and meaning that are widely recognized or otherwise validated, preserved, studied, emulated, and passed on. They are the stuff of textbooks and classroom instruction, learned journals, monographs, public lectures, art exhibits, items in the news media. Throughout their existence, they remain at all times subject to rules of formation that are hidden or otherwise inaccessible to "speakers" and "listeners" alike.

The domain of statements may be further qualified by their existence within a specific discursive formation or discipline. Discourse analysis within an accepted discipline is particularly useful, for it casts in relief the internal rules that operate within that discursive formation and highlights the non-contingent role played by truth and meaning. As Foucault argues: "A discipline is not the sum total of all the truths that may be uttered concerning something; it is not even the total of all that may be accepted, by virtue of some principle of coherence or systematization, concerning some given fact or proposition" (1972b:223).

Just because a statement may consist of a truth about plants, for example, that does not necessarily qualify it as part of the recognized discipline known as botany. It must first be seen to be among possible truths and then be validated by the rules of formation at work within that field: "In short, a proposition must fulfill some onerous and complex conditions before it can be admitted within a discipline; before it can be pronounced true or false it must be . . . 'within the true'" (Foucault 1972b:224). I take this same approach and apply it to the Western science or discipline of Islam and the Muslims—that is, to the serious speech that I call the "anti-Islam discourse."

As a result, I treat primarily the statements of those who have put themselves forward as Islam experts and that are *accepted* as such in distinct historical epochs or eras as the raw data for analysis. From time to time, I may also examine popular or other lay manifestations of this expertise. However, the discourse on Islam has been since its very formation in the eleventh century the exclusive realm of such experts, in the face of whose expertise the public at large has had little choice but to act as passive, trusting receptors.

Such expert statements can be found in a wide variety of Western sources, including those that in a different methodological context and a different analytical framework might be considered "secondary" ones: works on the history of science, philosophy, or religion; ethnographic and anthropological texts; news items; bureaucratic reports; and statements made by politicians and government functionaries. These sources are the primary canon of the anti-Islam discourse, for in them we can see the discursive formation in full cry. Other documents I consider resemble more traditional primary sources—for example, the memoirs of colonial administrators in British-ruled Egypt and India, Montesquieu's philosophical and literary writings, accounts of Urban II's call to crusade and other political speeches, and essays by leading Renaissance humanists.

As should be clear by now, I am not particularly interested in the veracity—the seriousness, if you will—of claims by serious speech to either meaning or truth, although at times it may be useful to put forward alternative understandings or interpretations that surface periodically but that remain outside "the true." Rather, my primary aim is to explore how the discursive claims are produced and deployed in the first place, only to be set aside later—as if on a library shelf—and then hauled down again in the furtherance of the discourse and at the behest of new social actors or institutions. I propose to do this by examining what Foucault calls the "modes of existence" of such statements as the most fruitful way of understanding the workings of the anti-Islam discourse: "The analysis of statements . . . questions them as to their mode of existence, what it means to them to have come into existence, to have left traces, and perhaps to remain there, *awaiting the moment that they might be of some use once more*; what it means to them to have appeared when and where they did—they and no others" (1972a:109, emphasis added).

In addition to my analysis of discursive statements about Islam, this work also invokes a more traditional approach to the matter of the Islam expert: How does he or she benefit from the prevailing discourse? However, these two avenues are perhaps not as far apart as one might expect when first contemplating the interaction of the classical world of Max Weber and the post-structuralist milieu of Michel Foucault. Weber reveals throughout his works the importance he places on his subject's notion of reality and on that subject's point of view, what constitutes his *verstehende Soziologie* (interpretive sociology), which takes into account insight into the individuals' behavior rather than attributing such behavior to idealized types or positivist abstractions (Turner 1974:39).

Nevertheless, Weber does make significant room for the social power of ideas and their ability to shape and direct human behavior. Weber's (1965:51–52) insights are not diminished by his own entanglement in the anti-Islam discourse, which leads him to insist that "early Islam" was a hedonist religion carried out by the warrior classes. In his understanding of the Orient, Weber here was following neatly in the footsteps of the classical European thinkers of the nineteenth century—Adam Smith, John Stuart Mills, Karl Marx, and others (Turner 1974; Matin-Asgari 2004). Writing on the social psychology of world religions, Weber notes: "Not ideas, but material and ideal interests directly govern men's conduct. Yet very frequently the 'world images' that have been created by 'ideas' have, like switchmen, determined the tracks along which action has been pushed by the dynamic of interest" (1958:280). Although clearly less interested than Foucault and the post-structuralists in the epistemological context of discursive formations, Weber acknowledges that ideas, like railway "switchmen," can also be determinant of social action.

Weber's sociology fits neatly within my own framework in several other ways. First, he argues that one's worldview and its accompanying motivations are molded by the self-interest of one's social strata. Second, he defines social action as that which "takes account of the behavior of others and is thereby oriented in its course," a position that downplays or even excludes subjective behavior of any one particular social actor (1947:89; see also Turner 1974:41). Third, Weber is not particularly interested in "an objectively 'correct' meaning or one that is 'true' in the metaphysical sense," a central characteristic that distinguishes "the empirical sciences of action," including sociology, from such "dogmatic" disciplines as jurisprudence, ethics, and logic (89–90). Taken together, then, many of the central elements of Weber's classical project dovetail nicely with my own inquiry into the ways that varying social groups, herein defined as Islam experts, have deployed the same anti-Islam discourse to advance their own interests in concert with one another, even as the context and meaning of those interests may have changed over the centuries.

Chapter 2 discusses my theoretical approach to the anti-Islam discourse. Chapter 3 explores the formation of Islam as discourse—thus addressing the first of my underlying analytical questions: How was this discourse created? It also lays the groundwork for the discussion of the social, intellectual, and political influences that this discourse has exerted ever since.

Chapters 4, 5, and 6 take a thematic approach, breaking down the anti-Islam discourse into a number of component parts and placing each in its appropriate social and historical context. The central themes they investigate are Islam and science, Islam and violence, and Islam and women. These themes are among the most prominent elements of the public discourses surrounding Islam, but the list is by no means exhaustive.[11] *Islam Through Western Eyes* then concludes with a proposed alternative reading of relations between Islam and the West and suggestions for future research.

2

FOUCAULT'S TOOLBOX

> Archaeological description is precisely . . . an abandonment of the history of ideas, a systematic rejection of its postulates and procedures, an attempt to practice a quite different history of what men have said.
>
> MICHEL FOUCAULT, *THE ARCHAEOLOGY OF KNOWLEDGE*

THE WESTERN STUDY of Islam and Islamic movements has been dominated in recent years by the disciplines of political science, international relations, history, and others, but space for new approaches to the field needs to be staked out. *Islam Through Western Eyes* seeks to respond to a call for just such a new approach issued by sociologists Philip W. Sutton and Stephen Vertigans in 2005. Lamenting the academy's failure to recognize and then explain in any satisfactory way the contemporary "growth of practicing Muslims, the establishment of Islamic states and the emergence of radical Islamic social movements," Sutton and Vertigans write in *Islamic Resurgence: A Sociological Approach*: "Sociological analysis potentially brings something unique to our understanding of this important phenomenon by connecting Islamic history to changes in the figuration of international states, the rise of political and violent forms of Islam alongside widespread beliefs in 'civilized' values and 'superior' (and 'inferior') civilizations. In short, the absence of a thoroughgoing sociological perspective leaves our understanding of resurgent Islam relatively fragmented and therefore partial" (2005:2).

As these authors recognize, most efforts to date to address contemporary Islam and the Muslims within a sociological framework, albeit indirectly rather than head on, have so far yielded little and have often clouded the issues more than they have clarified them. Thus throughout most of the twentieth century, the popularity and longevity of secularization theory—the notion that increased economic development necessarily brings with it decreased levels of religiosity—within the social science corpus and among sociologists of religion in particular virtually ensured that inquiries into what is commonly termed an "Islamic revival" or "Islamic resurgence" would see it as an unexpected development to be explained in terms of reaction to or escape from economic, political, or physical hardships.

By effectively correlating a rise in secularization with the emergence of this Western notion of modernity, the established approach dictates that growing Muslim religiosity and expanding Islamic movements be seen as deviant or reactionary phenomena restricted to marginalized populations (Sutton and Vertigans 2005:27). This characterization has introduced into the study of non-Western societies serious distortions across many distinct disciplines. The postmodern experience challenges the embedded notion that there is a single, grand narrative that defines the nature and direction of progress, modernity, and development for all societies alike (S. Thomas 2005:11). Yet as Robert Keohane has acknowledged, "The attacks of September 11 reveal that all mainstream theories of world politics are relentlessly secular with respect to motivation" (2003:272).

The root of the problem lies in the same Enlightenment notions of progress that so heavily imbue the works of such pioneering social scientists as Karl Marx, Émile Durkheim, Max Weber, and Sigmund Freud. All saw religious expression as significant but somehow outside the main flow or direction of modernizing societies (Berger 1999:2–4; Beyer 2006:97–98). One of the central concerns running throughout Weber's work, for example, is the notion of rationalization, as measured by the degree to which intellectual coherence and consistency over time replace magical elements in a society's approach to religion. This *Entzauberung*—best understood as "disenchantment," in the sense of the loss of mystery—lies at the heart of Weber's sociology of knowledge and describes a process whereby charismatic and prophetic knowledge is gradually reinterpreted and rationalized, first by a new stratum of acolytes and priests and later by intellectuals and bureaucrats who reflect the dominant forces in society at large (Gerth and Mills 1958:51–65; Swatos and Christiano 1999:212).

In *The Sociology of Religion*, Weber writes: "As intellectualism suppresses belief in magic, the world's processes become disenchanted, lose their magical significance, and henceforth simply 'are' or 'happen' but no longer signify anything. As a consequence, there is a growing demand that the world and total pattern of life be subject to an order that is significant and meaningful" (1965:125). This growing demand for meaningful order and the accompanying demystification of the world, then, represent "secularization"—a process that increasingly came to be seen as both a social good and a universal phenomenon against which all societies could be measured and assessed. Weber himself appears to have had in mind a rather fluid definition of "secularization," particularly in its application to the study of religion.[1]

In the hands of Weber's heirs, however, secularization theory evolved from the vague assessment of church–state power relations or the extent of religious authority to the full-blown "claim that, in the face of scientific rationality, religion's influence on all aspects of life—from personal habits to social institutions—is in dramatic decline" (Swatos and Christiano 1999:214). Underpinning much of this development was the influential work of Talcott Parsons (1977), who adopted an evolutionary approach grounded once again in an Enlightenment notion of development and progress. The result is effectively an approach to religious history in which the "stages" of development are defined in advance (Swatos and Christiano 1999:218–219). This advance definition falls into the trap of what Paul M. Sweezy (1953) once dismissed as the predilection among social theorists for "the present as history" (cited in Mills 1959:146).

Classical secularization theory has beaten a retreat over the past decade or more amid growing recognition of rising levels of religious activity throughout the world and across virtually all traditions as well as among New Religious Movements (e.g., Stark and Bainbridge 1985; Greeley 1989; S. Thomas 2005). One of the theory's earlier supporters, Peter Berger, has since acknowledged that proponents of secularization were wrong in their assertion of a necessary, causal link between modernity and a decline in religiosity on both the societal and individual level: "The world today . . . is as furiously religious as it ever was, and in some places more so than ever. This means that a whole body of literature by historians and social scientists loosely labeled 'secularization theory' is essentially mistaken" (1999:2; quoted in Sutton and Vertigans 2005:27). Moreover, Berger (1999:4) notes, religious communities have not been forced to adapt to secularity in order to survive, as the theory predicted; rather, those that have thrived in the modern world are precisely those that have resolutely refused to do so. Rodney Stark's (1999) contribution to a special issue of the journal *Sociology of Religion* devoted to secularization theory was titled succinctly "Secularization, R. I. P." Despite this retreat, the residual influence of secularization theory on the study of Islam has generally remained intact.

The rise of globalization theories among social scientists has likewise bolstered the prevailing view of Islam and contemporary Muslims—frequently characterized as "fundamentalist"—as both reactive and reactionary. In general, such theories commonly focus on economics, politics, and culture as separate realms, although some seek combinations of the three. At their core, however, they take the industrialized Western nation-state and its associated societal forms as the yardstick against which to measure all others. This approach, in turn, yields a decidedly Eurocentric view and tends to ignore or downplay the perspective of those taking part in Islamic movements (Sutton and Vertigans 2005:89). As a result, Islamic and other religious movements tend to be seen as resistance to Western values or materialism or culture in general (Robertson and Lechner 1985; Waters 1998). Zygmunt Bauman, for example, ties globalization directly and intimately to fundamentalism: "Fundamentalist tendencies . . . reflect and articulate the experience of people on the receiving end of globalization" (1998:3; quoted in Sutton and Vertigans 2005:90).

Yet, Sutton and Vertigans point out, these Islamic movements are "far more sophisticated than Western theorists give them credit for, and they are themselves part of the globalizing processes which they seek to direct. They need to be given far more attention within globalization theories" (2005:90–91). That they are not given more attention reflects the underlying assumption of most globalization theories that the West is culturally and economically creative, whereas other civilizations and cultures lack yet secretly yearn for this same dynamism (Sutton and Vertigans 2005:175). In *Islam Through Western Eyes*, the chapters focusing on particular themes, especially chapter 4 on Islam and science, reveal the debilitating impact of this theoretical blind spot.

Globalization theories, like the secularization theories before them, also suffer from a basic methodological shortcoming when applied to Muslims: the weight of the traditional view of Islam as the "independent variable" that can account for the salient characteristics of Muslim societies, including levels of socioeconomic or political development (Abootalebi 2000:ix, 2003:155).

This approach again focuses attention on exclusion rather than on inclusion, on what is missing in the Islamic world rather than on what is present but largely ignored or simply unseen by the Western gaze—a process that both emerges from and sustains the anti-Islam discourse: "Muslim societies are still considered to lack essential features associated with the dynamic development of the West, including rationality, liberalism, democracy, and as a consequence are considered inferior" (Sutton and Vertigans 2005:26).

The remarkable resilience and unchanging nature of the anti-Islam discourse over the past millennium also pose a significant challenge to the traditional Western history of ideas and to the philosophy of history in general. The primary difficulty surrounds the very notion of change, something fundamental to the way history has been conceived in the Western experience. This conception holds as much for the church fathers as for the *philosophes* of the Enlightenment and the postmodernists, even as the nature of that change—generally but not exclusively held up as "progress"—becomes increasingly complex.

For Augustine, history was essentially a straight-line progression, from the flawed society of man to that shining metropolis on the hill, literally the "City of God." The eighteenth-century Italian philosopher Giambattista Vico added a layer of complexity when he proposed a threefold development in the history of nations: an age of gods, an age of heroes, and an age of men. Vico's complex and idiosyncratic system, laid out in his *Scienza nuova*, was generally ignored by his contemporaries. It was, however, later rediscovered and remains influential to this day. Of particular interest to this study, Vico made ample room for the activities of man and society as the appropriate object of study: "But in the night of thick darkness enveloping the earliest antiquity, so remote from ourselves, there shines the eternal and never failing light of a truth beyond all question: that the world of civil society has certainly been made by men, and that its principles are therefore to be found within the modifications of our own human mind" (1968:331).

Of course, the Western idea of history has undergone significant evolution since the days of Giambattista Vico, but there has been no substantive departure from its central engagement with notions of change: from G. W. F. Hegel to Marx and his revisionists and on to the postmodern era. Later critiques of Enlightenment historiography do not generally dispute this notion of historical progress so much as they rebel against the flawed way in which earlier practitioners sought to justify it. These thinkers cast their own efforts in terms of restoring historical "realism" (White 1973:47–48). Marxist dialectical materialism, for example, represents an attempt not to eliminate this notion of progress but to rationalize it: "It [dialectical materialism] reveals the transitory character of everything and in everything; nothing can endure before it except the uninterrupted progress of becoming and passing away" (Engels 1941:12).

In the same vein, Thomas Kuhn's landmark study of revolutions in science rises and falls on the dynamic of one paradigm driving out another as an accumulation of new data, in the form of anomalies, vitiates the incumbent approach and literally forces scientists, often against their own innate conservatism, to accept another set of problems and viewpoints. When the shortcomings of the conventional view become too big to ignore, Kuhn argues in *The Structure of Scientific Revolutions* (1962), a shift in paradigm is in order. In fact, it is unavoidable: "Paradigms gain their status because they are more successful than their competitors in solving a few problems that the group of practitioners has come to recognize as acute" (Kuhn 1996:23). In response to his critics, Kuhn later modified some of his terminology, but his essential observations about the nature of scientific change remained intact. Much of the controversy centered on his definition of the term *paradigm*, and in later writings Kuhn (1970:2n.1) noted that perhaps *theory* would have been a better choice. For my purposes, *paradigm* remains perfectly viable.

But what if there is no change? What if we find none of the transformations of discursive formations that the modern French philosophers, following Gaston Bachelard, refer to as "discontinuities"? What if there simply is no paradigm shift? What if the anti-Islamic discourse shows none of the attributes of the traditional history of ideas, but instead appears to violate the "laws" of intellectual physics?

This lack of change in the theory of Islam is, I contend, pretty much what has happened. The outlines of possible new paradigms have emerged, but so far none has prevailed. Despite the intervening centuries and the military, commercial, and cultural communication that they naturally entailed—not to mention countless studies, monographs, news items, and other statements about the Muslim world—the Western "conversation" about Islam remains very much rooted in its medieval beginnings. Kuhn would teach us that the shortcomings contained in an initial paradigm constructed one thousand years ago on the bases of Crusades propaganda and a complete lack of first-hand knowledge of Islam would have succumbed long ago to its manifest anomalies. In its place, we would expect to find a more insightful, more useful, and ultimately more helpful way of looking at and thinking about Islam and Muslims. That shift has not happened. Instead, we have entered the twenty-first century much as we exited the eleventh—with a deadly crisis of relations between Islam and the West, of which today's war on terrorism, which our leaders tell us may never end, is but the most acute symptom.

In response, I propose to modify traditional intellectual history by using a broader approach in order to better understand the workings, maintenance, and consequences of the anti-Islam discourse. Revisiting the three elements of my analytical framework—the formation of the discourse, its operation, and its social and institutional beneficiaries—allows me to relocate the problem to more fruitful ground. And that is the aim of this work.

This relocation does not, however, mean losing sight of the historical content or of the utility of historical analysis in general. Bauman's evocatively titled work *Liquid Fear* flirts with the danger of doing just that. Bauman notes that in response to modernity, particularly at its virulent, globalizing worst, the world's monotheistic faiths have fallen back on a polarizing, black-and-white worldview as a means of final defense. He then adds: "Indeed, the Manichean vision of the world, the call to arms in holy war against satanic forces threatening to overwhelm the universe, the reducing of the Pandora's box of economic, political and social conflicts to an apocalyptic vision of a last, life and death confrontation between good and evil: these are not patterns unique to Islamic ayatollahs. On our fast globalizing planet, the 'religionization' of politics, of social grievances and battles of identity and recognition, seem to be the global tendency" (2006:113–114).

Although perhaps a plausible enough description of today's world, Bauman's characterization fails to hear the clear echo of the same sentiments, fears, and attitudes that were present at the very creation of the anti-Islam discourse one thousand years earlier and that have been nurtured ever since. Rather than a response "commissioned, customized and tailor-made to satisfy the longings fed by negative globalization," to use Bauman's (2006:115) phrase, we clearly have here deep-seated and lasting forces, ideas, and conceptualizations that cannot simply be explained away by the latest twists and turns of modernity.

As C. Wright Mills reminds us, the essential unity of history and sociology is central to proper social studies. "No social study that does not come back to the problems of biography, of history and of their intersections within a society has completed its intellectual journey," he writes at the outset of his manifesto *The Sociological Imagination* (1959:6). Such an approach can move the researcher in new directions and generate fundamental questions of acute interest to the social scientist: What is the structure of the society under consideration? Where do we place this society in human history, and how does it differ from other eras? And what kinds of men and women prevail in this time and place? "Whether the point of interest is a great power state or a minor literary mood, a family, a prison, a creed—these are the kinds of questions the best social analysts ask. They are the intellectual pivots of classic studies of man in society—and they are the questions inevitably raised by any mind possessing the sociological imagination" (Mills 1959:7).

Recent decades have seen a growing recognition among social scientists of the importance of language and its steady transformation from a relatively neutral or transparent means of communicative exchange to an object worthy of study, either as part of other, established disciplines or in its own right (Fairclough 1992:2). The result has been a proliferation of competing definitions and theoretical approaches to the analysis of discourse.[2] However, two distinct camps can be discerned quite readily: those grounded primarily in linguistics and concerned with "extended samples of either spoken or written language" and those based chiefly in social theory and addressing "different ways of structuring areas of knowledge and social practice" (Fairclough 1992:3).

Among the latter trend is so-called critical discourse analysis, which sees discourse—here defined as language used in speech and writing, listening, and reading—as "social practice" (Fairclough and Wodak 1998:258) or as "practical, social, and cultural phenomenon" (van Dijk 1998a:2). Theoretical approaches within critical discourse analysis, however, vary widely, depending largely on the degree to which they rely on the linguistic characteristics of texts and statements (Fairclough and Wodak 1998:271–280).

At one end of the spectrum lies critical linguistics, developed in Great Britain in the 1970s (Halliday 1978, 1994; Fowler 1991), with its close attention to grammatical usage, choice of vocabulary, and the ways in which one text influences the production of a subsidiary one—for example, how a government report might become an item in the news (Fairclough and Wodak

1998:263–264). At the other end—some might say straying well outside the spectrum's confines altogether—stands the work of Michel Foucault, in which linguistic analyses of texts and statements play no significant role, and broader epistemological and philosophical questions predominate.

As to his own working definition of the term *discourse*, Foucault writes in *The Archaeology of Knowledge*: "I believe I have in fact added to its meanings: treating it sometimes as the general domain of all statements, sometimes as an individualizable group of statements, and sometimes as a regulated practice that accounts for a number of statements" (1972a:80). And it is the latter meaning—the rules that oversee the production and reproduction of statements as constitutive of knowledge as well as their subsequent transformation into a discipline—that is central to both Foucault's thinking and my own analysis of the anti-Islam discourse.

But what, exactly, does Foucault mean by *archaeology*? As with many things concerning his work, there is no one single and straightforward answer, so it may be better first to address what archaeology is *not* by contrasting it—as the author does himself—with the traditional notion of the history of ideas: "Archaeological description is precisely . . . an abandonment of the history of ideas, a systematic rejection of its postulates and procedures, an attempt to practice a quite different history of what men have said" (1972a:138).

In his inaugural lecture to the Collège de France, delivered in 1970, Foucault spells out four distinct differences that characterize his method.[3] First of all, archaeology is not intended to impose unities on the unruly diversity of discourses, whether a work, a period, or a theme. Nor does it seek to reveal hidden meanings, uncover influences, or ascribe innovation or originality to individuals; it is not an interpretive discipline. Likewise, it is not the pursuit of "the point of creation" (Foucault 1972b:230).

Unlike archaeology, all these activities are hallmarks of the history of ideas as commonly constructed and practiced. Yet, for Foucault, they are not worthy of serious, "grown-up" researchers:

> It is not legitimate, then, to demand, point-blank, of the texts that one is studying their title to originality, and whether they really possess those degrees of nobility that are measured here by the absence of ancestors. . . . But to seek in the great accumulation of the already-said the text that resembles "in advance" a later text, to ransack history in order to rediscover the play of anticipations or echoes, to go right back

to the first seeds or to go forward to the last traces, to reveal in a work its fidelity to tradition or its irreducible uniqueness, to raise or lower its stock of originality . . . these are harmless enough amusements for historians who refuse to grow up. (1972a:143–144)

In contradistinction to such historical practice, archaeology takes differences and disunities seriously, making no real attempt either to explain them away or to establish a systemic relationship among them, but only endeavoring to describe them. This approach inverts the usual values, not by increasing differences but simply by declining to reduce them: "For the history of ideas, the appearance of difference indicates an error, or a trap. . . . Archaeology, on the other hand, takes as the object of its description what is usually regarded as an obstacle: its aim is not to overcome differences, but to analyze them, to say what exactly they consist of, to differentiate them" (Foucault 1972a:171).

This approach to differences gives Foucault's work the unique power to identify "minor" statements and other obscure data overlooked by traditional investigation, a quality that computer scientists and physicists approvingly call "granularity," and to restore to them their true, full value. "Foucault's genius," writes the philosopher Ian Hacking, "is to go down to the little dramas, dress them in facts hardly anyone else had noticed, and turn these stage settings into clues to a hitherto unthought series of confrontations out of which, he contends, the orderly structure of society is composed" (1986:28). In this vein, my thematic chapters identify and explore a number of the miscellaneous facts left "homeless" by the anti-Islam discourse.

Archaeology can also explain why it is that certain things can be thought and said about Islam and the Muslims and certain other things cannot. In other words, it reveals the ways in which the anti-Islam discourse operates. In *The Archaeology of Knowledge*, Foucault makes clear the central distinction between his method and the more linguistic approach common to forms of critical discourse analysis: "The question posed by language analysis of some discursive fact or other is always: according to what rules has a particular statement been made, and consequently according to what rules could other similar statements be made? The description of the events of discourse poses a quite different question: *how is it that one particular statement appeared rather than another?*" (1972a:27, emphasis added). In a special English-language foreword—which Foucault proposed calling "Directions for Use"—to another major methodological work, *The Order of Things: An Archaeology of the Human Sciences*, he comments: "I should like to know whether the subjects responsible for scientific discourse are not determined in their situation, their function, their perceptive capacity, and their practical possibilities by conditions that dominate and even overwhelm them" (1994b:xiv).

The utility of this approach can be demonstrated by returning to Pope Benedict XVI's address to German intellectuals in 2006, in which we can now begin to see the workings of the anti-Islam discourse more clearly. Aside from the spectacle of one of Urban II's direct successors lecturing Muslims on the subject of holy war, the pontiff found himself hopelessly entangled in two of the central threads of the West's established narrative, violence and the nature of God, with the delicate matter of sex perhaps understandably ignored. Yet his polemic is fatally flawed on several counts.

For one, the Qur'anic verse barring "compulsion in religion" (2:256)[4] is in fact a later revelation from the Medina period, by which time Muhammad was a significant political and military leader and increasingly able to enforce his will; it was not made, as the pope argued, from a position of weakness and then somehow forgotten or set aside when Muhammad's fortunes improved. Moreover, Islam never presents anything like an unequivocal or unwavering endorsement of religious violence; rather, notions such as *jihad* and other concepts commonly seen by many Muslims and non-Muslims alike as fundamental to the faith and thus immutable reflect the social and political context of specific time and place. I return to this subject in detail in my discussion of Islam and violence in chapter 5.

Nor must Muslims take a backseat to any of the other People of the Book in terms of their faith's underlying rational characteristics. The very language of the Qur'an makes repeated appeal to man's rationality. A significant number of verses refer to the order inherent to God's universe and to man's capacity to recognize and exploit this order for his own needs, such as keeping time: "He [God] it is who appointed the sun a splendor and the moon a light, and measured for her stages, that you might know the number of the years, and the reckoning [of time]. . . . He details the revelations for people who have knowledge" (10:6).

According to an analysis by Franz Rosenthal (2007:19–21), the Arabic word for "knowledge" (*ilm*) and its derivative forms account for almost 1 percent of the Qur'an's 78,000 words and are among its most frequently used terms and phrases, a linguistic feature that highlights just how important the concept was for the first Muslims. Rosenthal recognizes the importance of knowledge and wisdom for the ancient Graeco–Roman world but adds: "Yet, nobody would wish to argue that the attitude toward knowledge in the Ancient world as a whole or in any particular region or epoch of it was inspired and sustained by the same single-minded devotion that existed in medieval Islam. . . . Nor was the sphere of religion ever fused with that of knowledge as inseparably as happened later on in Islam" (336–337).

As Foucault would most assuredly have pointed out, such muddling—for instance, that of Pope Benedict—is inescapable. It is also largely beside the point. The pope was "misled" not by a few errant facts or mistaken interpretations by his experts, but by the existence of an anti-Islam discourse that allows for no conclusions or statements about Muslims other than that Muslims are prone to violence by their faith and irrational to boot. In other words, there was nothing else the pope could say; he was quite literally overwhelmed by a thousand-year-old discourse.

Nor is it only popes, politicians, and the public at large who are seduced by the siren call of the prevailing discourse; expertise and scholarship provide no surefire defense, as we can see in one example involving the historian Bernard Lewis. Lewis has long advocated a reading of Islam as an authoritarian and rigid faith—and thus implacably antimodern. He writes in *The Political Language of Islam*: "The duty of obedience to legitimate authority is not merely one of political expediency. It is a religious obligation, defined and imposed by Holy Law and grounded in revelation" (1988:91). Yet this view is based in large part on his particular reading and translation of a key verse in the Qur'an (Afsarrudin 2008:127). By translating an important phrase in verse 4:59, "ulu 'l-amr minkum," as directing believers to "obey those in authority *over* you" rather than as the more literal "those in authority *among* you," Lewis obscures the verse's egalitarian intent and focuses instead on Islam's supposed authoritarian nature (Afsaruddin 2006b: 53–54, 2008:127).

Foucault's work is not without its difficulties, and his commentators and critics have raised objections that are either epistemological or political or quite often both. Particularly troubling for many is Foucault's insistence on the total autonomy of discourse to produce statements in accordance with rules that are outside the consciousness of the speakers themselves and that are recognizable only to the archaeologist. Such autonomy threatens to cast all knowledge as relative and all serious thought as an illusion on the part of the thinker. It puts in doubt the place for political and social activism and, for some, raises the specter of what might be called "cryptofunctionalism," universally condemned by such critics as fundamentally conservative (Hoy 1986:7). Finally, it appears to pose the relativist question of how the archaeological discourse can ever hope to evade its own illusions.[5]

In response, in some measure at least, Foucault went on to introduce a second order of analysis that reaches beyond what is available to pure archaeology and takes into account the conditions and context, including any institutional and social constraints, in which statements are produced. Foucault termed this new addition to his toolbox "genealogy," and he outlined three key questions at its core: "How series of discourse are formed, through, in spite of, or with the aid of these systems of constraint; what are the specific norms for each; and what were their conditions of appearance, growth, and variation" (1972b:232). By now, the echo of my own analytical questions surrounding the anti-Islam discourse should be clear: How was this discourse formed? How does it operate? And which institutions and groups have benefited and continue to benefit from its preservation and perpetuation?

None of the criticisms directed at Foucault on either philosophical or political grounds renders his toolbox any less useful for my own purposes. His epistemological shortcomings—if they are, in fact, shortcomings and not just reflections of his readers' own hopes, expectations, and ideological beliefs—are most acutely felt against the backdrop of the grand postmodern search for a new science of man, a response to the Aristotelian question of whether a proper science of the individual is even possible. Here I am deploying his techniques against a more modest yet vitally important target: How is the Western "science" of Islam carried out? And what are its consequences?

Foucault's analytical strengths may clearly be drawn on here without any danger that relativism will infect all of Western knowledge. In fact, what some commentators have termed his unserious attitude toward the truth can be turned into an analytical asset, for it allows me to focus on the workings of the anti-Islam discourse without the distraction of necessarily having to arbitrate the truth or falsity of all of its claims. As noted earlier, this study is more interested in what the discourse tells us is true and what is not or cannot be true about Islam and the Muslims.

Foucault summarizes his own thinking in this regard in the foreword to the English edition of *The Order of Things*: "What I would like to do . . . is to reveal a *positive unconscious* of knowledge: a level that eludes the consciousness of the scientist and yet is part of scientific discourse, instead of disputing its validity and seeking to diminish its scientific nature" (1994b:xi, emphasis in original). This research program is perfectly reasonable, and I attempt to emulate it.

Edward Said's *Orientalism* demonstrates the power of Foucault's analytical methods for cultural and social studies. This landmark work, which defines Orientalism as "a style of thought based upon an ontological and epistemological distinction between 'the Orient' and (most of the time) 'the Occident'" (Said [1978] 2003:2), relies heavily on Foucault's notion of discourse, a fact that Said acknowledges at the very outset of the book (3). *Orientalism* also serves as both an invaluable precursor and something of a way station for *Islam Through Western Eyes*. Said's effort has deeply shaped the thinking of countless investigators across a range of fields and helped clear the way for this work. Yet it focuses on only one specific segment—the content-rich heyday of the European colonial era and its American-dominated aftermath—of the broader narrative arc that I take as my own field of study, which stretches from the discovery of Islam by the Christian West around the eleventh century into the foreseeable future. By placing the phenomenon of Orientalism in the context of the anti-Islam discourse as a whole and by extending it backward and forward in time, I hope to build substantially on Said's work.

These differences in scope and frame of reference naturally lead to some notable differences in approach and ultimately in findings. For Said, the Orientalist discourse is both precursor and handmaiden to Western colonial domination of the East, and he dates the beginning of its formation in earnest to the late eighteenth century, when European ideas and images of the Orient began to take on the urgency and immediacy that surrounds one culture's direct, physical subjugation of the Other. Although *Orientalism* concerns only the West's experience of the East, the East itself remains a physical space made up of real nations and cultures whose "lives, histories, and customs have a brute reality obviously greater than anything that could be said about them in the West" (Said [1978] 2003:5).

Thus Said finds it necessary to qualify somewhat the implied notion of the East as nothing more than an intellectual or cultural construct: "It would be wrong to conclude that the Orient was essentially an idea, or a creation with no corresponding reality" ([1978] 2003:5).[6] He therefore seeks to ground the Orient of the Orientalist imagination in something resembling a real time and place; it is only the epistemological context—that is, the West's apprehension and understanding—that gives specific meaning to the objective reality of the Orient.

In contrast, I see the crucial formation of the broader anti-Islam discourse as taking place *outside* the confines of any such "corresponding reality." In other words, it is virtually untethered from any corresponding conditions of Muslim religious, social, or political life, none of which was known in the West at the time of the discourse's formation. This quality is central to the anti-Islam discourse's unwavering form, power, and tenacious hold on the Western imagination over the course of a millennium. In this way, this discourse is distinct from those laid out by Said in *Orientalism* or treated in *Inventing the Middle Ages: The Lives, Works, and Ideas of the Great Medievalists of the Twentieth Century* (Cantor 1991) and *Inventing Eastern Europe: The Map of Civilization on the Mind of the Enlightenment* (Wolff 1994). All three propose reconceptualizations—that is, new ways of looking at what might be called established facts—rather than probe inventions from scratch.

A second consequence of Said's periodization is the privileged place he accords to Western power within the discursive formation he calls "Orientalism": "To believe that the Orient was created—or, as I call it, 'Orientalized'—and to believe that such things happen simply as a necessity of the imagination, is to be disingenuous. . . . The relationship between Occident and Orient is a relationship of power, of domination, of varying degrees of a complex hegemony" ([1978] 2003:5). I would not wish to deny the important place of power in general or to reject the argument that ever since Napoleon's invasion of Egypt in 1798 the East–West dynamic has been shaped by particular power relations. Nevertheless, it is important to recognize that this domination of the East by the West was not the case at the formation of the anti-Islam discourse. In the first place, medieval Christendom lagged behind the Muslim world by virtually any measure—cultural, scientific, military, and economic. Second, the formation of the discourse took place, as chapter 3 recounts in detail, without any real knowledge or firsthand experience of Islam or Muslims. And third, what power there was in the relationship was surely to the disadvantage of Christian Europe, which saw in Islam an existential, civilizational threat; for its part, the world of Islam felt it could safely ignore the invading Crusaders for decades before mobilizing to expel them.

Said does part company with Foucault over one important aspect of the latter's approach to discourse analysis, the so-called problem of the author. For Said, Foucault's stress on the autonomy of discourse and the unseen rules that bind the authors of statements downplays or removes any question of "profit, ambition, ideas, the sheer love of power" (1994b:117). Edward Said, like Jürgen Habermas and a number of Foucault's other critics, sees this tendency to set aside the author and read everything as text as a threat to political and social action, intervention, and resistance (Ochoa 2006:52–53).

As a result, Said seeks to identify the peculiar features of individual texts by individual authors rather than to see them largely as the undifferentiated and *undifferentiable* production of the discursive formation in question. This task leads him to an approach familiar to more linguistic-based elements of critical discourse analysis: "Accordingly my analyses employ close textual readings whose goal is to reveal the dialectic between individual text or writer and the complex collective formation to which his [Foucault's] work is a contribution" ([1978] 2003:24–25).

The example Said offers to support this strategy is instructive. He notes that such was the reception of Edward William Lane's *An Account of the Manners and Customs of the Modern Egyptians* (2003), first published in 1836, as so authoritative that no one then writing about the Orient, not just about Egypt, could fail to borrow from it even when such borrowings were clearly inappropriate, unreliable, or otherwise irrelevant. Thus passages about Egypt are transposed verbatim into another author's work about village life in Syria: "Lane's authority and the opportunities provided for citing him discriminately as well indiscriminately were there because Orientalism could give his text the kind of distributive currency that he acquired. There is no way, however, of understanding Lane's currency without also understanding the peculiar features of his text" (Said [1978] 2003:23).

Rather than see this phenomenon as demanding unique attention for the putative author, as does Said, it would seem more instructive and informative to treat Said's "ensemble of texts" as a product of the entire discursive formation of Orientalism. Put another way, the remarkable "currency" that Said attributes to *Manners and Customs of the Modern Egyptians*—its ability to meld effortlessly with other, seemingly unrelated Orientalist texts—stems from the power of the discourse and its rules of formation rather than from any necessary attribute of the author himself. Foucault's (1972a:55) approach to discourse analysis, after all, effectively removes the author in an effort to provide direct access to the deeper epistemological phenomena. Given the explanatory power of archaeological analysis, the particularly broad sweep of statements that compose one thousand years of anti-Islam discourse, and the resilience of its rules of formation, I see no compelling reason to follow Said in this regard.

However, such differences are relatively minor. Both *Orientalism* and my own investigation are in the final analysis studies of Western society and culture, despite their deep investment in things Eastern. The object of investigation, whether the more limited notion of Orientalism or the anti-Islam discourse as a whole, is but a useful means to watch the West as it watches the Other; it is these processes of scrutiny, the collection of facts, and the dissemination of knowledge about Islam and the Muslims that are most important—not the content of that knowledge. Said seeks to ground his investigation in the structure of power underpinning more than two hundred years of colonial and postcolonial domination, whereas I aim to locate mine in a broader social and intellectual context that supports a range of subsidiary discursive formations and practices, of which Orientalism is but one notable facet among many.

As discussed earlier, Max Weber's (1965:125) notion of the fundamental disenchantment, or *Entzauberung*, that characterizes modern societies naturally leads to a demand for "order" and "meaning," and what was once mystery becomes governmental reports, bureaucratic data, and media coverage. The social manifestation of this phenomenon, in terms of Western views of Islam and the anti-Islam discourse, lies with the serial Islam experts who have defined the Muslims for the rest of us over the centuries. Initially the Latin theologians' virtually exclusive domain, this discourse was over time gradually reinterpreted and rationalized, first by intellectuals (the humanists, the *philosophes*, and Orientalist scholars) and then by bureaucrats (the colonial administrators, diplomats, and ministerial appointees).

Here Weber offers another useful insight about our ability to identify and analyze those social layers that exercise particular influence on the beliefs of the times: "Those strata which are decisive in stamping the characteristic features of an economic ethic may change in the course of history. And the influence of a single stratum is never an exclusive one. Nevertheless, as a rule one may determine the strata whose styles of life have been at least predominantly decisive for certain religions" (1958:268). In this light, it is worth restating that the anti-Islam discourse has always been an elite affair in which an uninformed public has no other recourse—nor does it generally seek any—than to put itself in the hands of the experts. The later rise of mass media and the advent of public-opinion surveys have done nothing to cast doubt on the top-down nature of the West's predominant Islam narrative; as we have already seen, "elite" opinion is reliably reflected in "mass" opinion on the subject.

Robert K. Merton has applied one of Weber's best-known, if most often abused theses—the relationship between the rise of Protestantism and the rise of modern capitalism—in his own study of the interplay among science, faith, and society in seventeenth-century England. In *Science, Technology, and Society in Seventeenth-Century England*, Merton argues that intellectual movement away from the fields of philosophy, theology, and art and toward the study of science in the past four hundred years can be ascribed at least in part to social and cultural factors, an argument that leads him to pose questions not too distant from my own: "Which social processes are involved in shifts of interest from one division of human activity to another? What, indeed, is the nature of the sociological conditions that are associated with pronounced activity in any one of these domains?" ([1938] 1970:3). In "Puritanism, Pietism, and Science: Testing a Hypothesis," chapter 6 of this work, Merton finds the values of Puritanism "congenial," if not necessarily essential, to the development of scientific values, a finding not dissimilar to Weber's, albeit in a slightly different context.

But Merton is wary of what he sees as the overreliance of Weber and other Continental thinkers on the ideas and attitudes of social elites at the expense of a more "American" focus on mass public opinion. "This [overreliance] leaves untouched, and untouchable, the independent question of the extent to which these beliefs set down in books express the beliefs of the larger and, so far as history goes, inarticulate population," wrote Merton (1968:449) many years after his initial study of science and society in England. With this qualification out of the way, he focuses on the essentials of the sociology of knowledge: "It is primarily concerned with the relations between knowledge and other essential factors in the society or culture" (510).

This approach, then, requires consideration of other important questions: What exactly do we understand as "knowledge"? And do different types of knowledge involve different types of relationships to social structures? Merton attacks the matter this way: "The question is, of course, whether these

diverse kinds of 'knowledge' stand in the same relationship to their sociological basis, or whether it is necessary to distinguish between spheres of
knowledge precisely because this relationship varies for the various types"
(1968:521). Social theorists have offered a number of answers to these and
related questions. Definitions of knowledge, for example, range from the
broadest category, that of "culture" in general, to much more specific modes
of thought and intellectual activity.

One of the most useful approaches for understanding aspects of the anti-
Islam discourse can be found in the work of Karl Mannheim, who excludes the
exact sciences from his understanding of knowledge but includes "historical,
political and social science thinking as well as the thought of everyday life"
(Merton 1968:524)—the very types of knowledge that should most interest
us in the context of the anti-Islam discourse. With this in mind, Mannheim's
Ideology and Utopia unfurls his approach to the understanding of knowledge:
"The principle thesis of the sociology of knowledge is that there are modes
of thought which cannot be adequately understood as long as their social
origins are obscured" (1936:2). Here we can see an underlying compatibility
with Foucault's later approach.

But Mannheim has more to offer. His sociology of knowledge appears particularly well equipped to take into account the seemingly ahistorical stasis
of the anti-Islam discourse: "It is never an accident when a certain theory,
wholly or in part, fails to develop beyond a given stage of relative abstract-
ness and offers resistance to further tendencies toward becoming more
concrete, either by frowning upon this tendency towards concreteness or
declaring it to be irrelevant. Here, too, the social position of the thinker is
significant" (1936:276).

Finally, the importance that Mannheim ascribes to the intelligentsia not
only fits neatly with my own notion of the Islam expert but also suggests how
it is that such a group's ossified outlook can become entrenched in social and
political terms: "In every society there are social groups whose special task
it is to provide an interpretation of the world for that society. . . . The more
static a society is, the more likely it is that this stratum will acquire a well-
defined status or position of a caste in that society" (1936:10).

Mannheim had in mind such social groups as the Brahmins and the medieval Latin clergy, but the same phenomenon holds true for the "caste" of
practitioners of the anti-Islam discourse whose oracular utterances have
rarely faced serious examination or challenge. For a recent example, one has

to look no further than Bernard Lewis and Fouad Ajami and their assurances to the White House that ordinary Iraqis would welcome the U.S. invasion of their country. Ajami, for example, boldly predicted, "We shall be greeted, I think, in Baghdad and Basra with kites and boom boxes" (quoted in von Drehle 2002). Vice President Dick Cheney (2003) invoked similar assurances from Lewis when he told the public that American forces would be "greeted as liberators" by the Iraqi people.

Mannheim's sociology of knowledge has not always received the respect it deserves, largely due to consistent criticism of his work's epistemological aspects—a critique not unlike the one Foucault faced later. This criticism is the familiar problem of relativism, which Mannheim's critics see as flowing from the notion that all knowledge, which by definition must include his own theory, is socially determined and thus cannot be evaluated as true or false by any knowable standard of validity. Alexander von Schelting's (1936) review of the German edition of *Ideolgie und Utopie* (1930) helped set the tone for this line of criticism in the English-speaking world (see also Merton 1968:551–558 and Hartung 1970).

Yet Mannheim's thinking on the subject, presented comprehensively in the English edition of *Ideology and Utopia* (1936), clearly recognizes this danger and takes it into account. As A. P. Simonds argues, Mannheim has as his ultimate goal an understanding of the interaction of thought and being, a notion central to any sociology of knowledge: "By looking closely at Mannheim's manner of formulating the question, and in considering this in the light of his arguments . . . about the nature of meaning and its communication, it is possible to see that his object is the interpretation of thought, not its reduction to some non-meaningful 'base'" (1978:21).

Simonds's reading of Mannheim is the one that I employ here. It provides a useful avenue of exploration into the anti-Islam discourse and allows ample room, without necessarily devolving into crude reductionism, for interpretive analysis of the underlying social structures that have supported this discourse. In this way, it resembles Weber's classic work on the Protestant ethic and the rise of modern capitalism more than it does Marx and Engels's scientific materialism. Moreover, the controversy over relativism and other elements of Mannheim's epistemology leaves essentially intact much of what Merton, himself a strong critic of this alleged relativism, calls Mannheim's "substantive sociology of knowledge" (1973:31)—that is, the relationship between thought and social structure. Mannheim himself at times distinguished between the two related ventures: "One can accept the empirical results without drawing the epistemological conclusions" (1936:239). It is also worth noting, as I have already shown in the case of Pope Benedict XVI, that the truth-value of the anti-Islam discourse is not fundamentally at issue; only its formation, longevity, and power need be considered.

Considerations of method and theory, as Mills has argued convincingly, must not be allowed to distract the social scientist from completing the job at hand; they are tools, not ends in themselves. For Mills, method concerns above all else "how to ask and answer questions with some assurance that the answers are more or less durable." Theory, meanwhile, demands close attention to the words one uses, especially their logical relationship: "The primary purpose of both is clarity of conception and economy of procedure, and most importantly just now, the release rather than the inhibition of the sociological imagination" (Mills 1959:120).

Second, Mills asserts the absolute need for social scientists to risk thinking Big Thoughts and not to carve research questions into minor issues that effectively exempt the existing political and social order from serious reexamination and criticism—a lesser task that he assigns to judges, social workers, teachers, and such: "The social scientist who spends his intellectual forces on the details of small-scale milieux is not putting his work outside the political conflicts and forces of his time. He is, at least indirectly and in effect, 'accepting' the framework of his society" (1959:78). Thus the scale of my inquiry—one thousand years of Western thought—is deliberately, if somewhat dauntingly, ambitious.

Mills also helps highlight the central problem of the anti-Islam discourse, reflected in Western thought's inability to accommodate alternative ways of looking at the question even long after the old ways have proved bankrupt: "When we try to orient ourselves—if we do try—we find that too many of our old expectations and images are, after all, tied down historically; that too many of our standard categories of thought and of feeling as often disorient us as help to explain what is happening around us; that too many of our explanations are derived from the great historical transition from the Medieval to the Modern Age; and that when they are generalized for use today, they become unwieldy, irrelevant, not convincing" (1959:166).

Peeling back the separate layers of mystery that conceal the West's Islam discourse—Is any word for such a venture more apt than *archaeology*?—

represents a necessary first step toward understanding the damage that this discourse has wrought over the centuries, from the Crusades' sectarian violence to Orientalist colonialism's exploitation and degradation to today's anti-Muslim war on terrorism. Here, then, is the true battleground for the Western understanding of Islam and the Muslims, for it is in the production, presentation, and maintenance of statements on Islam and the Muslims that the discourse has triumphed. It is here that any proper study of Islam must begin—at the very beginning. And that means, first, a return to the most fundamental questions of all: Just what do we mean by "Islam"? And why do we mean this instead of something else?

3

THE WESTERN IDEA OF ISLAM

It is safe to speak evil of one whose malignity exceeds whatever ill can be spoken.

GUIBERT DE NOGENT, CHRONICLER OF THE FIRST CRUSADE

SOMETIME IN 1076, Pope Gregory VII (r. 1073–1085) wrote a most respectful letter to the Muslim ruler of what is today eastern Algeria. Addressing the Hammadid emir as "Anazir, king of the province of *Mauretania sitifensis* in Africa," the pope agrees to consecrate a local bishop to tend to the spiritual needs of the emir's Christian subjects. Gregory also thanks the king, known in Arabic as al-Nasir (r. 1062–1089/1090), for accompanying his request with gifts and word that he had freed a number of Christian prisoners as a goodwill gesture. All this is, of course, the act of an accomplished diplomat and experienced man of world affairs on the part of the pope.

Yet Gregory, the dominant figure of his day in Latin Christendom, seamlessly crosses over from the demands of politesse to the realm of theology: "In truth, such charity we and you owe more particularly to our own than to the remaining peoples, for we believe and confess, albeit in a different way, the one God, and each day we praise and honor him as the creator of the ages and the ruler of this world" (2002:204). And he proposes to establish possible commercial and political ties to Anazir through a pair of trusted aides who were "brought up with us in the Roman palace from almost their very youth" (205).

Gregory's pontificate placed him at the forefront of the church's struggle with the rising power of nascent European states unleashed by the gradual disintegration of the Carolingian Empire once led by Charlemagne. These new states—including what we would more or less recognize today as Germany, France, and England, among others—were headed by monarchs who sought centralized control over all aspects of social and economic life within their realms. Conflict with the Catholic Church's traditional claims to final, universal authority flared in particular over the appointment of senior clerics, who enjoyed dual roles as spiritual leaders and enormously rich and powerful local landowners. At the same time, the economic needs of the religious establishment in a feudal economy had led to the creation of large foundations with great landholdings of their own, remaking many a high church officer in the image of the lay landed elite. The struggle between church and state for the final say over such matters became the dominant issue of eleventh-century Europe.

Pope Gregory's response was a militant one. He moved aggressively to limit lay authority over the investiture of bishops and other senior clerics; to clamp down on the practice of simony, the trade in clerical offices that had arisen to meet the demand for such powerful and lucrative posts; and to enforce existing requirements for clerical celibacy as a way of preventing these positions from becoming hereditary family holdings independent of church control. All these measures were linked by a central theme running throughout Gregory's thought: the imperative to assert and strengthen papal prerogatives as matters of right and law rather than of theological requirement or religious duty. To complement his social and economic policies, Gregory VII also elevated the innovative theological concept of armed struggle in the interest of the faith—under the ultimate leadership of the popes—to the center of official church thinking. This was the origin of the doctrine of Christian holy war.

Gregory had had a long-running interest in warfare on behalf of the faith, and at one point he proposed the creation of a papal fighting force from among the warring European knights, the Militia of St. Peter, to combat heresy and enforce the church's claims against its secular rivals. The pope and his most loyal supporters, the *fideles beati Sancti Petri*, recognized that their ambitious reform project was certain to provoke concerted political opposition that could be countered only by adequate armed force. Although force of arms was clearly a temporal matter, the church reformers of the eleventh century introduced a uniquely spiritual component directed at lay recruits—

the notion of absolution of sins for those who battled in the name of the papacy. This component created a potent mix of penance and violence that would one day animate the Crusades (Tyerman 2006:46–47).

Sympathetic church intellectuals such as Bishop Anselm of Lucca, well versed in canon law, combed through the works of the church fathers, especially Augustine, for theories of just war that could be invoked in support of Gregory's endeavors. Anselm's redaction of Augustine's views yielded the twin notions of sanctified warfare commanded by God and God's direct intervention to ensure ultimate victory for true believers (Riley-Smith 1986:6; Asbridge 2004:28). Another papal ally, John of Mantua, reworked Jesus's famous admonition to one of his followers to sheath his sword as the Roman soldiers closed in to arrest him in the Garden of Gethsemane: "Put your sword back into its place; for all who take the sword will perish by the sword" (Matthew 26:52).

In the hands of John of Mantua, Jesus did not direct his disciples to surrender their swords or to disavow violence altogether, but only to await a more opportune moment to strike. The allegorical message was clear: such a time was finally at hand under the leadership of Pope Gregory VII (Asbridge 2004:29). Bishop Bonzio of Sutri, meanwhile, widely celebrated the image of the Christian holy warrior who would battle heretics and schismatics and protect the weak and downtrodden among the pious (Tyerman 2006:47–48). The same reformers also realized that the church had to restore its position of moral and temporal authority and to draw closer to the common people as part of its broader resistance to the secular power of kings (Riley-Smith 1986:4–5). What better than a volunteer papal army that would allow ordinary believers to defend the faith while providing for the remission of their worldly sins in return?

Not surprisingly, Gregory's strained relations with the monarchs of Latin Christendom were complicated by his growing calls for a military campaign, which he aspired to lead in person against heretics, "Saracens," and loosely defined "pagans." Lacking military forces of his own, the pope was left to rely for men and matériel on the support and goodwill of the very secular rulers whose political, social, and economic powers he now sought to rein in. Gregory was especially eager to aid the Byzantine Christians against the attacks by Saracen forces, in large measure as a way of extending Rome's influence over the rival Eastern empire. In a letter to Count William of Burgundy dated February 2, 1074, the pope asks for troops to be sent to Italy to confront the

Normans, a campaign he hoped would serve as a prelude to a march toward Constantinople: "We also hope that a further advantage may, perhaps, accrue from it: namely, that when the Normans are brought to peace we may cross to Constantinople to bring aid to Christians who are grievously afflicted by the most frequent ravagings of the Saracens and who are avidly imploring us to extend them our helping hand" (2002:51).

In a separate appeal dated March 1, 1074, to "all who are willing to defend the Christian faith," the pope reports that a visitor from "the lands beyond the seas" had informed him that "a race of pagans has strongly prevailed against the [Eastern] Christian empire and with pitiable cruelty has already almost up to the walls of the city of Constantinople laid waste and with tyrannical violence seized everything; it has slaughtered like cattle many thousand Christians" (2002:55). This statement was almost surely a belated reference to the decisive defeat of the Byzantines at Manzikert two and a half years earlier at the hands of the Muslim Seljuq Turks. A further sense of the pope's military ambitions may be seen in a letter to Henry IV of Germany three months later. Gregory here announces that he has already succeeded in rousing "Christians everywhere . . . that they should seek by defending the law to lay down their life for their brothers." He says that fifty thousand "men from Italy and from beyond the Alps" are ready to march at his command, and he asks Henry to safeguard the church during his planned absence (123).

According to traditional historical accounts, Pope Gregory's general commitment to the idea of holy war, his zeal in expanding papal prerogatives by force if necessary, his emphasis on indulgence for Christian holy warriors, his desire to extend Rome's influence eastward, and his denunciations of pagans and Saracens alike cast him in the role of father of the anti-Muslim Crusades launched two decades later by Pope Urban II (r. 1088–1099), his former aide and protégé. The literature on the origins of the Crusades is, of course, extensive. Writing in the eighteenth century, Edward Gibbon (1910:6, 35) sees Gregory as animating the entire enterprise against the Muslims. Steven Runciman's classic *History of the Crusades* praises the pope's "imaginative statesmanship" in laying out the new policy of holy warfare (1951–1954, 1:99). Recent studies take a somewhat more measured and nuanced view (Riley-Smith 1986; Asbridge 2004; Tyerman 2006).

Gregory VII, then, becomes a significant link in a logical—and chronological—chain of events culminating in Urban's call to the anti-Muslim Crusade in November 1095 in the French town of Clermont. Thus Jonathan Riley-Smith opens *The First Crusade and the Idea of Crusading* with the following summary of Western historical consensus: "There is general agreement that the [First] Crusade was the climacteric of a movement in which the eleventh-century Church reformers, locked in conflict with ecclesiastical and secular opponents, turned to the knights of the Christian West for assistance. Pope Urban's message to the faithful at Clermont is believed to have been the synthesis of ideas and practices already in existence—holy war, pilgrimage, the indulgence" (1986:1).

On the level of archaeological analysis, however, things look quite different, especially if, following Michel Foucault, we suspend the overriding search for historical unities. First of all, we can see from his official correspondence that Gregory VII is clearly casting the Saracens as a threat to individual Christians—even "many thousand Christians"—but never as an existential danger to Christendom as whole. Second, he is often confused about the nature of the enemy and assigns the adversary, whether described as "pagan" or "Saracen," no particular ideological content beyond a general hostility to Christian interests. For example, he accuses the "pagans" who now rule most of Spain of "ignorance of God" (1990:6–7), clearly not recognizing their direct religious and ethnic affinities with the Muslim Arabs and Berbers of North Africa, home to his interlocutor Anazir.

More confusion arises when we see how Gregory elsewhere distinguishes Saracens and pagans as he bemoans the levels to which the church has sunk of late: "Its ancient colors are changed, and it has become the laughingstock, not only of the Devil, but of Jews, Saracens, and pagans" (1990:195). He is also more than prepared to paint rivals closer to home—the Normans, the Lombards, or even the troublesome citizens of his adopted Rome—as far greater concerns than any pagan or Saracen and to blame Europe's secular rulers for fostering a culture of violence, instability, and war for profit:

> But now everyone, as if smitten with some horrible pestilence, is committing every kind of abominable crimes without any impelling cause. They regard neither divine nor human law; they make nothing of perjury, sacrilege, incest or mutual betrayal. Fellow citizens, relatives, even brothers, capture one another for the sake of plunder, extort all the property of their victims and leave them to end their lives in misery, a thing unknown anywhere else on earth. Pilgrims going to or returning from the shrines of the Apostles are captured, thrust into prison, tortured worse than by any pagan and often held for a ransom greater than all they have. (39–40)

Gregory VII's letter to the Muslim king of "*Mauretania sitifensis* in Africa" is clearly one of those minor statements—what Ian Hacking calls "the little dramas" (1986:28), discounted by conventional accounts—that when examined by the Foucauldian archaeologist help reveal society's deeper structures, thought, and culture. What is perhaps most striking about this particular letter is the way it suggests a basic level of theological and doctrinal understanding of Islam—amid some confusion over the identity of the Muslims—on the part of the pope and his circle, the likes of which would only rarely reappear until the modern era, if then.

As we have seen, Gregory grasps the nature of Muslim belief in the one God, whom he identifies with the deity worshipped by the Christians and, by extension, the Jews. In another passage of his letter to Anazir, he seeks to curry favor with the king by astutely reprising the Muslims' own view that their spiritual lineage goes back to Abraham: "For God knows that we love you sincerely to the honor of God, and that we desire your own welfare and honor both in the present life and in that which is to come; and with heart and lips we beseech that God himself will bring you, after the long continuance of this life, into the blessedness of the bosom of the most holy patriarch Abraham" (2002:205).

In *Madness and Civilization: A History of Insanity in the Age of Reason*, Foucault addresses the Western discourse of madness by seeking "that zero point in the course of madness at which madness is an undifferentiated experience. . . . To explore it we must renounce the convenience of terminal truths, and never let ourselves be guided by what we may know of madness" (1988:ix). Likewise, when we set aside "what we may know" of the Crusades, we can see that for Pope Gregory VII, Islam was not an enemy-in-waiting and certainly not a threat to the very survival of his church. Despite the pope's relatively acute sense of some of the basic tenets of Islam, for the broader society Islam remained much an "undifferentiated experience," with no particular ideological content and barely discernible among a sea of generalized threats to the world of Latin Christendom that included rebellious Normans, marauding Viking bands and other pagan barbarians of various stripes, mysterious Saracens, distant Persians, and, worst of all, the ever-present danger of Christian heretics closer to home.

Within just two decades, when Urban II publicly issued the call to the First Crusade, such a letter from a pope to a Muslim leader would, by the new rules of the new discursive formation, become unthinkable—un*writable* even—and would remain so for many, many centuries to come. This sequence, then, helps us to zero in on Foucault's "zero point," in this case that moment at which the idea of the Muslims becomes bound up irrevocably with the West's discourse of Islam.

The formation of this anti-Islam discourse, like the history of madness, is the history of difference imposed from without. Any internal attributes of Islam, its meaning for its adherents, its worldview, its religious dogmas, and so on—that is, Islam qua Islam—are irrelevant and can be safely ignored. Thus Foucault might just as easily be addressing the West's emergent narrative of Islam and the Muslims instead of madness when he writes in *The Order of Things*: "The history of madness would be the history of the Other—of that which, for a given culture, is at once anterior and foreign, therefore to be excluded (so as to exorcise the interior danger) but by being shut away (in order to reduce its otherness); whereas the history of the order imposed on things would be the history of the Same—of that which, for a given culture, is both dispersed and related, therefore to be distinguished by kinds and to be collected together into identities" (1994b:xxiv).

Later in this chapter, I explore the West's "Othering" of the Muslim: the ways the once familiar was first made alien and strange; the ways Islam was isolated and otherwise "shut away"; and the ways Western discourse imposed from without its own demand for orderly identities on this new-found Other. But first I must examine the Muslim's relatively uneventful sojourn through Western consciousness as "undifferentiated experience"—from Muhammad's revelations, beginning in 610 in accordance with Muslim tradition, until shortly before the first Christian mobs began setting off to "reclaim" the holy city of Jerusalem from the Muslims at the end of the eleventh century.

Abiding uncertainty over just who the Muslims might be and where they might fit within God's divine plan for humankind has left a curious trail through the annals of Latin Christendom. Chronicles, letters, and other documents from this early period serve up a hodge-podge of designations that reveal a mixture of roughly equal parts indifference and ignorance about the subject at hand. This state of affairs was not helped by the generally low level of learning in the West. The disorder that swept in with the barbarian invasions of the western Roman Empire from the fourth century had gravely weakened formal education and undermined the preservation and pursuit of knowledge. Science, philosophy, geography, medicine, and many other fields suffered badly. There were a few isolated outposts—chiefly monasteries in Ireland, northern England, Catalonia, and southern Italy—where the monks labored to keep some scraps of classical learning alive. Yet the results were meager.

When medieval Christians thought about the Muslims at all, they generally assigned them to one of two broad categories, either ethnic or biblical. The former designations included Arabs, Moors, Persians, and Turks. The latter drew from familiar scriptural history: Saracens, descendents of Abraham's wife, Sarah; Hagarenes, from the line of Sarah's insubordinate bondwoman Hagar; and Ishmaelites, from Hagar's son Ishmael. As is clear from Gregory VII's own correspondence, these terms were hopelessly confused in even the most acute medieval mind. Any cultural, sectarian, or ethnic distinctions among the Muslims were likewise lost on the Latins. In one account of his call to crusade, for example, Pope Urban II denounces, incorrectly as it happens, the infidel enemy in Jerusalem as "Persians." The modern English terms *Muslim* and *Islam* did not appear until the early seventeenth century (Tolan 2002:xv n.1).

This early confusion and uncertainty are understandable. The Christian West at the time faced far greater and more immediate dangers than any posed by the remote and distant Muslim empire, which had spread outward from Arabia with remarkable speed after the death of Muhammad in 632. Byzantine-controlled Damascus fell to the Arabs in 635, and the Persian capital Ctesiphon, just two years later. Alexandria surrendered in 641. Muslim forces reached India by 643 and Spain by 711. They decisively defeated the forces of the Tang dynasty for control of Turkic western China at the battle of Talas in 751. Despite these swift conquests, medieval Europe initially regarded the Arabs as little more than a nuisance, akin perhaps to the Vikings, the Magyars, and other barbarians who periodically raided the settled lands or harried local shipping. For centuries, they remained largely free of religious animus or other ideological content in the eyes of Christian Europe. Little or no inquiry was made into the nature of their society, its faith, or its practices.

Not even significant territorial gains on the Iberian Peninsula by a Muslim force of Arabs and Berbers in the early eighth century, followed by regular forays into France from their base in Narbonne or even a successful raid on Rome and the sack of St. Peter's Cathedral in 846, could disturb this general lack of concern on Europe's part. In his *History of the English Church and People*, the Venerable Bede recounts one such attack with equanimity, reinforced by his faith in God's protection and confidence in ultimate Christian victory: "In the year of our Lord 729, two comets appeared around the sun, striking terror into all who saw them," signs that Bede, who died six years after the comets appeared, took to mean that mankind was "menaced by evils" both day and night (1968:330). These evils were, he suggests, the arrival of the Arabs and unexplained troubles in his native Northumbria: "At this time, a swarm of Saracens ravaged Gaul with horrible slaughter; but after a brief interval in that country they paid the penalty of their wickedness" (330). A later Carolingian chronicle, the *Annales regni francorum* for 793, lists a Saracen foray into the south of France and a revolt by local Saxons as equally noteworthy, if not terribly troubling, events of that year (cited in Rodinson 1987:4).

Bede's relative equanimity on the subject of the Saracens was only partly a product of the enormous distance between his Northumbrian monastery and the heart of emerging Arab power to the east. It also reflected his own understanding of the state of affairs in the Holy Land, now under the control of the Muslim Arabs, as collected in his *De locis sanctis* (Wallace-Hadrill 1962:4–5) and later excerpted in his *History*. The former work itself was based on another text of the same title by the Irish monk Adamnan of Iona, and both rely on the personal account of a recent pilgrimage to Jerusalem by the *Galliarum episcopus* Arculf, tentatively dated to between 679 and 682, approximately forty-five years after the Muslim conquest (Meehan 1958:11).

Throughout his account, Arculf paints a rich portrait of Christian religious life and provides detailed descriptions of his visits to all of the important holy sites in Jerusalem, Bethlehem, and environs, unimpeded by their Muslim overlords. He praises the "king of the Saracens, Mavais by name"[1] for arbitrating a dispute over ownership of Christ's burial shroud by ruling against the Jews—still the traditional spiritual enemy in spite of the Muslims' rise to power—and in favor of the Christians (Adamnan of Iona 1958:55). Later, recounting life in the imperial city of Damascus, the visiting bishop notes: "The king of the Saracens holds the principality and has his court there, and in the same place a great church has been raised in honor of the holy John the Baptist. In this city . . . even the unbelieving Saracens have constructed a church" (99). For Arculf, a Christian bishop traveling alone through Muslim territory, the only real difficulty throughout his extensive journey appears to have been his efforts to return home, for he is reported shipwrecked "by a violent storm off the western coast of Britain," ultimately a fortuitous event that first brings him into contact with Adamnan, his future amanuensis (Bede 1968:294).

Greater proximity to the Muslims, however, did not necessarily spark greater Christian intellectual or theological interest in Islam or even enhance understanding of these newcomers. The same may also be said for the Byzantine Empire, which saw its territory and power beginning to erode in favor of the neighboring Muslims from the mid-seventh century. The Christian experience in both Muslim-ruled Spain and Orthodox Byzantium instead helped lay the groundwork for a later Western anti-Islam discourse that had very little to do with what Muslims actually said, did, or believed. What ultimately emerged was a rigid and long-lasting corpus of polemical and apologetic works, defensive by nature and not overly concerned with anything but ridiculing the Muslim faith and discouraging conversion on the part of Christians and cultural Arabization in general.

Muslim expansionism in Spain in the early eighth century—chiefly through exploitation of local divisions, well-timed threats, and astute diplomacy rather than by outright armed conquest—failed to promote anything like serious inquiry into this new phenomenon on the part of Latin Christendom. Nor did it prompt undue alarm on behalf of the large indigenous Christian population of Spain, which soon found numerous cultural, economic, and even political advantages to life under Muslim rule. Even church ideologues and polemicists were for the most part far more concerned with perceived Christian heresies and the threat of accretions from Jewish practice than with the presence of Islam on the peninsula (Wolf 1986:281–284). Rival Berber and Arab factions in southern Spain routinely found that their own Muslim faith did not prevent local Christian forces from seeking alliances with them into the eleventh century (Blanks 2002:259).

Early Christian chronicles from Spain identify the followers of Islam strictly as Arabs, Saracens, or Ishmaelites. Terms of religious identity, in particular those that would have defined the Muslims in direct opposition to Christians—such as *pagan*, *infidel*, and *gentile*—are markedly absent (Wolf 1986:283, 1990a:36–37). Two chronicles from post-invasion Spain, known as the *Arabic-Byzantine Chronicle of 741*—the oldest extant document of its type—and the *Mozarabic Chronicle of 754*, offer useful windows on the local elite's thinking about these newcomers to continental Europe, including some of the earliest references to the Prophet Muhammad. Yet both documents paint a thoroughly anodyne picture of the Arabs as Muslims, concentrating almost exclusively on political developments and generally steering clear of religious discussion.

An account in the *Chronicle of 754* of the Arab military successes against the Byzantines, for example, is cast in the language of political rebellion and liberation from the Orthodox "yoke" and is notably devoid of religious overtones, despite the defeat by the upstart Muslims of Emperor Heraclius, champion of the Eastern Christians: "The Saracens rebelled . . . and appropriated for themselves Syria, Arabia, and Mesopotamia, more through trickery than through the power of their leader Muhammad, and devastated the neighboring provinces, proceeding not so much by means of open attacks as by secret incursions. Thus by means of cunning and fraud rather than by power, they incited all of the frontier cities of the empire and finally rebelled openly, shaking the yoke from their necks" (Wolf 1990b:113–114).

The *Chronicle of 754* is elsewhere more than prepared to praise individual Muslim rulers of al-Andalus as well as the Arab caliphs in far-off Damascus and to condemn others according to their performance in office. We are told that Yazid, caliph from 680 to 683, was "the most pleasant son of Muʾawiya" and was "very well liked by all of the peoples of the land that were subject to his rule" (Wolf 1990b:123–124). A local governor, Uqbah ibn Hajjaj (r. 734–740), comes in for praise for his sensible financial management and modest style: "He very energetically enriched the fisc by various means and lived austerely on his private income. He condemned no one except according to the justice of his own law" (147). The same criteria are also applied to the former Visigoth Christian masters of Spain, with no sign that their respective religious affiliations played any part in the author's assessments (Wolf 1990a:37–38). Religious themes are likewise notably lacking from the chronicle's treatment of the defeat of Roderic, the last king of the Visigoths, by the advancing Arabs, an event that it ascribes to internal political rivalries among the Christians and to the king's own overweening ambition.

In a rare exception to the general view of the Muslims' prophet, the author of the *Chronicle of 741*, an unknown Christian who may have served in the local Arab administration, briefly describes Muhammad as "a prescient man" with prophetic powers: "Today the Saracens worship Muhammad with great honor and reverence as they affirm him to be an apostle of God and a prophet in all of their sacraments and scriptures" (quoted in Wolf 1990a:35–36). But the author's successor, who draws heavily on the earlier document for much of his core material, drops virtually all references to the Arabs' religious identity, makes only the briefest passing mention of Muhammad, and declines to portray the Franks' victory—later celebrated throughout Christendom—over the Arabs at Poitiers in anything like sectarian terms. In the *Chronicle of 754*, the victors are roundly praised as steadfast and brave, but the defeated Arabs are neither ridiculed nor vilified: "The northern peoples remained immobile like a wall, holding together like a glacier in the cold regions, and in the blink of an eye annihilated the Arabs with the sword" (Wolf 1990b:145).

This early chronicle tradition is notable in one other important respect—its readiness to create a space for the Arab rulers of Spain and the Arabs in general in the grand sweep of world history. The use of the chronicle style was well suited to recounting major events in the history of contact between Christians and Muslims, such as the defeat of Heraclius and the conquest of al-Andalus, without having to address the contentious and potentially explosive issue of religious identity and rivalry. But the simultaneous use of the chronologies of the Byzantine emperors, the biblical "date" of creation, the reigns of the Arab caliphs, the Spanish era, and the Muslim religious epoch, dating from Muhammad's flight to Medina in 622, in the *Chronicle of 754* suggests an inclusive world-view on the author's part—or at the very least a fatalistic recognition that the Muslims, like the other players in this drama, were here to stay (Collins 1989:60).

When early sectarian tensions did flare in al-Andalus, it was often the local Arabized Christians, the Mozarabs, who were most instrumental in defusing them. Faced with an attempt, beginning in 851, by militant Christian clerics and activists to foment a rebellion by seeking persecution and even death through a public campaign of blasphemy against the Prophet Muhammad, the assimilated Mozarabs of the imperial capital, Córdoba, effectively disowned this so-called martyrs' movement. For the Mozarabs, who were fluent in Arabic and intimately familiar with the faith and culture of the ruling Arabs and Berbers, this refusal to approve of the Christians' rebellion was not simply a calculated effort to maintain their comfortable places in a thriving society and economy. It was also an expression of their fundamental understanding of Islam. How could such a campaign, they demanded of the militants and their clerical supporters, be considered a legitimate act of martyrdom when the Muslims, like their Christian and Jewish subjects, worshipped the one true God and followed a law revealed by one of his prophets? After all, Muslim law treated Jews and Christians as fellow People of the Book, allowing them to retain their property and according them considerable autonomy in exchange for political loyalty and payment of an annual poll tax. In their eyes, this treatment made it acceptable to cooperate with the Muslims and delegitimized the so-called martyrs (Wolf 1986:290).

But the very real threat of assimilation and mass conversion to Islam throughout al-Andalus could not be ignored forever. It eventually provoked a significant backlash among the local clergy, which increasingly engaged in a concerted effort to attack any notion that Islam and Christianity could coexist in the same theological, social, and cultural space. They were also intent on rolling back the tide of Arabization, which had already made huge inroads into the language and culture of the local Christian population. In the ninth century, the bishop of Córdoba famously lamented the fact that Arabic was threatening to replace Latin, the language of the Catholic Church, in daily usage among his fellow Christians: "Hardly one can write a passable Latin letter to a friend, but innumerable are those who can express themselves in Arabic and can compose poetry in that language with greater art than the Arabs themselves" (quoted in R. Hillenbrand 1994:115).

The bishop's deepest fears were well founded: the common use of Arabic helped break Latin's stranglehold on Europe's literary speech, paving the way for the rise of the vernacular languages and the great works of "national" writers. Miguel de Cervantes Saavedra used the device of a lost text by an Arab author, Sidi ben Hamed, to frame his story of Don Quixote, and Dante's description of paradise and the inferno clearly reflect Islamic traditions then in European circulation.

Sacred history would play an important role in the imagination of the Spanish Christians, for it offered a familiar and easily defined space in which to orient the sudden arrival of the Muslims.[2] Polemicists reached back into the church's rich textual tradition to help imagine and frame the emerging new enemy. This tradition was none other than the rich trove of obscure references, terrifying predictions, and arresting imagery contained in the Book of Revelation at the end of the New Testament and in the older Book of Daniel.[3] Adoption of the Christian apocalyptic tradition both to understand and to define the Muslims and in particular the notion that Muhammad represented the Antichrist—or at the very least the false prophet of whom Jesus had earlier warned his followers—began to take root in Spain (Williams 1993).

Eulogius of Córdoba, who died in 859, may have been the first Latin author to label Muhammad the Antichrist, based on the Muslims' refusal to accept Christian teachings that Jesus, whose prophecy they openly acknowledge, was the son of God. Muhammad was also denounced as a false prophet and a heresiarch (Wolf 1986:291–293). Apocalyptic theologies and their application to the Muslims had already enjoyed a long history in the increasingly isolated Byzantine lands that directly bordered the dynamic and expansive empire of Islam (Meyendorff 1964; Kaegi 1969).

Despite the efforts over the centuries by church leaders and intellectuals to stamp out literal readings of the apocalyptic literature, this tradition would prove immensely useful as a central pillar of anti-Muslim propaganda. Among the most prominent critics of this tradition was Augustine, who sought to defuse any notion of coming apocalyptic crisis by presenting the Last Days as a slow, steady process of penitence and self-discipline in this life rather than a theological Big Bang at the end of time (E. Weber 1999:44–45). The apocalyptic tradition's hold on the popular imagination, however, was not diminished. Later events in the Near East helped cement the link between the still-mysterious world of Islam and the Latin Christians' worst terrors. In 1009, the Muslim caliph ordered the destruction of the Holy Sepulcher in Jerusalem, an act associated in the European imagination with the persecution of believers that foretold the End of Time. Coming so soon after the millennial symbolism surrounding the year 1000, this act appeared to tie the Muslim control of the Holy City to the coming of the apocalypse (Blanks 2002:259–261).

Rumors of tighter Muslim restrictions on access to the city by the steady flow of Christian pilgrims and even of physical harassment directed at religious travelers only exacerbated these sentiments. Some said that Peter the Hermit, one of the populist rabble-rousers who helped lead the People's Crusade to its disastrous end outside Constantinople in 1096, was ill treated by the city's Muslim overlords on an earlier pilgrimage to the Holy Land. Anna Comnena, daughter of the Byzantine emperor Alexius, reports that Peter suffered "many things at the hands of the Turks and Saracens" before struggling back to Europe (1928:248). In another version of Peter's story, Jesus comes to Peter in a dream and directs him to warn Christian Europe of Muslim perfidy (Blake and Morris 1985).

By tapping into this potent apocalyptic tradition, the emerging anti-Islam narrative significantly increased the odds of its own long-term survival, a phenomenon that Richard Fenn sees very much at play in our own age: "Modernity intensifies the hatreds that separate the East from the West, but it is apocalyptic beliefs that solidify the enmity between the Islamic and Christian worlds into passions that are enduring, intractable, and above all hell-bent on a bloody finale" (2006:28).

At the other end of the Christian world, in the eastern lands of Byzantium, the coming of the "godless" Arabs, particularly their conquest of Jerusalem and the surrounding Holy Land, was also cast in terms of sacred history: as a scourge from heaven that would ultimately be turned back by renewed Christian rectitude. Sophronius, patriarch of Jerusalem, bemoans the recent loss of Bethlehem in his Christmas sermon of 654, and he attributes the defeat to divine retribution for the sins of his fellow believers. Strikingly, Sophronius makes no mention of the religious faith of the invaders or of their spiritual leader, Muhammad (Kaegi 1969:139–140). Other Eastern theologians preferred to see the crisis strictly in terms of their own internal doctrinal disputes, mostly over the nature of Christ, and members of the persecuted Nestorian and Monophysite communities, now living in formerly Byzantine lands, found a new freedom of worship under the Muslims that had been sorely lacking under the heavy hand of orthodoxy enforced from Constantinople.

Despite their newfound intimacy with the Arabs and the enormity of the long-term threat to Byzantine theological and imperial interests, Orthodox thinkers remained confident that the danger was only a fleeting one, and they made no real attempt to inquire about the religious beliefs of their Muslim rivals. Those in a position to know better, such as the bureaucrat-turned-monk John of Damascus, either were unable to grasp fully the significance of what they had learned or preferred to keep such knowledge to themselves. According to traditional accounts, John came from a family with many years of high-level administrative service to the Muslim court in Damascus, and his De haeresibus betrays a certain intimacy with some aspects of Muslim belief, chiefly Islam's rejection of Christ's divinity and of his suffering on the Cross. Yet he commingles these aspects with accusations of idol worship at the Ka'ba and infection with the Arian heresy that so concerned the orthodox Christian thinkers of his day. In fact, John finds a place for Islam among the Christian heresies.[4]

The Saracens, John writes, were idolaters until the days of Heraclius, who ruled Byzantium from 610 to 641: "From that time on a false prophet appeared among them, surnamed Mameth [Muhammad] who, having casually been exposed to the Old and New Testament and supposedly encountered an Arian monk, formed a heresy of his own" (1972:133). John, like many other Orthodox writers, then links the pre-Islamic practice of idolatry among the Arabs to Islam itself, with the Ka'ba in Mecca said to be the venue for continued worship of a stone image of Aphrodite: "They venerated the morning star and Aphrodite, whom they called 'Habar' in their language, which means 'great'" (133). This description is clearly a jumbled reference to the common Arabic phrase "Allahu akbar," or "God is most great," which Muslims use frequently and in many different contexts. Nevertheless, John refrains from presenting the Muslims in eschatological terms or linking their appearance to the existing apocalyptic traditions. Moreover, his accusation that Muhammad was a "forerunner of the Antichrist" does not differ in form or substance from the accusations that he and his fellow Orthodox thinkers regularly directed against those more traditional heresiarchs, the Nestorians (Sahas 1972:69; Tolan 2002:55).

As in Spain, the Orthodox clergy were concerned primarily with quashing any notion of commonality between Islam and Christianity rather than with engaging their rivals in scholarly, theological disputation. Thus they repeatedly asserted that Muslims were idol worshippers, which their own personal experience and knowledge over the centuries could hardly have confirmed. As late as 1178, the Byzantine emperor Manuel I ran afoul of the religious hierarchy when he ordered that an official rite for Muslims converting to Christianity no longer include an anathema against "the God of Muhammad," an implicit imperial recognition that the two faiths worshipped the same divinity. The emperor won a narrow victory, but only after church leaders again asserted that the Muslim God was in fact an idol "of hammer-beaten metal" (quoted in Meyendorff 1964:124–125). However, for Latin Christendom as a whole, such controversies brewing in far-off Byzantium or cut-off Spain were very much on the fringes of both sacred and secular geography, and Islam remained largely an "undifferentiated experience," one that would take on meaningful shape and definition only with the advent of Christian holy war and the Crusaders' march on Jerusalem.

Islam, then, was virtually a blank canvas for Latin Christendom of the late eleventh century. The two best sources of reliable intelligence on the Muslims, the Christian elites of al-Andalus and Byzantium, had been unable to exploit their privileged positions of proximity to the Arabs and to offer up anything of real value on Islam or the Muslim peoples. Their need to combat conversion or assimilation as well as other domestic pressures instead produced strong polemical and apologetic traditions. Besides these factors, the experience of these communities on the fringes of Christian European consciousness was too remote to make much immediate impact. Instead, they would act as deep reservoirs of pejorative imagery, polemical rhetoric, and apologetic strategies around which the West's dominant Islam discourse would later coalesce.

For now, the imperatives of holy war demanded an easily grasped and emotionally compelling enemy worthy of a grand cause and the enormous mobilization of men, money, and matériel such a campaign would entail. In the relatively brief period between Pope Gregory VII's sympathetic correspondence with the Muslim "King Anazir" in 1076 and the launch and prosecution, beginning just two decades later, of the First and Second Crusades, the essential "Othering" of the Muslim was virtually complete. No longer "undifferentiated experience," Islam and the Muslims now took on a specific ideological role as the ultimate enemy of Christendom.

This new discursive formation, what I have identified as the anti-Islam discourse, can clearly be seen taking shape in the episodic accounts of Pope Urban II's public call to crusade, delivered in late 1095 to the church council in Clermont. There are no surviving copies of the pope's text, but chroniclers recounted his declaration of holy war numerous times over the ensuing decades, and these tellings and retellings—along with their historical, social, and theological accretions—present us with the steady unfolding of the new anti-Islam discourse as it begins to take on the recognizable features of its final, mature stage.

This lack of a verbatim text is no real obstacle. In fact, it is immaterial, and it may even be a distinct advantage, for the anti-Islam discourse that Pope Urban ushered in remains visible to the archaeologist sifting through the discursive deposits left behind in the chronicles of Fulcher of Chartres (1941, 1970); the account of Robert the Monk (2005), also known as Robert of Rheims; the anonymous *Gesta francorum et aliorum Hierosolymytanorum* (1945, 1962), the earliest of the group and an extremely popular source for later writers; versions by Balderic, archbishop of Dol, and by Guibert, abbot of Nogent; as well as the work of their many successors, imitators, and commentators.

Or as cultural historian Norman Daniel, a pioneering student of Western images of Islam, remarks in a somewhat different context in his analysis of Crusades propaganda:

> In Urban's preaching we find new notions, more especially new sentiments, that correspond to ideas immediately and henceforth in

general use. From this point of view it matters more what Urban was understood to have said than what he actually did say. We shall say little to distinguish the propagandist from the consumer of propaganda, because the one is usually, and simultaneously, the other. We are concerned only to identify the main lines of persuasion and self-persuasion which thenceforward men of all types accepted as defining their official motivation. (1989:40)

None of the surviving accounts of Pope Urban's declaration of holy war was recorded at the time of the Council of Clermont or in the immediate days thereafter. In fact, none predates the launch of the First Crusade in 1096 or even the successful Christian siege of Jerusalem in July 1099. The *Gesta francorum et aliorum Hierosolymytanorum*, written by a knight traveling with Bohemond of Taranto, one of the leading Crusades commanders, dates from around 1100. Robert the Monk's account may have been written as much as a decade after that. Thus all are shaped either directly or indirectly by the experience of religious war and informed to varying degrees by the momentous events precipitated by the pope's famous speech some years earlier.

This gap between the speech at Clermont and the chronicles that recount it, of course, provides these and other writers with the rare chance to justify *in advance* the violent conduct of the subsequent campaign, which saw the massacre of Jews in central and eastern Europe, the rampant killing of unfamiliar Arab Christians in the Near East, as well as the deaths of many Muslims, including unarmed civilians, at the hands of the Crusaders. It also permits the presentation of the substantial territorial gains initially made by the Latin forces as the liberation of holy sites and the struggle against spiritual pollution by the unclean pagans. The epic *Chanson d'Antioche*, for example, relates how Christ on the Cross predicted the coming of the Crusaders one thousand years later: "My friends, the people are not yet born who will avenge my death with their steel lances.... They will regain my land and free my country" (1998:305).

An examination of the multiple chronicles as the collective product of a new discursive formation reveals a number of interrelated themes and ideas that, taken together, present for the first time in Latin Christendom the singular identity of the Muslim as Other. Gone is the fellow worshipper of the same God, "albeit in a different way," and the recipient of good wishes for an eventual return to the "bosom of the most holy patriarch Abraham," seen in the correspondence of Gregory VII. In his place now is the "godless" defiler of Christian sacred precincts, tormentor and torturer of true believers, idol worshipper, and usurper of lands rightfully belonging to Latin Christendom. In other words, the Muslim is no longer undifferentiated experience. Instead, he is assigned distinct characteristics that make him the opposite of all that is "Christian" and a legitimate target of holy war, whose death or destruction carries with it promises of the remission of sins for those willing to take up the Cross.

The earliest of these texts, the *Gesta francorum*, devotes little space to Urban's speech at Clermont, comprising in all just several paragraphs; the bulk of the work is a firsthand narrative of the military campaign itself, ending with the conquest of Jerusalem in July 1099 and the follow-up victory at Ascalon one month later. Throughout the narrative, the author does not hesitate to present the horrors of warfare. Nor does he cover up the misdeeds of his fellow Christians, including incidents of cannibalism in the Syrian town of Marra and the slicing open of Muslim corpses in a frenzied search for hidden gold coins: "So they cut up the corpses, because bezants were to be found concealed in their stomachs. Others cut their flesh up into morsels and had them cooked for eating" (*Gesta francorum* 1945:77).

Even after victory in Jerusalem and a celebratory mass at the Holy Sepulcher, the bloodshed continued with the slaughter of the defeated Muslims on the Temple Mount, where they had been promised protection by the commander of the Crusader forces: "The following morning our people climbed the roof of the Temple [of Solomon], attacked the Saracens, men and women and decapitated them with drawn swords. Some threw themselves from the top of the Temple. . . . No one has ever heard and no one has ever seen such a slaughter of the pagan people; pyres, like [hay] stacks, were set up, and nobody, save God alone, knows their number" (*Gesta francorum* 1945:88).

The *Gesta francorum* casts Urban's appeal exclusively in terms of Christian redemption and Christian duty: "Whoever wishes to save his soul should not hesitate humbly to take up the way of the Lord, and if he lacks sufficient money, divine mercy will give him enough. . . . Brethren, we ought to endure much suffering for the name of Christ—misery, poverty, nakedness, persecution, want, illness, hunger, thirst, and other [ills] of this kind" (1962:xlixx).

The *Gesta francorum* contains no suggestion that the campaign is a life-and-death struggle against an infidel or a heretical enemy. In fact, it does not yet clearly identify or define the Muslim enemy. This state of affairs begins to change with the next account of Urban's address at Clermont, *A History of the Expedition to Jerusalem* (1970) by the French churchman Fulcher of Chartres. It is not clear exactly when Fulcher wrote the first edition of his history, although internal textual evidence and its periodic reliance on the *Gesta* and another similar works as primary sources suggest that he began in late 1101 or early 1102 and completed it around 1106 (Ryan 1970:18–21).

In his account of the Council of Clermont, Fulcher tells us that the pope identified the enemy simply as "the Turks, a Persian people" who have "killed or captured many people, have destroyed churches, and have devastated the Kingdom of God." Urban then warns his audience that the Turks are intent on conquering "God's faithful people much more extensively" if they are not held in check. And he reminds his listeners of their religious duty to stand up to such a menace: "Oh what a disgrace if a race so despicable, degenerate, and enslaved by demons should thus overcome a people endowed with faith in Almighty God and resplendent in the name of Christ! Oh what reproaches will be charged against you by the Lord Himself if you have not helped those who are counted like yourselves of the Christian faith!" (Fulcher of Chartres 1970:66).

Yet Fulcher presents the call to crusade as only one part—and by no means the central part—of the matters before the Council of Clermont. Rather, the pope's overriding message is, according to Fulcher's account, one of urgent need for the radical reform of society and the church, and Fulcher relegates the pope's appeal to crusade to the third chapter of his opening book I. In the preceding chapters, we instead see the pope castigating the Christians for their violent behavior toward one another, denouncing the moral degeneracy of daily life as a whole, and upbraiding the clergy for its abject failure to lead by example.

As an interesting instance of the broader discourse at work today, it is worth pointing out that Fulcher's presentation prompts his modern English translator, Frances Rita Ryan, to note with "surprise" that the call to crusade does not feature more prominently in the account of Clermont: "Rather surprisingly, we learn that most of the business seems to have dealt with decrees proposed by Pope Urban as the leader of the Cluny reform movement in the Church. Not until the third chapter does Fulcher set forth the call for the First Crusade and its enthusiastic reception" (1970:25).

Any reticence on the part of the pope—or, more precisely, on the part of the Latin propagandists who popularized his speech at Clermont and the First Crusade in general—to identify the Muslim masters of the Holy Land with all that is evil in the world or to present a catalog of their crimes against innocent Christians is wholly gone by the time Robert the Monk puts pen to parchment, around 1107 or later. This account corresponds to a renewed, if brief, upsurge in enthusiasm in Europe, particularly in Robert's native France, for a fresh Crusade as well as to a period of postwar reflection in which the full implications of the first campaign against the Muslims were coming more sharply into focus. In fact, Robert was commissioned by his abbot to produce his *Historia Iherosolimitana*, essentially a redaction and rewriting of the *Gesta francorum* with the incorporation of some additional information, to whip up support for a new military expedition (Sweetenham 2005b:6). Other works on the First Crusade began to appear around the same time, with the same goals in mind.

That "vile race" of Turks or Persians in Fulcher of Chartres's earlier account is now an enemy completely outside the pale, ritually unclean and utterly cut off from God himself. Thus Robert the Monk, who in *Historia Iherosolimitana* reports that he personally attended the Council of Clermont but wrote of it many years later, presents Pope Urban as juxtaposing Robert's fellow Franks, "men chosen and beloved of God," against the "race of Persians," "a foreign people and people rejected by God" (2005:79). In Robert's hands, the pope then produces a laundry list of terrible crimes suffered by Christians at the hands of the Muslims—one torture is markedly reminiscent of the *Gesta's* earlier account of Christians slitting open Saracens to search for gold coins that they may have swallowed—and demands that the Latin princes set aside their internal quarrels and march to the Holy Land:

> They throw down the altars after soiling them with their own filth, circumcise Christians, and pour the resulting blood either on the altars or into the baptismal vessels. When they feel like inflicting truly painful death on some they pierce their navels, pull out the end of their intestines, tie them to a pole and whip them around it until, all their bowels pulled out, they fall lifeless to the ground. They shoot arrows at others tied to stakes; others again they attack having stretched out their necks, unsheathing their swords to see if they can mange to hack off their heads with one blow. And what can I say about the appalling treatment of women, which is better to pass over in silence than to spell out in detail? . . . [L]et the Holy Sepulcher of our Lord the Redeemer move you—in the power as it is of foul races—and the holy places now abused and sacrilegiously defiled by their filthy practices. (80)

It is only after this list of Muslim atrocities is laid out that the pope begins to take up his domestic-reform agenda with an appeal for civil peace and moral conduct among the Christians themselves, an aspect that is emphasized from the start in the older *Gesta francorum*. But even here Robert the Monk has Urban return immediately to the language of war and conquest; the pope praises the Franks' martial prowess and reminds them that Jerusalem is a land "more fruitful than any other, almost another Earthly Paradise" (2005:81) in contrast to the hardscrabble life and poor prospects that many face here at home. "When Pope Urban had eloquently spoken these words and many other things of the same kind, all present were so moved that they untied as one and shouted, 'God wills it, God wills it' " (81).

Reading the *Gesta francorum* alongside its successor texts, especially Robert the Monk's *Historia Iherosolimitana*, brings the West's emerging discursive formation of Islam into sharp relief. The *Gesta* is foremost a chronicle of a violent and arduous military campaign, written by a military man, and it bears witness to the atrocities of war committed by both sides: "You could not find stronger or braver or more skilful soldiers" (1962:21). The *Gesta* has little time for theological speculation, for the religious implications of the First Crusade, for the guiding hand of the papal court, or for the role of the Crusaders as religious pilgrims rather than as warriors. Its narrative is not one of Christian sacred history running its course or of the recovery of "Christian" territory, but rather of the age-old saga of men at war.

The *Historia Iherosolimitana*, by contrast, places the theological narrative front and center. Thus Robert the Monk lovingly locates Pope Urban's address at the Council of Clermont in what he sees as its rightful place as the dramatic starting point of the entire venture and the glory it would bring with the conquest of Jerusalem. The religious aspects of crusading now take clear priority over purely military ones, and the campaign's central goals— conquering the "holy" land and cleansing hallowed sites of the pagan Saracens' "unclean" presence—are linked firmly to notions of sacred history and religious competition (Sweetenham 2005a:21–22).

For Robert the Monk, the Muslims were not a worthy enemy to be admired in any way but more like animals to be slaughtered and perhaps pitied for finding themselves on the wrong side of God. "That was how the Turks were gloriously defeated by the Franks; their jabbering voices, the grinding of their teeth and noise of their daily insults were no longer heard," he writes of one Christian victory outside the walls of Antioch in early 1098. "The

Turks look on from the high walls and lofty towers, weeping bitterly, tearing their cheeks and pulling out their hair. They start to beg the help of Mahommed, their master; but Mahommed could not bring back those Christ had destroyed through his soldiers" (2005:134–135).

—❦○

Robert's redaction of the *Gesta francorum*, like his fellow chroniclers' revisionist works in the early twelfth century, sealed the Othering of the Muslim among the political, intellectual, and religious elite of Latin Christendom. The followers of Islam were now irretrievably outside the bounds of civilized society, reduced in status to little more than animals. They were almost universally depicted as idolaters and thus cut off from any possibility that they worshipped the same God as the Christians. Any common ground—the begrudging respect of one soldier for another seen in the *Gesta*, for example, or the different manner of approaching the same deity that Gregory VII refers to—was now lost. In such an atmosphere, it was unthinkable to consult Muslims about their own practices or beliefs.

The Muslims' newfound alterity had a number of important social consequences. As Foucault writes of the emerging discourse of madness in *The Order of Things*, Islam was now something to be excluded "so as to exorcise the interior danger" that might be done to the Christian West and to be shut away "in order to reduce its otherness" (1994b:xxiv). Christendom responded to increasing contacts between Muslim and Christian, particularly as a result of the expanding Christian conquest of al-Andalus, with ever tighter restrictions on Muslim social and religious life—a process that concluded with the ultimate act of isolation and exclusion: the wholesale expulsion of the Muslims from the Iberian Peninsula.[5]

In 1179, the Third Lateran Council barred Muslims from holding Christian slaves, and the Fourth Council of 1215 imposed a range of new measures designed to safeguard the Christians' physical—especially sexual—purity and spiritual integrity. These measures included regulations to require Muslims to dress in distinctive clothing so there could be no accidental "mixing" of the two communities, to banish Muslims from the public space during Holy Week, and to bar Muslims from holding positions of authority over Christians (Tolan 2002:189–198). In the mid-thirteenth century, King Alfonso X of Castile prepared an idealized legal code, which he never enforced, that envisioned the almost complete separation of the Muslim and Christian communities under his rule. Here, again, the emphasis was on the prevention of religious contamination—conversion to Islam was banned, but so was any act of Muslim worship within the sight of Christians—and of physical contamination in the form of sexual relations (Tolan 2002:189–190). Alfonso X's attempt at radical social engineering, an idealized apartheid aimed at some of his most educated and productive subjects, is all the more notable given his historical reputation as a patron of Islamic arts and sciences.

These moves toward isolation and exclusion of the Muslims and the accompanying ignorance of things Muslim on the part of the West created the necessary conditions for the rise of a new social actor, whose role has remained virtually intact to this day. This actor is, of course, the Islam expert, the predominant carrier of the idea of Islam and thus the central social figure in the anti-Islam discourse. In its ideal type, the Islam expert acts as the trusted intermediary between the familiar world of Us and the disquieting world of Them. This expert, unwittingly subject to the rules of the dominant discursive formation, tells us what to think and what *not* to think about Islam; in the absence of any real countervailing information, the expert's word generally goes unchallenged and is accepted at face value. There is ultimately little alternative.

In the earliest centuries of the anti-Islam discourse, this role was commonly filled from among the ranks of the educated Christian clerical class. Later eras saw the rise of the humanist theoreticians of the Renaissance; the nineteenth-century armies of philologists, anthropologists, and literary critics who created the Orientalist underpinnings for Western colonial domination of the Muslim world; and today's array of journalists, commentators, pundits, and political leaders.

The early prototype of the Islam expert is the curious figure of Petrus Alfonsi, a Jewish convert to Christianity whose experience of life among the Muslims in his native Spain provides material for a crucial chapter in his *Dialogue Against the Jews* (2006), otherwise devoted to a polemic against his former coreligionists. Petrus was born in Huesca, a small border city under Muslim control that was seized by Christians in 1097. In keeping with the traditions of his relatively prosperous Jewish community, he received a solid education that included Arabic and Hebrew, Jewish religious studies, as well as mathematics, astronomy, and medicine. He converted to Christianity in 1106 (Resnick 2006:11).

Dialogue Against the Jews, completed around 1109 and presented in the form of an exchange between the author as both a Jew, under the name of "Moses," and a Christian convert named "Petrus," devotes one of its twelve chapters to the "faith of the Saracens." From its opening lines, this fifth chapter establishes Petrus Alfonsi's credentials as an expert on the Muslims, one able to present and explain the faith to Latin Christendom: "I wonder why," asks Moses, "when you abandoned your paternal faith, you chose the faith of the Christians rather than the faith of the Saracens? . . . For you were always, as I said, associated with them and you were raised among them; you read [their] books, and you understand the language" (Petrus Alfonsi 2006:146). Moses then goes on to offer a generally accurate account of many of the central teachings and practices of the Muslims, before repeating the same query: "Since from childhood, no less, you have known that these things and many others, which would take too long to enumerate, were written and held in the greatest veneration by the entire race of Saracens, then why have you followed the Christian rather than the Muslim religion?" (150).

In response, Petrus lays out his central case against Islam: what appears on the surface to be a fully rational "law" is in fact a cover for idol worship, falsehood and deceit, sexual depravity, Muhammad's boundless personal ambition, and forced conversion at the point of the sword. Other elements of Muslim practice, he argues, are mere devices to set Islam apart artificially from the faith of the Christians and Jews. These devices include the banning of wine and the five daily prayers, the latter of which Petrus argues is simply a compromise between the three prayers of the Jews and the seven codified for Christians by the Rule of St. Benedict.

In its attack on Islam, the *Dialogue Against the Jews* takes particular aim at the person of Muhammad, and it dismisses Moses's suggestion that converting to Islam would have allowed Petrus to "better enjoy the felicity of the present life" as well as that of the afterlife. "One thing," Petrus responds tartly, "remains uncertain to you, I reckon: how useless I will judge that doctrine that they call Muhammad's. When, though, you have heard this life and character summarized in my narration, then you will easily be able to discern whether I do or do not know what is true about him" (2006:150–151).

According to Petrus, Muhammad's rise to power and influence was not divinely inspired; he performed no miracles and was not a true prophet, and thus it would not be "appropriate" to follow his law. Instead, Petrus presents Muhammad's success as the product of calculated ambition, fueled by his own inordinate sexual appetites and aided by a Christian heretic and two renegade Jewish advisers, who helped manufacture a religious message designed to win over followers: "And these three mixed together the law of Muhammad, each one according to his own heresy, and showed him how to say such things on God's behalf which both heretical Jews and the heretical Christians who were in Arabia believed to be true; whereas those who were unwilling to believe of their own free will nevertheless were forced to believe for fear of the sword. But we do not know of any other prophecy of his nor any miracles, as we heard about Moses, Joshua, Samuel, Elijah, and Elisha who, we read, performed many miracles" (2006:152).

A true prophet would not only perform miracles and correctly foretell the coming of momentous events but also lead a life of exemplary probity. None of this, says Petrus, applies to the leader of the Muslims, who could not contain his own sexual desires and who used his religious teachings, such as the permissibility of polygamy, to gratify them and those of his male followers: "Muhammad loved women a great deal and was too much the voluptuary, and, just as he claimed, the power of the lust of forty men dwelled in him. And also, especially because the Arabs were very dissolute, he pandered to their desire, so they would believe" (2006:161).

Nor could Muhammad succeed without the use of force, in contradiction to the revelations recorded in the Qur'an: "That Muhammad commanded [them] to despoil, capture, and slay the adversaries of God until they decided to believe or pay tribute, is not among the acts of God, nor did any of the prophets command that anyone be forced to believe, but he commanded this himself out of a desire for money, in order to destroy his enemies" (Petrus Alfonsi 2006:159). Petrus then presents a series of quotations from the Qur'an opposing the use of force, including the well-known injunction—cited in a completely different context by Pope Benedict XVI almost one thousand years later—against "compulsion in religion" (2:256). "Why, then, did he order [them] to despoil, capture, and coerce the nations to believe by force, and why does he claim that all these are the paths of God? Tell me, Moses, why do you order me to believe a law which contradicts itself?" (Petrus Alfonsi 2006:160).

In the *Dialogue Against the Jews*, we can see the basic outlines of the anti-Islam discourse in its adult form, incorporating elements from the established polemical tradition cultivated in Petrus's native Spain. It raises the specter of past idol worship and decadence among the Arabs: "A purity resulting from the ablution of the members, however, was important to the worshipers of the planet Venus, who, wanting to pray to her, prepared themselves as if they were women, coloring [their] mouths and eyes" (Petrus Alfonsi 2006:156). It also locates Islam among the Christian heresies bedeviling church orthodoxy, in this case as the work of the Jacobites.[6] Muhammad is presented as a deceiver, a false prophet even, driven by sexual fantasies and a lust for power and violence. And the very essence of the religion is now grounded in force and coercion, dressed in an outward message of peace and conciliation.

Yet *Dialogue Against the Jews* does more than establish the central tenets of the anti-Islam discourse; it reveals the scope, power, and operation of the discursive formation itself. Easily overlooked in the text's polemical excess is the dispassionate and generally straightforward account of many of the Muslims' core beliefs and practices that opens the work's discussion of Islam. They include belief in the One God and Muhammad as his prophet, the five daily prayers, the fast of Ramadan, and the hajj pilgrimage. Also noted, albeit in cursory fashion, are the Muslim dietary laws; legal procedures pertaining to marriage, property, and related matters; as well as the ban on the consumption of wine. In other words, the author of this seminal anti-Islam text is far from ignorant of the ways of the Muslims. After all, he has lived among them for years and knows their habits, customs, and sacred language. Yet virtually none of this knowledge informs the central narrative.

As we shall see with succeeding generations of Islam experts, facts on the ground that do not accord with the discourse are not treated as facts at all; they may be ignored, distorted, or never truly mastered in the first place. This trend becomes all the more dominant as the works of Islam experts gradually give rise to Islam as a "discipline." In his "Discourse on Language," Foucault (1972b:224) points out that for a fact even to be considered, it must meet the criterion of the dominant discourse. Moses's detailed account of Muslim belief in *Discourse Against the Jews*, then, is not "within the true" and thus can be safely ignored, whereas Petrus's polemic meets the requirements of the anti-Islam discourse and thus may be accepted, retained, and preserved.

Dialogue Against the Jews placed the imprimatur of the leading Western expert, in this case an Arabic-speaking former Jew from once-Muslim Spain, on the anti-Islam discourse that first emerged with the advent of the Crusades. An examination of these texts allows us not only to track the formation and operation of this discursive formation, but also to apply the third element of our analytical framework by returning to the question posed at the outset: Cui bono?

In the case of Robert the Monk, this application is a relatively simple matter: his abbot directed him to rework the standard account of the First Crusade, the *Gesta francorum*, and to invest it with enthusiasm for a renewed military campaign against the Muslims. Robert and his fellow authors of the immediate post-Crusade period also had to account for the atrocities against the Jews, Eastern Christians, and defeated Saracens at the hands of the Christian forces and to justify—in advance—the destruction or seizure of land and property in a far-off realm. In their hands, Pope Urban II's message of the pressing need for social, religious, and political reform inside Latin Christendom gets pushed to the background, and the speech at the Council of Clermont becomes instead an urgent appeal for holy war against the polluting presence of the animal-like Muslims in lands now deemed to be Christian by right.

For his part, Petrus Alfonsi casts his lot with the increasingly dominant forces of Christendom by renouncing his Jewish faith under the sponsorship of no less than the bishop of Huesca and the king of Aragon, from whom he took his new Christian name. Petrus tells us that he was baptized in 1106 by Bishop Stephen and received "at the sacred font" by his godfather, Alfonso I, "the glorious emperor of Spain" (2006:40). He was soon celebrated not only as an expert on things Muslim, but also as an adept of Arab science, which dwarfed the low level of contemporary European learning.

Petrus goes out of his way to deny any connection between rising Christian power and his own decision to convert: "[Some have] accused me of vainglory and falsely claimed that I had done this for worldly honor, because I perceived that the Christians' nation dominated all others" (2006:41). However, it is worth noting that his own personal advancement and the advancement of the anti-Islamic discourse that so informs *Dialogue Against the Jews* went hand in hand. Sometime after completing his *Dialogue*, Petrus moved to England and later to France, and in both locales his level of scientific learning, unremarkable in the Arabic cultural milieu of his homeland, astounded his new hosts and reinforced his fame and influence. For a time, he attached himself to a small circle of scholar-monks in England's West Country who were interested in the latest ideas in astronomy and mathematics beginning to trickle in from the Arab world, and he may have served as court physician to King Henry I.

Petrus's wanderings and his storied scientific achievements helped establish the popularity of the *Dialogue Against the Jews* in different parts of

Christian Europe and made him the leading source of information on Islam (Southern 1962:35n.2; Kedar 1984:92; Tolan 2002:154). Today the *Dialogue* is extant in an impressive sixty-three manuscripts and another sixteen adaptations. An abbreviated version incorporated into a popular work of the mid-thirteenth century, the *Speculum historiale* of Vincent de Beauvais, survives in another two hundred copies. At times, only the chapter on Islam was transcribed (Tolan 2002:154), which underscores the centrality of the anti-Muslim discourse for Latin Christendom as opposed to the older but less pressing "problem" of the Jews.

Among Petrus Alfonsi's most important and influential readers was Peter the Venerable, the abbot of Cluny and head of a vast religious empire that at its height comprised more than six hundred monasteries and thousands of monks (Kritzeck 1964:3). In 1142 during a visit to Spain, Peter paid a team of scholars, who held out for an exorbitant fee, to translate the Qur'an and several other religious texts from Arabic into Latin as raw material for his own polemical works, the *Summa totius haeresis Saracenorum* and the *Contra sectam sine haeresim Saracenorum*, the latter an apparent attempt to refute the teachings of Islam and to entice Muslims to convert to Christianity.

Peter the Venerable's conclusions are all in keeping with the anti-Islam discourse, which by this time was already well established. Like many of his contemporaries, he casts Muhammad as a sex-mad fraud: "In order that he could more easily attract to himself the carnal minds of men, he loosed the reins on gluttony and impurity, and he himself having at the same time 18 wives, including the wives of many others, committing adultery as if by divine command, he added to himself a larger number of damned ones by his example, as it were, as a prophet," Peter recounts in the *Summa totius haeresis Saracenorum* (quoted in Kritzeck 1964:137). Elsewhere, Peter puzzles over whether the Muslims were heretics or brute pagans before concluding halfheartedly that they should probably be counted among the former, given their veneration of Jesus as a great prophet (Kritzeck 1964:137–144).

But Peter the Venerable has bequeathed us more than just a useful retelling of the anti-Islam narrative, dressed up in the scholarly tradition of textual analysis and presented in the grand style of the church fathers. He has revealed one of the unseen aspects of the anti-Islam discourse: its formation took place long before the West had any meaningful knowledge of Islam or real interaction with Muslims. Writing as the church was preparing to launch the Second Crusade, Peter cannot help wondering aloud why the military campaign against the Muslims might not, instead of just killing them, be preceded or at least accompanied by a serious attempt to convert these heretics to the true faith. It is in this context that Peter makes his fateful confession: "A flame was enkindled in my meditation. I was indignant that the Latins did not know the cause of such perdition, and by reason of that ignorance could not be moved to put up any resistance; for there was no one who replied [to it] because there was no one who knew [about it]" (quoted in Kritzeck 1956:180).

The radical social and religious reforms backed by Pope Urban II and his circle culminated in the call to crusade at Clermont in November 1095 and the ensuing preparations for the invasion of the Holy Land, then under Muslim control. Here is the "zero point" of the West's discourse of Islam, and it marks a break with an earlier time when the Muslims' place in the European imagination and consciousness was still largely vague and unformed. The ambitious mobilization of Christian Europe, demanded by wartime exigencies of the First Crusade and by the church's broader social and political needs, required an identifiable and distinct enemy. From now on, the Muslim Other would be imbued with qualities in direct opposition to Christian values. Chief among these qualities were the notions of Islam as irrational, inherently violent, spread by the sword and maintained by force, and sexually perverse.

In short, the Muslims were transformed from an inchoate, if at times deadly, nuisance to an existential threat to Latin Christendom encompassing the annihilation of true Christian values, beliefs, and practices. Yet this discourse was fashioned with little or no reference to actual Muslims and forged with no real understanding or recognition of what they believed or said or did. None of these details was of much concern to the reformist church intellectuals and ideologues who were the first direct beneficiaries of this new narrative. Nor would they be to the subsequent generations of Islam experts who have drawn on the same narrative to advance their own interests ever since. The result has been a fateful decoupling of the anti-Islam discourse from the nondiscursive reality of Islam and a broad distortion of the Western understanding of the Muslims on virtually all fronts, from the eleventh century to the present day.

4

ISLAM AND SCIENCE

I shall scarcely be persuaded that anything good can come from Arabia.

FRANCESCO PETRARCH, *LETTERS OF OLD AGE*

PERHAPS NO OTHER realm of the Western experience has been as jealously guarded as that of modern science and its stepsister, technology. To be "modern" today—at least among elites worldwide—is to be totally enmeshed in a worldview shaped by the products and processes of science and technology. Those who command their secrets and wield their powers—or at least feel that they do so—literally rule the world. The West's military, economic, and political predominance relies on the continued mastery and effective monopoly of science. Enforcement measures include global restrictions on military technology transfer as well as the nuclear arms–control regime that safeguards, albeit imperfectly, the developed world's privileged grip on such weaponry. Western pharmaceutical, agricultural, and software firms vigorously sell high-priced drugs, genetically modified seeds, and computer programs to the rest of the world while retaining the fundamental technology for themselves.

For the most part, humanity worldwide wants many of these technological advances and has been more than willing to accept science and technology on Western terms.[1] This acceptance has extended the reach of modern science around the world without regard for national boundaries or for non-Western intellectual, cultural, and religious traditions. As a result, the discourse of science and the practice of the scientist are recognizably the same everywhere. One would be hard pressed to make a serious claim for the existence today of a "Hindu astronomy" or a "Chinese mathematics," intellectual categories that made perfect sense in bygone times. The field of medicine provides a rare exception, for traditional approaches remain popular and viable in a number of cultures, including those of China, India, and the Islamic world, where they compete, often quite effectively, with Western biomedicine (Lyons 2009b).

In the Muslim world, beginning with the so-called modernizing trend of the nineteenth century, the pull of modern science has produced a general consensus on the need to catch up to the West, with little time set aside for debate over the broader implications for society, science, or faith (Iqbal 2002:xv–xix). Islamic science, grounded in the Islamic intellectual tradition and its theory of knowledge and practice of scholarship, can now be spoken about only in the past tense. All that remains are attempts by some religious conservatives to endorse creationism or to find the roots of all scientific discoveries in the sacred texts of Islam—both signs of the enduring importance of the need to be "scientific."

Given the enormous value of this monopoly, it is not surprising that the West has sought to maintain its control over the source of modern science. Thus the predominant discourse has enshrined the birth and subsequent history of modern science in a series of mythlike events, including the heresy trial of Galileo, the Renaissance, and the scientific revolution. Likewise, it celebrates totemic achievements, such as penicillin, the A-bomb, the space race, and DNA sequencing. Protecting this hegemony requires the elimination of all other possible contenders, a cause that has generally been well served since the nineteenth century by the discipline commonly known as the "history of science," with its propensity to measure other, non-Western scientific traditions—Mayan, Chinese, Islamic, and so on—solely by the yardstick of modern and specifically Western science.

One of the most troublesome aspects of this claim on science as Western birthright, however, is what we might call the problematic of Muslim science.[2] After all, from the eighth century well into the Renaissance, the Muslims led the world in creative works of science and produced many of the ideas and technologies that are today inextricably bound up with our common, accepted notions of Western civilization: the algebra of Muhammad ibn Musa al-Khwarizmi (ca. 780–ca. 850) and the perfection of trigonometry; the pioneering chemistry of Gaber (ca. 721–ca. 815); the medical teachings and psychological insights of the Persian polymath Avicenna (980–1037); the geographical works of Muhammad al-Idrisi (1099–1166); the rationalist philosophy of Averroës (1126–1198); the engineering marvels of Abu al-Jazari (1136–1206); and the theoretical innovations in mathematical astronomy of Nasir al-Din Tusi (1201–1274) and others at the Maragha observatory—to name just a few of the most prominent examples uncovered to date. Even more important than any individual work was the Arabs' conceptual breakthrough, which goes to the very heart of the contemporary West: the realization that science can grant humans power over nature (Lyons 2009a:103–124).

Much of our modern technical vocabulary comes straight from Arabic, along with the scientific understanding such terms embody: from *alcohol*, *alembic*, and *azimuth* to *zenith* and *zero*. The Western diet owes a considerable debt to Muslim agronomy, which supplied such foods as apricots, oranges, hard wheat, and artichokes. Similarly indebted are our nautical terminology and commercial language—*admiral*, *sloop*, *barque*, *tariff*, *arsenal*, and *douane* (Watson 1983:21–80; Kramers 1990:97; Abulafia 1994:1). Likewise, those masters of early secular European literature Dante, Cervantes, and Chaucer were well aware of Islamic philosophy and science and of the religious imagery of Muslim culture. As George Sarton (1927–1948, 2:1:1), one of the first Western historians of science to begin to take the Islamic intellectual tradition seriously, once noted, science and philosophy flourished across the Muslim world far longer than it did among either the Greeks or the medieval Latins (see also Iqbal 2002:127).

And therein lies the problematic: Given the enormous power and undeniable achievements of Islamic science over the centuries, at a time when Christian Europe faced a deeply impoverished intellectual landscape and had to borrow extensively from the Muslims, how can modern science be said to represent the natural and exclusive product of the Western experience?

Several Western strategies have evolved in the face of this and related questions. The simplest and still the most prevalent strategy is to downplay or ignore outright Islamic achievements in science and philosophy as—to recall Michel Foucault's useful phrase—outside "the true." College textbooks intended for use in survey courses often adopt this tactic, as do the Western mass media and, as a result, much of the general public. Widespread news coverage in 2007 of a discovery by Western mathematicians that medieval Iranian architecture displayed sophisticated geometric patterns that were understood in the West only five hundred years later illustrates just how woeful our knowledge of Islamic science really is. One of the researchers even suggested that the Islamic designers almost certainly did not understand the underlying science of what they were doing at the time (Wilford 2007). And to see this strategy at work, one has only to recall the recent Gallup Organization (Abdo 2006a) finding that a majority of Americans believe that Islam has contributed little or nothing of value to the world. In other words, the problematic of Islamic science can be resolved simply by denying that it ever existed in the first place.

Of course, outright denial has generally not been open to the Western discipline of the history of science, which nonetheless still suffers from serious shortcomings when considering the Islamic scientific tradition. The history of science cannot, for example, account for much of what we now know about Islamic science—in particular, recent findings that significantly extend the scope and extend forward the timeline of Muslim scientific achievement—any more than it can offer cogent reasons for its eventual decline or even date that decline with any rigor or precision (Iqbal 2002:127–152; Saliba 2007). Instead, this history is caught up in the gravitational pull of the anti-Islam discourse that has sustained the predominant Western view of the Muslims and their world for a thousand years.

The history of science is perhaps particularly prone to such distortions, for—in contrast to, say, the history of philosophy—it tends to assess and evaluate any historical achievement or text almost exclusively in terms of its contribution or similarity to the ideas of accepted modern conceptions of science (Pines 1986:352; Berggren 1996:266). This approach, in turn, dictates the range of sources and the types of evidence considered legitimate and controls the production of Western statements about Muslim science. Two key distortions emerge as a result: first, a predetermined narrative of the Muslims as "caretakers" of the classical Greek tradition until Europe was ready to take up the torch and, second, self-selection of only those medieval Muslim works that can be cast as precursors to modern science and thus as worthy of consideration, study, and preservation (Berggren 1996:266).

In a critique of such approaches to the Islamic scientific tradition, George Saliba (2007:1–3) identifies the main strands of what he calls the "classical narrative": the lack of any substantive pre-Islamic Arabic tradition on which to build an indigenous science; the consequent need for the Muslims to rely exclusively on translated works and other borrowings from more advanced civilizations nearby (that is, the Greek, the Sasanian, and the Hindu); the Muslims' essential recapitulation of the classical Greek experience, with few real innovations and certainly no radical transformation of the idea of science itself; the short-lived nature of an Islamic Golden Age of science and philosophy that soon enough gave way to the onslaught of religious reaction; and, finally, the swift rise of an autonomous European tradition, known as the Renaissance, at the start of the West's solo journey toward today's modern science. To this list should be added the notion that relations between science and religion are inevitably characterized by conflict, as in the West's account of its own scientific revolution. In Islam, by contrast, principles of the faith are tied directly to the sciences and to philosophy, the three composing a seamless whole in which all knowledge is legitimate as long as it remains within the framework of the Muslim worldview as laid out in the Qur'an. After all, such prominent philosophers as Avicenna, Averroës, and Maimonides were also great physicians, the last a Jew who wrote his philosophical works in Arabic and served as personal doctor to Saladin (Nasr 1983:64, 184).

At the heart of this classical narrative lies one of the central tenets of the Western discourse of Islam: the fundamental hostility of Muslims toward rational thought, seen as the mirror opposite of prevailing Western attitudes. And it is this notion that has run in various guises throughout statements about Islamic science ever since the subject first began to attract serious Western scholarly interest.

In *The Rise of Early Modern Science: Islam, China, and the West* ([1993] 2003), the sociologist Toby Huff provides an excellent exemplar of the contemporary discourse, especially in that it defines and then seeks to address the problematic of Islamic science. This work is particularly useful for my purposes here because it reflects the established Orientalist canon and rests on long-accepted Western interpretations for its underlying data set (for other critiques of Huff, see Rashed 1994:332–348; Saliba 1999a, 1999b; Iqbal 2002:143). Cast in the specific terms of this study, it reflects fully the anti-Islam discourse. Thus Huff writes: "The problem of Arabic science has at least two dimensions. One concerns the failure of Arabic science to give birth to modern science; the other concerns the apparent decline and retrogression of scientific thought and practice in Arabic-Islamic civilization after the thirteenth century" ([1993] 2003:47).

All the central arguments advanced by Huff's sociological approach to the problematic of Islamic science ultimately recapitulate one of the core elements of the anti-Islam discourse: the notion that the Muslims' inherent opposition to rational thought prevented their once-great scientific enterprise from attaining Western heights. In this schema, the rise of an orthodox religious thought—associated by Orientalist scholars since the nineteenth century with the work of the towering medieval theologian Abu Hamid al-Ghazali—acts as an impermeable firewall to the development of the spirit of free inquiry and autonomous institutions, such as universities, that inevitably led to modern science. In contrast to the Islamic world and its tradition of enforced orthodoxy, says Huff, the West enjoyed centuries of "unfettered" pursuit of rational thought: "This [Western] flight of the imagination, if you will, was both sponsored by and motivated by the idea that the natural world is a rational and ordered universe and that man is a rational creature who is able to understand and accurately describe that universe" ([1993] 2003:1).

As to the vexing matter of explaining the decline of science within Islam, Huff offers a revealing corollary to his earlier argument, further steeped in the Western discourse: the historic patterns of conversion to Islam gradually eroded the number of non-Muslims, steadily depleting the pool of scientific and philosophic talent not constrained by religion, until an antiscience tipping point was reached somewhere around the thirteenth century: "[W]ith this new wave of conversion to Islam, the percentage of freethinkers [that is, non-Muslims] who were not fearful of the corroding effects of the foreign sciences also dramatically declined, and this dynamic probably had negative consequences for the pursuit of the natural sciences and intellectual life in general" ([1993] 2003:47n.2).

This same general thrust—of ultimate failure and inevitable decline vis-à-vis a modernizing West—takes on more polemical tones in the hands of Bernard Lewis, whose *What Went Wrong? Western Impact and Middle Eastern Response* (2002) was completed but not yet published when terrorists struck the World Trade Center and the Pentagon. In a brief preface added after the attacks, Lewis asserts a direct, causal link between those events and what he sees as the Muslim world's systemic shortcomings in its prolonged encounter with the West: "This book was already in page proof when the terrorist attacks took place in New York and Washington on September 11, 2001. It does not therefore deal with them, nor with their immediate causes and after-effects. It is however related to these attacks, examining not what happened and what followed, but what went before—the longer sequence and larger pattern of events, ideas, and attitudes that preceded and in some measure produced them" (vii).

Like Huff, Lewis blames Muslims' refusal to accept or even recognize what he calls the "underlying philosophy and socio-political context of . . . [Western] scientific achievements." Further, Lewis sees in this refusal the genesis of anti-Western anger and resentment that boiled over so many centuries later in September 2001: "The relationship between Christendom and Islam in the sciences was now reversed. Those who had been disciples now became teachers; those who had been masters became pupils, often reluctant and resentful pupils" (2002:81).

The West's interaction with Islamic science has enjoyed a lengthy, complex, and colorful history, characterized by distinct periods of ebb and flow dating back at least to the tenth century, when Christian Catalonia slowly began to absorb and then transmit to the rest of Europe such innovations as the astrolabe, the Hindu–Arabic number system, and even the game of chess from the neighboring cultural superpower Muslim al-Andalus (Burnett 1997:3). There soon followed an intensive period of Western enthusiasm and affinity for Muslim science and philosophy, succeeded by an even more intensive period of assimilation and even outright expropriation before the emergence of the longest and final phase, essentially one of denial of Muslims' intellectual contributions, which largely persists to varying degrees in many works besides those by Huff and Lewis.

As one would expect, given the vagaries of cultural transmission, these phases often lack distinct boundaries and display considerable overlap and even significant, if temporary, reversals. Yet the overarching trajectory undeniably asserts—often with remarkable speed and severity—the West's prevailing anti-Islam discourse, effectively diluting and even devaluing the originality, creativity, and staying power of Muslim science and philosophy. This dilution in turn distorts the Western social sciences with regard to the Muslim world and perpetuates the notion of a looming clash of civilizations by highlighting the Otherness of the Muslim and obscuring considerable areas of scientific and philosophical commonality between Eastern and Western traditions.

How, then, to account fully for both the shifting dynamics of the Western reception of the Islamic scientific tradition over the centuries—from affinity to expropriation to denial—and the general narrative arc stretching back from the present to the formation of the anti-Islam discourse itself? The answer lies with application of an analytical framework that reveals not only the formation and operation of the classical narrative of Islamic science, but also its social and institutional beneficiaries. The approaches spelled out in chapter 2 provide the necessary tools to account for this relationship and to locate it in terms of the totalizing discourse of Islam: Foucault's principle of *reversal* as part of his broader archaeological method and the analytical question: Who benefits?

In Foucault's hands, the reversal of meaning allows us to see behind the discourse itself and to gain a better understanding of its modes of operation and rules of production. By freeing ourselves from the unity commonly assumed in meaning, for example, we can free ourselves to ask questions that are hidden or otherwise overlooked or ignored. In *Madness and Civilization: A History of Insanity in the Age of Reason*, Foucault deploys this strategy to focus not on madness as an object itself, but on the shifting ways in which the very idea of madness has been applied. This focus reveals how the term was reinvented at different times to serve different goals (Shumway 1993:17). Elsewhere in the same text, he practices the reversal of value: the freeing of the mad after the French Revolution was commonly seen as a humanitarian act of liberation from the horrors of imprisonment, when in fact it doomed many to even greater misery on the streets (Shumway 1993:17).

In the case of Islamic science, different social groups periodically expropriated the Western discourse to serve different ends, so that it generally remained within the same broad outlines until its emergence in its final form beginning in the nineteenth century. In chapter 7, I discuss how reversing the traditional concept of the inevitability of tension between theology and science, a holdover from the Western experience, opens up fruitful new ways to explore and understand the Islamic scientific and philosophical tradition.

Toward the end of the twelfth century, a wandering English scholar signaled the arrival of a new era in European learning, one that saw the replacement of traditional Western sources of authority with newfound riches of Islamic science and philosophy, now within Christian reach in and around Spain,

Sicily, and the Crusader states of the Near East. Recounting his intellectual pilgrimage to Spain upon his return home sometime around 1175, Daniel of Morley wrote in his *Philosophia*, also known as *De naturis interiorum et superiorum*: "When some time ago I took myself away from England for the sake of academic study and spent some time in Paris, there I saw beasts seated in scholarly chairs with grave authority. . . . These masters were so ignorant that they stood as still as statues, pretending to show wisdom by remaining silent. But when I heard that the doctrine of the Arabs . . . was all the fashion in Toledo in those days, I hurried there as quickly as I could, so that I could hear the wisest philosophers of the world" (quoted in Pym 2000:41).

Daniel later made his way back to England with "a precious multitude" of Arabic books, extending a budding Western tradition in peripatetic scholarship and intellectual tourism. More significant, he imported an entire cosmology fully grounded in "the doctrine of the Arabs," in this case the Aristotelian teachings of the ninth-century Baghdad astrologer and philosopher Abu Ma'shar, commonly known in Latin as Albumazar.

Daniel was by no means the first student from Christian Europe to abandon outmoded Western teachings and seek out Arabic science. That honor may well go to his fellow Englishman Adelard of Bath, who left behind his traditional education at the cathedral schools of France and traveled to the Crusader principality of Antioch in Asia Minor sometime around 1109 (Cochrane 1994:32–37; Lyons 2009a:89–105). In a popular essay, *Questions on Natural Science*, Adelard hectors his fellow Europeans for their blind adherence to intellectual orthodoxy and announces that Arabic science has freed man to explore the natural world with his own faculties: "For I have learned one thing from my Arab masters, with reason as guide, but you another: you follow a halter, being enthralled by the picture of authority. For what else can authority be called other than a halter? As brute animals are led wherever one pleases by a halter, but do not know where or why they are led, and only follow the rope by which they are held, so the authority of written words leads not a few of you into danger, since you are enthralled and bound by brutish credulity" (1998:107).

Daniel of Morley's own teacher in Spain, Gerard of Cremona, the prolific translator of Islamic scientific and philosophical texts, was himself drawn to al-Andalus in search of a firsthand look at an Arabic version of Ptolemy's great astronomical textbook, the *Almagest*. Gerard was to live the rest of his life in Spain, where he was responsible in full or in part for the translation of more than seventy Arabic texts. A eulogy published by his students on his death in 1187 notes that he, too, had turned to the Muslims' works after a mastering what little the West had had to offer: "For the love of the *Almagest*, which he could not find at all among the Latins, he went to Toledo; there, seeing the abundance of books in Arabic on every subject, and regretting the poverty of the Latins in these things, he learned the Arabic language, in order to be able to translate" (quoted in E. Grant 1974:35).

Among the translations attributed to Gerard and his disciples were medical textbooks and surgical manuals, including Avicenna's great *Canon of Medicine*—which was later printed in Venice in 1515 and remained a standard European work into the seventeenth century—and assorted treatises on alchemy and chemistry, astrology, astronomy, mathematics, optics, and the science of weights (d'Alverny 1982:453). In an important shift away from the purely technical concerns of the earliest translators, Gerard of Cremona began to open up the West's intellectual horizons through the introduction of a broader range of Greek philosophy and natural science as well as through the writings of the Arab philosophers and scientists themselves.

This process was virtually completed by another traveling scholar, the enigmatic polymath Michael Scot, whose translations around 1230 of Averroës's commentaries on Aristotle forced Christian Europe to confront directly an alien system of metaphysics and cosmology. In the course of a colorful career dotted by allegations of sorcery and black magic, Michael emerged as the West's first expert on Aristotle; the translator from the Arabic of important astronomical and metaphysical works; mentor to Fibonacci (ca. 1150–ca. 1250), one of the West's greatest mathematicians; and an author of original works on astrology, human anatomy, physiology, and physiognomy.

Pioneers such as Adelard of Bath, Daniel of Morley, Gerard of Cremona, and Michael Scot were all part of an influential new Western cohort of scholars that grew out of social, economic, and political changes that had begun to emerge in tenth-century Europe. Chief among these changes were the development of a money-based economy and the associated rise of proper towns and cities at the expense of a slowly unraveling feudal order (E. Grant 1996:34). Peasants escaping bondage to the land peopled these new towns, where they could pursue independent lives as merchants or artisans and take advantage of economic updrafts from expanding foreign trade and the emergence of city life itself. These new urban communes gradually began to organize to defend their interests against the nobility, the Crown, and the church.

Before that, Europe had had nothing to approach the great Muslim urban centers of Damascus, Baghdad, and Cairo, where wealthy and well-ordered societies could provide financial, social, and institutional support for learning and scholarship (Wiet 1971:3–4). Western education, by contrast, remained the province of the so-called cathedral schools, relying on outmoded texts and a narrow curriculum to churn out a trickle of future clerics and clerks for church and state. All that now began to change with the rise of the towns. Students and teaching masters, who at first met only informally, followed the lead of artisans and other urban professionals and came together to found independent corporations to regulate membership, limit competition, and protect their livelihood. The totality of members of any guild or profession was called a *universitas*, the origin of our modern term *university* (Haskins 1957:9; E. Grant 1996:34).

Adelard of Bath, Michael Scot, and the rest of Europe's new intellectuals were characterized by a high degree of mobility within the normally rigid world of medieval Europe as well as by their distinct urban origins (Le Goff 1993:5–6). They represented a broad-based social movement, as witnessed by the range of nationalities among the leading translators in Spain: German, English, French, Italian, and Slav. And, much to the alarm of the church's entrenched interests, who feared their loss of monopoly over learning, they were more open to new ideas, new experiences, and new technologies than were their colleagues in the staid cathedral schools. This openness prompted one twelfth-century monk to complain bitterly about these new "professional" students: "They are wont to roam about the world and visit all its cities, till much learning makes them mad; for in Paris they seek liberal arts, in Orleans classics, at Salerno medicine, at Toledo magic, but nowhere manners and morals" (quoted in Haskins 1957:82–83).

The new urban scholars were direct beneficiaries of the exciting and innovative ideas now available from the Muslims, and, as a result, they actively promoted Islamic science. In the hands of these independent and inquisitive intellectuals, "knowledge workers" in today's parlance, the translation movement quickly became a significant export industry. Arabic texts were gathered mostly in Spain, but also in Sicily and the Near East; rendered into Latin by multiethnic, multiconfessional translation teams often using the local vernacular as an intermediary language; and then dispatched to the cathedral schools and budding universities in France, England, and Italy (MacKay 1977:88; Burnett 1994:1044).

Spain saw little direct benefit from this process despite its status as the richest Western repository of Muslim learning. Perhaps blinded by the crusading zeal that characterized the so-called Reconquista, its leaders were largely unable to mobilize this unique resource. The later expulsions of first the Jews, who were heavily Arabized, in the late fifteenth century and then the Muslims in the early seventeenth deprived the now-Christian territory of many of its best-educated and most-skilled residents. Many ended their days in the Ottoman Empire, and tradition has it that the sultan thanked his Spanish counterparts for sending him such valuable new subjects.

Outside Spain, however, mastery of Muslim learning proved a powerful aid to social advancement. Adelard of Bath, the son of a midlevel Benedictine functionary, used his status as England's leading Arabist to become tutor, adviser, and, it appears, personal astrologer to King Henry II. Taking advantage of his standing at court, Adelard used part of his astronomical text *On the Use of the Astrolabe* to lecture Henry on the ideal model for his kingdom: it should be ruled by a philosopher-king, for philosophers speak the truth and are guided by reason; it should tolerate all religious faiths; and it should recognize the authority of the Arabs—that is, the scientists and thinkers—and not that of the church (Burnett 1997:46). Michael Scot's extensive knowledge of Arabic science and philosophy secured his appointment as personal physician and counselor to Frederick II of Sicily, the Holy Roman Emperor. Frederick underwrote Michael's translations of Averroës and Avicenna and arranged for them to be forwarded to "you men of learning" in the Italian universities for dissemination and study (quoted in van Cleve 1972:303; see also Huillard-Breholles 1852–1861, 4:I:383).[3]

This royal patronage effectively made Michael Europe's leading public intellectual and represented a huge step up from his early years when he supported his scholarly life as an itinerant musician (Thorndike 1965:12). Such was his reputation for learning—he was said to know Hebrew as well as Arabic and to be well versed in medicine, mathematics, and astronomy—that he even managed to win financial support from both Frederick and Frederick's great rivals, the popes (Haskins 1927:274–275). Other scholars and translators, such as Daniel of Morley, were supported by direct commissions from leading bishops or given benefices from church properties, effectively to fund their research. The fact that so many translations bear dedications to local bishops and other churchmen who had clearly underwritten the work of the translation teams is another indication of the church's early role in the transmission of Arabic texts. Adelard of Bath, for example, dedicated one of his major works to the bishop of Syracuse, who may have helped arrange his travel to southern Italy and on to the Near East.

Yet so strong was demand for what Adelard called the *studia Arabum* that this new breed of scholar was increasingly independent of the church. Many of their works, both translations and original texts, flew in the face of Catholic orthodoxy, and few of these early scholars were prepared simply to do the church's bidding. When Peter the Venerable, the abbot of Cluny and one of the most powerful men in Christendom, wanted a team of scholars to translate the Qurʾan into Latin for the first time, he had to resort to "a large remuneration" to convince them to suspend their studies of Islamic astronomy (quoted in Kritzeck 1956:180). Despite this remuneration, Robert of Ketton, the lead translator of the Qurʾan, remained less than enthusiastic. He tells us in his preface that he was willing "to overlook in the meantime, my principal study of astronomy and geometry" to take part in the translation but remained determined to return at once to the work that had drawn him to Spain in the first place—understanding the Islamic science of the stars (quoted in Kritzeck 1964:62).

This enthusiastic reception of things Islamic was not, however, without serious reservations, even among the most enthusiastic Western adepts of Arabic science and philosophy. Robert of Ketton's translation of the Qurʾan—which was actually more of a paraphrase than a direct rendering of the Arabic—and its subsequent early manuscript tradition betray many aspects of the anti-Islam discourse. This discourse is immediately evident in the title of the work, *Lex Mahumet pseudoprophete* (*The Religion of Muhammad, Pseudo-Prophet*). Robert's preface then refers to Islam as *lex letifera*, or a "death-dealing religion," and the enemy of all Christendom (quoted in Burman 2007:13–15). These references came from the same Robert of Ketton who had such love for Arabic astronomy and alchemy that he grumbled about interrupting his studies of them to translate the Qurʾan for Peter the Venerable.

The earliest surviving manuscript of this Latin Qurʾan from the twelfth century carries on in the same tradition. Annotations in the margins such as "liar" and "extremely stupid" provide a running commentary, and some of the chapters, or suras, are given derogatory headings, including "Enveloped in absurd lies and the characteristic repetition of incantations" (quoted in Burman 2007:60). Other notations link Muhammad to the devil and assert that Islam relies on the promise of sexual gratification to win over converts:

"Note that he [Muhammad] everywhere promises such a paradise of carnal delights, as other heresies have done before" (quoted in Tolan 1998:356). A drawing in one of the margins depicts "Mahumeth" with the head of a man and the body of a fish, a possible reference to the predominant Christian view that Islam was a hodge-podge of beliefs and practices (d'Alverny 1947–1948:81–82; Cahn 2002:51–53).

Even those not venturing directly into questions of religion took refuge in the predominant Western narrative of Islam and the Muslims. Roger Bacon, the thirteenth-century English scholar who so admired the Muslim practice of philosophy—"Philosophy is drawn from the Muslims," he once decreed—also denounced what he saw as the unbridled lust that characterized Muslim life (Atiya 1962:220). The Muslims are, he asserts in *Opus majus*, "absorbed in sensual pleasures because of their polygamy" (1927:815).[4] One anonymous scribe concluded his laborious copy of a Latin translation of Albumazar with a personal note of protest: "finished, with praise to God for his help and a curse on Mahomet and his followers" (quoted in Tester 1987:153).

Initial reaction to Islamic science, mostly in the form of new technologies such as the astrolabe, the abacus, and the Hindu–Arabic number system, was less equivocal among the West's traditional clergy and the public at large, with black magic regularly invoked as the true source of such innovations. In *History of the Kings of England*, William of Malmesbury, a twelfth-century monastic librarian, denounced the new technologies that the future pope Sylvester II had first brought from Muslim-influenced Spain 150 years earlier: "There he learned what the singing and flight of birds portended, there he acquired the art of calling up spirits from hell" (1815:199). William also dismissed Sylvester's mathematical ideas as "dangerous Saracen magic" and attributed his election as pontiff, on the cusp of the millennium in 999, to a pact with the devil. A thirteenth-century tradition called the learned Sylvester "the best necromancer in France, whom the demons of the air readily obeyed in all that he required of them by day and night, because of the great sacrifices he offered them" (quoted in Burnett 1997:16).

Far more threatening to the West's traditional order were the arrival in the early twelfth century of Arabic astrology, which many saw as a threat to Christian ideals of free will, and the Muslims' rendering of Aristotelian physics and cosmology that accompanied it. It had been one thing for the Western elite to marvel at the practical uses of the Muslims' astrolabe, algorism, and related technologies, for none of them required a radical rethinking of

Christendom's dominant worldview—at least not at the relatively low level at which Europe's early adopters first approached them. And church authorities had already adopted Aristotle's methods of logical argumentation, the dialectic, because they were keen to use it to establish the truth of Christian revelation in their battle against heresy.[5] But all that began to change with the introduction of the Arab Aristotelians' natural philosophy. Here was an underlying metaphysics, a science of "being as being," that addressed many of the same questions, albeit in a very different way, as the traditional readings of revelation. It presented medieval Christendom with a competing "theory of everything" that could not be either digested and assimilated painlessly, on the one hand, or ignored outright, on the other.

Albumazar's ninth-century *Introduction to Astrology*, the full text of which appeared in Latin in 1133 and again in 1140, provided the West with the first major pathway into the Aristotelian tradition in natural science. Adelard of Bath had some two decades earlier translated Albumazar's own abridged version, the *Lesser Introduction to Astrology*. This early translation, essentially a practical handbook, helped ignite an appetite in the West for Arabic astrology and other occult practices, but it omitted the Aristotelian framework that made the full *Introduction to Astrology* such a powerful text. And it was this Arab-influenced apprehension of Aristotle rather than any immediate direct access to his natural philosophy that prompted the church to ban his teachings at the University of Paris, then the premier center of Christian theology, in 1210 to 1215 (Lemay 1958:xxvii).

The initial crisis at Paris induced by the Aristotle of the Muslim astrologers was soon followed by the appearance around 1230 of Michael Scot's translations of the great commentaries on Aristotle's metaphysics and natural science by the Muslim philosopher and jurist Ibn Rushd, known to the Latins as Averroës. Averroës's works provided Europe with some of its first access to an authentic Aristotle, freed of earlier entanglements with the occult. Yet this presentation posed an even greater challenge to the West, for it forced Christendom to reexamine critically many of its most closely held beliefs—on creation, on the nature of God, and on humanity's place in the universe.

Here, then, lie the origins and driving forces of the second phase—after the initial flurry of translations in Spain, Sicily, and the Near East—of the Western encounter with the Islamic intellectual tradition, that of assimilation and, more accurately, of expropriation of Arabic science and philosophy. This phase required an intensive effort to "Christianize" Aristotle, already champion of the church's dialectic, and to make his powerful natural philosophy and metaphysics safe for Western consumption (Lemay 1958:xxiii; Bullough 1996:46–47). And this effort meant, in effect, a campaign of intellectual "ethnic cleansing" that would attempt to strip out any traces of Muslim influence—now seen as a corruption of the original text—and to bequeath an acceptable version of Aristotle to his legitimate heirs in the Latin West. Over time, the vital contributions of the Muslim philosophers were pushed so far to the margins of Western intellectual history as to become almost invisible. A similar pattern would soon be repeated in other fields, including mathematics, medicine, and even literature. Each time, the anti-Islam discourse would provide the rules of procedure and the intellectual mechanism for this willful act of forgetting.

The beneficiaries of this second stage in the West's encounter with Muslim science and philosophy were no less than the Scholastics, exemplified by such figures as Albertus Magnus and Thomas Aquinas. Like the wandering scholars of a newly urbanizing Europe preceding them, the Scholastic monks and their sponsors found in Muslim science an avenue to power, prestige, and influence. The Order of Preachers, the Dominicans, in particular seized on the opportunities provided by the arrival of Muslim science and its disruptive powers in order to challenge their great rivals the Franciscans and to confront the rising influence of the secular intellectuals in the universities.

Beginning in the early thirteenth century, church authorities in Paris issued more than a dozen lists of banned ideas, largely of Arab origin and all meticulously detailed in the *Collectio errorum*. Yet the need for continued renewal of such bans betrays their very ineffectiveness; both the secular teaching masters and the theologians, it seems, routinely ignored them. Among the first to recognize the futility of such a quarantine was Thomas Aquinas's own Order of Preachers, and the Dominican charter of 1228 explicitly permitted its students to read the works of pagans and philosophers, if only "briefly" (van Steenberghen 1955:79–80). This permission was a powerful signal that at least some religious intellectuals recognized that the new learning was not about to fade away and must instead be mastered and then harnessed for the good of the church.

Three years later, Pope Gregory IX appeared to agree, and he called for the formation of a panel of experts to review the natural philosophy of Aristotle and his Arab commentators and to purge their errors: "But since, as we have learned, the books on nature which were prohibited at Paris in provincial council are said to contain both useful and useless matter, lest the useful be vitiated by the useless, we command your discretion . . . that, examining the same books as is convenient subtly and prudently, you entirely exclude what you shall find there erroneous or likely to give scandal or offense to readers, so that, what are suspect being removed, the rest may be studied without delay or offense" (*Chartularium universitatis Paresiensis*, 1:143–144; quoted in Thorndike 1975:34).

In the event, this papal commission never met. However, some of the leading Scholastics took up the campaign to purge the Arab Aristotle of errors and to Christianize its approach to the natural world—a difficult and deeply controversial effort whose long-term chance at success was established only with the canonization of Thomas Aquinas in 1323, almost fifty years after his death.[6]

In effect, Thomas worked out an intellectual and theological compromise that reserved for the church its most fundamental beliefs while freeing the new men of science to inquire into the natural world. This approach recognized explicitly the power and influence of Muslim science and philosophy in the West and saved the church from a dangerous confrontation with the forces of reason as unleashed by Arab influence. By providing a way out of the controversy over the arrival of Arabic learning, Thomas removed the Muslims as the fulcrum around which any ensuing Western struggle between faith and reason would turn. This displacement, then, hastened the departure of Muslim science and philosophy from Western historical memory.

Thomas's method and its lasting ramifications for the Western narrative of Islam can be best be seen in his subtle approach to the medieval controversy over the eternity of the world. This doctrine has a long history in the Christian tradition, drawing on the opening lines from Genesis: "In the beginning, God created heaven and earth." For the most part, Christians, following the Jews and followed later by the Muslims, understood this sentence to mean that the universe had a distinct starting point and was created "from nothing." In this traditional view, God made the universe at a time of his choosing and then controlled each and every event in it.

Such creation "in time," however, was not the predominant view in the Greek cultural sphere where early Christianity first flourished. Here, the influence of pagan philosophy remained a strong one. Writing in *Metaphysics*, for example, Aristotle says: "There is something which is always moved with an unceasing motion; but this is a circular motion. And this is not only evident from reason, but from the thing itself. So that the first heaven will be eternal. There is, therefore, something which moves. But, since there is that which is moved, that which moves, and that which subsists as a medium between these, hence there is something which moves without being moved, which is eternal, and which is essence and energy" (1801:280).

This "eternal something" is, of course, Aristotle's famous Unmoved Mover, a notion that clearly stands at odds with traditional readings of scripture. Nevertheless, the matter lay mostly dormant for centuries. The full implications of Aristotle's position—if they were even fully understood at the time—either did not really penetrate the early Christian consciousness or were conveniently ignored (Dales 1990:35–56).

The European encounter with Muslim learning, first in the philosophical inquiries of Avicenna and later in the commentaries of Averroës, upended this state of affairs. Little credited in the classical narrative but just as important, these and other Muslim thinkers paved the way for the eventual Western assimilation of philosophy and science. As pious Muslims and like their Christian readers, both Avicenna and Averroës were committed monotheists and thus much more interested than the pagan Aristotle in connecting metaphysics to their understanding of the one God.

Of particular importance were Avicenna's discussions of metaphysics and his notion of the soul, found in his comprehensive *Kitab al-shifa'* (*Book of Healing*), begun in 1021 (Hasse 2000:1). These excerpts were first translated into Latin in Toledo by 1166, but it took considerable time before their full impact was felt. Meanwhile, thanks to Michael Scot, Averroës's commentaries on *Metaphysics* and Aristotle's other works of natural philosophy made their way to Paris and other European universities. Averroës, as a brilliant philosopher in his own right and as a fellow monotheist, commanded enormous respect in medieval Europe. Such was his influence that Latin scholars commonly dispensed with his name and simply referred to him as "the Commentator," just as Aristotle was known in the same circles as "the Philosopher." No less a Western cultural icon than Dante accorded Averroës—along with Avicenna—his highest honor for non-Christians: the *Divine Comedy* (canto 4:129–144) assigns them both a place in limbo, alongside Aristotle and others in his "philosophic family."

This Western reading of Averroës, however, was based solely on those works that translators chose to render into Latin. There was enormous demand for Averroës's commentaries on Aristotle and for his medical texts, for example, but his equally important writings on the interrelationship between religion and philosophy as well as between faith and reason remained largely unexplored. His *On the Harmony of Religion and Philosophy* is preserved in several Arabic versions and one Hebrew translation. It apparently never appeared in Latin (Hourani 1967:40–41), although there is some evidence that Roger Bacon may have been familiar with its argument, if not with the actual text (Hackett 1988). As a result of this selective reading, Averroës's often subtle reasoning and careful conclusions were easily taken out of context and often applied in their more extreme forms.

Among his teachings, Averroës deftly laid out the case for the eternity of the world—that both time and matter are eternal and that the Creator had simply set the entire process in motion. Implicit in this Arabic philosophical tradition is the notion that God does not bother with the details of everyday life, that he remains steadfastly unaware of what the medieval theologians called "particulars." God is likewise effectively removed from day-to-day management of the universe. Instead, he relies on the universal laws of nature, which stem from his own perfection. Such notions, in the eyes of their many critics, contravened the scriptural promise of Judgment Day, when God would assess each person's adherence to the moral code spelled out by revelation. They also raised serious doubts about scriptural accounts of miracles. But they helped create the necessary opening for scholars to pursue and uncover the laws of existence, otherwise known as natural science.

By the mid-thirteenth century, the arrival of this new Arabic learning had touched off a free-for-all in Western theological and secular circles. The arts faculty at Paris, dominated by a new generation of Arab-inspired philosophers, was in open rebellion against church-imposed limitations on the scope of their inquiries. Thomas Aquinas's masters in the Order of Preachers dispatched their intellectual star to Paris in 1269 to try to quell the storm. As loyal servants of the church, the Dominicans were alarmed by the rising tide of philosophical speculation that seemed to infringe on traditional theological territory. Yet they were equally concerned that the conservative backlash, led by the rival Franciscans, would prevent the church from deploying the powerful new arsenal of natural philosophy against heretics, such as the Cathars of southern France.

Thomas, whose works generally display a deep respect for Avicenna and Averroës, had already sided decisively with his fellow theologians and thus against the Muslims in a dispute with the Parisian philosophers over the immortality of the soul.[7] But now his essay *On the Eternity of the World*, written in 1270, directs a powerful blow at the Franciscans. Thomas dismisses as "fragile" the notion that reason can demonstrate with certainty that the world was created in time. Proponents had argued that God was the cause of all things and thus must have come before the world that he created, thus establishing creation as an identifiable temporal act. Averroës (1954:65) had argued earlier in his own war of words with conservative Muslim theologians, *Tahafut al-tahafut* (*The Incoherence of the Incoherence*), that the traditionalists had failed to understand that both God's will and his creative actions must be instantaneous.[8]

Thomas now adopts the same line: "Since people are accustomed to think of productions that are brought about by way of motion, they do not readily understand that an efficient cause [that is, God] does not have to precede its effect in duration. And that is why many, with their limited experience, attend to only a few aspects, and so are overhasty in airing their views" (1964a:21). He also dismisses fears that this view would deprive God of his divine will, which likewise does not have to precede its effect in duration: "The same is true of the person who acts through his will, unless he acts after deliberation. Heaven forbid that we should attribute such a procedure to God!" (21).

Thomas concludes that on the basis of logic alone, Averroës may well be correct: the world is both eternal and created by God. What is more, this approach avoids the danger of making the world coeternal with God—a notion that Jews, Christians, and Muslims would abhor as polytheism. Thomas declares from the outset that it is an absolute article of Catholic faith that the world was created by God at a specific time, but he concludes that the traditionalists' failed attempts at philosophical argumentation do not help the Catholic cause: "Some of them are so feeble that their very frailty seems to lend probability to the opposite side" (1964a:22).

In *Summa theologiae*, unfinished at the time of his death in 1274, Thomas uses the notion of the eternity of the world to argue that preserving separate realms of science and revelation is vital to the protection of the faith: "That the world had a beginning . . . is an object of faith, but not of demonstration or science. And we do well to keep this in mind; otherwise, if we presumptuously undertake to demonstrate what is of faith, we may introduce arguments that are not strictly conclusive; and this would furnish infidels with an occasion for scoffing, as they would think that we assent to truths of faith on such grounds" (1964b:66).

In this way, Thomas Aquinas succeeded in effectively Christianizing the Arab Aristotle just as Averroës had succeeded in "Aristotelianizing Christianity"—the latter more commonly known as Scholasticism—and in ensuring the place for reason in late medieval Christendom (Bullough 1996:46–47). Under the Arabs' direct influence, Thomas staked out separate spaces for traditional church teachings and the new findings of the scientists emerging under the influence of the Muslim intellectual tradition.

Although many centuries passed before this Thomist compromise gained a firm hold, it still defines the Western rules of engagement between faith and reason. It also effectively naturalized Arabic science and philosophy and steadily removed its leading figures, in particular Averroës and Avicenna, as flashpoints in the episodic tensions between secular intellectuals and the church. From this point on, that battle would be fought almost exclusively on what was seen as wholly Western terrain. Given the enormous success of the so-called translation movement and European enthusiasm for science that the movement spawned, it is not surprising that Thomas also ushered in the beginning of the end of the explicit Western love affair with Arabic learning.

Within less than one hundred years of the saint's death, Francesco Petrarch, often called the father of Western humanism, pronounced a new and harsh verdict that still resonates within the classical narrative of Islamic science: "I shall scarcely be persuaded that anything good can come from Arabia; but you learned men, through some strange mental illness, celebrate them with great, and unless I am mistaken, undeserved trumpeting" (1992, 2:472). The medieval period of open assimilation and unabashed admiration for Muslim science and philosophy drew to a close as Europe turned to the predominant discursive notion that Muslims were wholly unsuited for scientific pursuits.

Petrarch's sickbed complaint, in a letter dated 1370 to the physician and astronomer Giovanni di Dondi, is more than a literary device to dismiss unwanted medical advice—that Petrarch abstain from drinking cold spring water and avoid certain foods, including apples. It is a heartfelt denunciation of all things Arab: "I hate the entire race. . . . There is nothing more charming, softer, more lax, in a word, more base" (Petrarch 1992, 2:471). Worse still, Arabic teachings had squelched Latin learning, particularly in medicine, and intimidated contemporary physicians into silence or mere imitation rather than fresh scholarly inquiry. Even the Greeks could not better the achievements of Latin culture, yet the "measly Arabs" were widely held up as paragons of learning who could not be equaled, let alone surpassed: "O infamous exception, O marvelous dizziness of things, O Italian intellects benumbed or quenched! I singularly weep over your talent, hemmed in by such narrowness" (473).

Petrarch's dim view of the Arabs' scholarly achievement is part and parcel of a boundless enthusiasm for renewing the West's zeal for a fresh Crusade, inflamed by a series of Christian setbacks in the East, as well as of his notion that the Muslims were weak, adulterous, effeminate, and unworthy stewards of lands rightfully Christian. The last Crusader statelet had fallen to the Muslim armies shortly before Petrarch's birth in 1304, and Ottoman expansion across Anatolia during his lifetime only heightened his sense of urgency (Bisaha 2001:284).

In a lengthy and rambling letter to Pope Urban V, written around 1367, Petrarch begins with an appeal for the liberation of the Eastern Christians from Muslim rule and warns of the danger posed to the West itself, largely through its own passivity and indifference: "You know the plight of your Christians throughout the East. Indeed the evil is close. Have you not heard how the unsoldierly peoples of Asia, whom our slackness makes valiant—especially the former Phrygians, now Turks—endlessly plunder wretched Greece and ravage the Cyclades that are scattered through the Aegean? Even if the Greeks deserve to pay for their stubborn persistence in rebellious sinfulness, the Turks are nevertheless crossing over from there toward us and true Catholicism" (1992, 1:254–255).

For Petrarch, then, the established anti-Islam discourse served a number of overlapping interests and ends. It offered a rhetorical language, a historical narrative, and a theological worldview in which to locate his renewed call to crusade. This discourse included such traditional elements as the diminution of the Muslims as "lax," "soft," and "unsoldierly"; the depiction of them as "Egyptian dogs" or other beasts desecrating Christian holy sites (Petrarch 1924:245); their alleged polytheism (Petrarch 1996:54–55); and dismissal of the Prophet Muhammad as "an adulterous and licentious fellow" and an "infamous robber," who fostered "wicked superstition" rather than a true religion (Petrarch 1924:247–248).

The same discourse also provided the early humanists with the ideal framework for their central project: the assertion of a direct and glorious link between their own cultural, political, and intellectual endeavors, the *studia humanitatis*, and those of a "classical" Greece and Rome. Such an effort clearly required the liquidation of the Muslim intellectual legacy, a task complicated somewhat by the preceding two hundred years of eager and explicit study and assimilation of Arabic science and philosophy on the part of Western scholars. That this strategy was a conscious one can be seen in the fact that Renaissance scholars were well aware of Arabic learning and often made use of it themselves, at the very least as preparation for their own work. Herbert Weissinger (1945:466) cites a number of examples, including a detailed and generally accurate accounting by the French humanist Louis Le Roy, dated 1594, of Arab achievements throughout the Middle Ages. The political philosopher Jean Bodin, writing in 1583, places the Arabs among the leading practitioners of the arts and sciences (Weissinger 1945:466).

But this strategy also required a renunciation of the Christian Middle Ages in general and of the methods and teachings of the Scholastics in particular. Only then could these new social and intellectual actors be freed to conjure up the idea of a "Renaissance" and with it an intellectual history that drew a straight line between the fall of Rome and mid-fourteenth-century Europe, with no inconvenient detours to include either "measly" Arabs or "medieval" monks (Weissinger 1945:462–467).[9]

The application of the anti-Islam discourse by the early humanists provided this new cohort of independent scholars with more than a compelling theory of history. It also offered a means of social and professional advancement in an urbanizing society still largely dominated on the one hand by the clergy—and in Petrarch's Rome that meant first of all the pope and the curia—and on the other by the princes and other great landowners. The *studia humanitatis*, encompassing rhetoric, grammar, poetry, history, and moral philosophy, became a pathway to political power and social influence as its practitioners increasingly found positions as secretaries to princes and senior clerics or as chancellors of the independent Italian republics. Many also served as private tutors to the wealthy households, inculcating their own cultural values and worldview in the minds of future leaders. By the mid-fifteenth century, the Italian universities began to welcome the humanists into their faculties and to pay well for their services, often from public funds. At the University of Florence, only professors of civil law earned more than the teachers of rhetoric and poetry (Grendler 2002:209–214). Informal humanist gatherings, or "academies," also flourished, often under the patronage of a wealthy figure or prominent member (D'Amico 1983:88).

As one would expect from an intellectual current that laid such stress on the value of grammar, rhetoric, literary style, and eloquence in general, language itself was a central concern for the humanists. And this meant the Latin of Cicero, as famously championed by Petrarch, and the Greek of the ancient philosophers and scientists, in particular Archimedes—another Petrarch favorite (Rose 1975:9). It most certainly did not mean "medieval" Latin, Italian or other vernacular tongues, or—God forbid—Arabic. Unlike their Muslim counterparts, the Western humanists did not look to their own scriptural language as their preferred model. Islamic humanism sought a return to the classical language of the Qur'an, and, to some extent, of pre-Islamic poetry (Makdisi 1989:180–182). The Italian humanists instead adopted Cicero as their standard; they had little time for medieval Latin or for the mastery of the Italian vernacular as displayed by Dante.

This cultivation of high-style Latin led to careers in the papal court and its ecclesiastical and secular circles, providing the early humanists with economic security and social position (D'Amico 1983:61). Under the humanists' influence, Virgil became the accepted authority in poetic style, and Vetruvius's De architectura, written in the first century B.C.E., was established as the last word in architectural theory and practice that guided the building of High Renaissance Rome (D'Amico 1983:125). Giorgio Valla of Piecenza, one of the leading humanist theoreticians, even proposed a unity of classical Latin, the Roman Empire, and the Catholic Church, with the medium of language binding the latter elements together for eternity—in spite of their of obvious philosophical, religious, and political differences (Johnson 1978:31–33; D'Amico 1983:119).

The study of Greek also flourished under the humanists' growing influence, a phenomenon no doubt aided by the continuing Ottoman expansion at the expense of Greek-speaking Byzantium, which forced a number of Greek intellectuals to seek safety and employment in the West, particularly in and around the papal court and in the Italian universities. Fueled in part by Petrarch's enthusiasm for the works of Archimedes—or, more precisely, by his endorsement of Cicero's enthusiasm for Archimedes—interest in Greek manuscripts, especially in mathematics, engineering, and even philosophy, ran high among wealthy patrons, collectors, and humanist scholars (Rose 1975:2–9; D'Amico 1983:121).

Senior church figures, including Pope Nicholas V and Cardinal Basilios Bessarion, stocked their personal collections with important Greek manuscripts, and both emerged as leading underwriters of translations of classical Greek works into Latin (D'Amico 1983:121; Grendler 2002:219). The fall of Constantinople to the Ottomans in 1453 unleashed a wave of Greek manuscripts on the West, many of which ended up in Nicholas's new Vatican Library. An inventory of library holdings after his death, in 1455, included 1,209 manuscript volumes, of which 414 were in Greek. Under Nicholas's predecessor, the same collection had housed just 2 Greek manuscripts out of a total of 340 volumes (Rose 1975:36–37).[10]

The humanists' pursuit of Greek manuscripts came to resemble the earlier intellectual gold rush that had seen such figures as Adelard of Bath, Daniel of Morley, and Gerard of Cremona set off in search of Arab wisdom. Now, however, the humanists were fueled by their new idea of history—captured, ultimately, in the very notion of a renaissance—and by a related quest for classical authenticity without the unwanted Arabs as intellectual middlemen. Western humanism from its very beginnings, then, was an attempt both to create a new theory of knowledge resting on what were now defined as exclusively Western sources—that is, classical Greek and Latin works—and to renounce any connections to the medieval Scholastics, who were so in thrall to the Muslim tradition (Cifoletti 1996:123; Høyrup 1996:110).

This logic can be seen at work in Valla's *De rebus expetendis et fugiendis*, an influential humanist encyclopedia completed in 1501 comprising translations and paraphrases of classical works. Along the way, Valla rigorously excludes any mention of Arabic learning, which is now the work of the unwanted Other—or, as the humanists would have put it, the work of barbarians (Rose 1975:48; Cifoletti 1996:123). The humanist scholars were also eager to apply their new methods of textual criticism to the medieval Latin translations, most made via the Arabic, and to restore the meaning of the Greek texts by working exclusively in the original language of Aristotle and Archimedes.

Such goals, however laudable they may appear on their face, contained a number of serious pitfalls that the humanists, blinded by their theory of history and bolstered by the established anti-Islam discourse, could not even imagine. Many of these shortcomings still plague the Western history of ideas, as reflected in the classical narrative of Muslim science. Foremost, in reducing the Arabs' role to little more than that of caretakers of an authentic

Greek and Roman classical tradition, the Renaissance humanists effectively eliminated the very real contributions to knowledge that the Muslim thinkers had made over the centuries. Second, they unwittingly reintroduced errors and re-created philosophical and scientific problems that had already been addressed within the Islamic tradition.

Third, by creating a vacuum once occupied by Arabic science, they allowed space for Western science to assert its primacy all the more easily, even going so far as to rewrite intellectual history, as was the case with the art of algebra (Cifoletti 1996). Finally, they forestalled and even precluded scholarly exploration of the full richness and depth of that same Muslim tradition, with the result that even to this day the state of knowledge about Islamic science and philosophy remains woefully incomplete. Hundreds of thousands of scholarly manuscripts produced over many centuries in Arabic, Persian, Turkish, and Urdu remain unstudied and largely forgotten (Savage-Smith 1988; Rashed 1994:2). It is difficult not to believe that a systematic analysis of this material would yield a very different picture of Muslim science than the one that predominates today. The same can be said of Islamic religious history, where only a tiny fraction of available manuscripts have been printed, let alone edited and studied (Makdisi 1981a:217–218). As a result, the anti-Islam discourse has been more than content to fill in the blanks.

Take, for example, the works of the Hellenistic astronomer Ptolemy, whose astronomical masterwork, the *Almagest*,[11] and study of cartography and geography, the *Geographia*, were important texts for both late-medieval and early-Renaissance scholars. Particularly prized among the Italian humanists was a Greek codex of the *Geographia* brought to Florence by the Byzantine scholar Emanuel Chrysolaras at the end of the fourteenth century; leading humanists of the day jockeyed for access to the text, and translations proliferated throughout the Renaissance (Rose 1975:26–27). Yet this rush to abandon medieval Latin translations made earlier through Arabic mediation in favor of Greek originals deprived Christian Europe of the many and substantial corrections and revisions that Muslim astronomers, mathematicians, and cartographers had made to these works over the centuries.

Influenced by ritual requirements, early Arab scholars were particularly keen to identify the *qibla*—the direction of Mecca in which to pray, bury their dead, and slaughter their animals—in cities and towns across the vast Muslim lands. They were also deeply interested in cartography and navigation, both to address the requirements of the pilgrimage, or hajj, and to make geopolitical and commercial gains, and in the ability to tell time and date in order to regulate the daily prayers and mark the month of Ramadan. All these issues could be addressed as problems in geometry and spherical trigonometry, and all required the determination of geographical coordinates—areas in which the Arabs had found Ptolemy's work to be deeply deficient as early as the ninth century. In fact, Islamic mathematicians and astronomers greatly improved on Ptolemy's calculations of the coordinates for around eight thousands cities, towns, and geographical features (Donini 1991:36–37; Kimerling 2002:20–21; Sezgin 2005:75–77).

The history of Western mapping of the Caspian Sea illustrates the point. Western cartographers, following Muslim examples, had successfully portrayed the Caspian's primary north–south orientation by the fourteenth century. Less than two hundred years later, under the influence of the new translations of Ptolemy's *Geographia* directly from the Greek, Europe's mapmakers set aside the fruit of Arab research and reverted to the classical representation of the Caspian as running east–west. Only two centuries later was the damage finally undone—eight hundred years after the Muslims had first accurately charted the Caspian (Sezgin 2005:541–542). In a similar vein, Renaissance Europe's refusal to recognize and then master the underlying achievements of medieval Arabic science led to the widespread notion that the earth's circumference was some 20 percent shorter than it actually is, an error not addressed by Western experimentation until the sixteenth century.[12] Christopher Columbus used this shorter distance in planning his exploration of the New World, an error with almost fatal consequences (Donini 1991:37).

The Muslim critique of Ptolemy's *Almagest* was even more profound, with attacks directed at its theoretical shortcomings, the methods and quality of its calculations, and its reliance on out-of-date observational data. Since their earliest translations, Muslim scholars had steadily corrected and revised the original Greek text, including a more accurate determination of the length of the solar year and improvements to other measurements (Saliba 2007:78–84). They had also introduced the trigonometric functions in place of the more cumbersome chords used in the Greek tradition (Saliba 2007:88). The resulting Arabic version and thus any accurate Latin translation from it, then, were clearly improvements over the authentic Greek original.

Over time, this Muslim critique broadened to encompass the so-called *shukuk* literature—literally, "objections" to Ptolemy's theoretical construct and its underlying cosmology (Sabra 1984:134; Saliba 2007:94–117). The central problem, the Muslims argued, was the failure of Ptolemy's planetary model to honor his own fundamental theoretical requirement: that all celestial objects move in uniform circular motion, with the earth at their center. Instead, Ptolemy had sought to account for anomalous observational data by introducing the notion of the "equant point," essentially an axis of rotation for some of the planets that did not pass through the center of the universe. In other words, he had violated the central requirement of classical astronomy as laid down by Plato and Aristotle and accepted for two thousand years: that all planetary motion was in the form of perfect, uniform circles. The oldest of the detailed *shukuk* works dates to the mid-eleventh century, one hundred years before Western translators in Spain struggled even to understand the mathematics and astronomy of the *Almagest* well enough to render it in Latin.

This critique of Ptolemy soon spread to the Muslim philosophers, including Avicenna and Averroës, who joined the astronomers and mathematicians in demanding that any cosmology both account for observed scientific data and remain in accord with its own internal rules and representation of reality. "The science of astronomy of our time contains nothing existent, rather the astronomy of our time conforms only to computation and not to existence," complained Averroës (quoted in Saliba 2007:179). Such a science, they argued, had to be both predictive and consistent—all hallmarks of what today is celebrated as the modern scientific method.

Scholars in the *shukuk* tradition also responded with proposed revisions to Ptolemaic astronomy, offering everything from modest improvements to wholesale overhaul of the entire system. In addition to addressing the shortcomings of classical astronomy, this tradition helped later Arab scientists mount the first serious challenges to the authority of Aristotelian physics (Saliba 2007:183). It also produced at least two approaches that Copernicus used later in his ultimately successful overthrow of Ptolemaic cosmology (Kennedy and Roberts 1959; Hartner 1973; Saliba 2007:193–232).

None of these developments, of course, would have been known to the humanist scholars and their patrons, determined as they were on preparing authentic translations from authentic Greek texts. Cardinal Bessarion, for example, dreamed of preparing a new translation of the *Almagest* but in the end had to hand over the project to two prominent mathematicians. In the event, the result was more an epitome than a full, usable translation, although it received more than its share of intellectual glory during the Renaissance (Thorndike 1963:144–145). The distorting effects of this humanist cult of Greek language and learning can still be seen in Western scholarship of Islamic learning. For example, Muslim philosophical and scientific terminology that can be identified as coming directly from the Greek is generally given precedence over original Arab concepts, categories, and ideas (Rashed 1994:1). This hierarchy, of course, strengthens the accepted notion of the Muslims as loyal torchbearers of classical Greek culture rather than as exemplars of creative forces in their own right.

Not simply content to invoke the anti-Islam discourse in the name of classical authenticity, as with the *Geographia* and the *Almagest*, the humanists also engaged in outright suppression of the Muslim tradition in order to achieve their social and intellectual aims. As Giovanna Cifoletti (1992, 1996) has shown, the French algebraists of the sixteenth century used the anti-Islam discourse to discredit Muslim scientific achievement and then gradually to insinuate into the Western narrative a decidedly non-Arab pedigree for their art. Here, the driving forces included the desire to establish a European—or, better yet, a French national—history of algebra and to raise the status of algebra above that of a simple, practical tool at the bottom of the social hierarchy, like surveying or commercial transactions, to a serious, theoretical discipline in its own right, thus also raising the status of its practitioners (Cifoletti 1996:125; Høyrup 1996:112). A similar pattern can be observed in the historiography of medicine (Crisciani 1990; Cifoletti 1996:125).

For the French algebraists and their Italian counterparts, the weapon of choice was the history of science; they steadily wrote the Arabs out of the history of algebra, providing a model for the later exclusion of Muslims from science in general as they told and retold the genealogy of what became known as the *ars magna*, or the "great art." As we have seen, Valla's humanist encyclopedia of 1501 excluded "barbaric" Arabic works from its account, thus paving the way for the later naturalization of the sciences as exclusively Western products. Four decades earlier, Regiomontanus (Johannes Müller von Königsberg), the first significant humanist mathematician and a member of Bessarion's circle, delivered his famous Padua lectures on the history of mathematics. No real mention was made of Muslim contributions to geometry or algebra. He instead ascribed the latter, which he called "the flower of mathematics," to the third-century Greek mathematician Diophantus, whose manuscript on the subject Regiomontanus said he had recently discovered

(Høyrup 1996:111). Even Arab advances in the art of arithmetic calculation were ignored (Høyrup 1996:111)—despite the fact that the very term then in common use, *algorism*, was a Latin corruption of the name al-Khwarizmi, belonging to the Muslim mathematical authority.

At first, however, most humanist accounts of algebra acknowledged the importance of al-Khwarizmi—the title of whose seminal text, *Kitab al-jabr wa'l-muqabala* (*Book of Restoring and Balancing*), gave the West the word *algebra*—or else ascribed it to Gaber, a reference to the eleventh-century scholar Jabir ibn Afl'a (Cifoletti 1996:127–128). However, the Muslim role was soon pushed to the periphery or presented as the source of unnecessary "difficulties" that had prevented the *ars magna* from assuming its rightful place in the Western intellectual pantheon. That role would eventually be eliminated altogether, particularly by the later French algebraists.

In 1559, Jean Borrel sought to do away with the word *algebra* completely and to locate the subject deliberately within the classical Greek notion of the art of calculation: "There remains to be added to the top, as a crown, that type of reasoning which is called popularly by the Arabic name of Algebra. I prefer to call it *quadratura*" (quoted in Cifoletti 1996:131). Borrel then presents what is soon to become the established Western verdict on Muslim science: "The utility and the intelligence of *quadratura* is accompanied by a specific difficulty, which derives more from the defect of its propagators than from the nature of the thing. For those, really ignoring the method of the disciplines, going far in the roughness of words and things, involve and trouble everything to the point that nothing could be more confused, and accumulating the clouds they obscure the senses of the readers" (131).

Three decades later, an influential treatise ascribed posthumously to the prominent humanist Petrus Ramus sidelined the Muslims altogether and provided an anachronistic and mythical origin to algebra. Algebra was now said to be the work of "an unknown mathematician" of Syriac origin—that is, non-Muslim Arabic, most likely Christian—who somehow shared his discovery with the ancient Greek hero Alexander the Great. As Cifoletti (1996:135) notes, with this transposition of historical settings—the Syriac references suggest the early Christian era, long after Alexander was dead—Ramus was now clearly operating in the realm of a founding myth, with a central valorizing role played by a glorious Greek culture.

Throughout this period, plenty of contemporary evidence of both historical and continuing intellectual intercourse between the Muslims and the

Europeans surrounded Ramus and his humanist colleagues. The publishers Dee and Commandino produced a translation in 1560 of a work on Euclid that they ascribed to "Machometo Bagdadino," or Mahomet of Baghdad, a clear reference to Muhammad ibn Musa al-Khwarizmi; Ibn al-Haytham's ground-breaking work on optics was printed in the West in 1572; and an Arabic version of Euclid's elements, said to be the work of the thirteenth-century mathematician Nasir al-Din Tusi, was published in Rome in 1595 (Høyrup 1996:115). Ramus himself had written an earlier treatise on algebra that does little more than reprise al-Khwarizmi and in general tends to emphasize the importance of the Arabs over the Greeks (Cifoletti 1996:132; Høyrup 1996:114–115).

Yet such evidence did nothing to slow the momentum of the anti-Islam discourse in its support of the humanist theory of history or its social, intellectual, and political aims. There could no longer be room for an Islamic intellectual tradition in a Europe that was fast reinventing itself under the banner of a renaissance of Greek and Latin learning. The arrival of the so-called Age of Discovery, with its implicit promise of economic, territorial, and geopolitical gains at the expense of non-Christian, non-European societies only accelerated this tendency. As Jens Høyrup suggests, European mathematicians could have moved away from classical teachings or discovered in the Muslim tradition fruitful avenues for future study, research, and advance. They did neither, says Høyrup: "In an age of incipient colonial expansion, however, such alternative histories or myths would have seemed awkward, perhaps even improper. The myth so fittingly prepared by Humanist mathematicians for a different purpose, to the contrary, was conveniently at hand and was generally adopted and handed down until the present or near-present time" (1996:115–116).

Initial Western perceptions of Islam, then, were formed by a Crusades-era propaganda that would have made the notion of Muslim learning largely ridiculous. As military, commercial, and political contacts increased, however, there followed an intense curiosity and enthusiasm for the *studia Arabum*, fueling the translation movement of the twelfth and thirteenth centuries and spurring a profound interest on the part of medieval Europe in the arts and sciences. This movement was soon displaced by a period of assimilation and expropriation of Muslim knowledge by the Scholastics, such as Albertus Magnus and Thomas Aquinas, before giving way to denial and outright exclusion of it at the hands of the humanists.

Ever since the Enlightenment, Western thinking has essentially ratified this state of affairs by declining to engage with many of the outstanding problems of Islamic science and instead posing variants of that popular rhetorical question: What's wrong with Islam? In its modern form, the classical narrative is prepared to acknowledge the existence of an Islamic scientific tradition, but it is then compelled to locate that tradition securely in a chronological strongbox, generally described as a delimited Golden Age from which decline was an inevitable product of its own essential Islam-ness (e.g., Hodgson 1974; Lewis 1976, 2002; Lapidus 2002; Huff [1993] 2003). When Islamic science exists at all, then, it becomes a problem in search of solution—When did it die off? Or, why did it fail to produce modern science?—rather than a subject to be explored, developed, and understood in anything like its own terms.

The outlines of the classical narrative of Islamic science emerged in recognizable form in the European Enlightenment. This was a time when Christian Europe began to sense political, military, and intellectual weakness on the part of its long-standing rivals to the east (Saunders 1963:702–703). The Ottoman Empire's final failed attempt to take Vienna in 1683, the loss of Buda in 1686, the Treaty of Carlowitz signed by the defeated Turks and the victorious Christian powers in 1699, the fall of the Safavid dynasty in Iran, and the sharp decline of the Mughal Empire in India soon afterward seemed to ratify this reversal in fortunes (Saunders 1963:703; Lewis 2002:16–18). The study of Islamic science soon enough found itself completely bound up with the larger Orientalist project, subordinating the Western assessment of Islamic intellectual achievement and its historical trajectory to the imperatives of European empire building.

Enlightenment thinkers and their Orientalist successors not surprisingly, given their own intellectual and philosophical inclinations, invoked the notion of human reason—or, with regard to the Muslims, the lack thereof—as the basis for the Western claim on science. After all, Borrel's humanist history of algebra had already pronounced the Muslims ill disciplined, coarse, and obscurantist, and the anti-Islam discourse had much earlier established the West as the antithesis of the Muslim Other. Who else, then, could rescue algebra and in fact all of science from the "defect of its propagators"?

In his scandalous and, as a result, wildly popular *Persian Letters*, first published in 1721 and reprinted ever since, Montesquieu deploys the imagined correspondence of two Persian visitors to Paris as a literary device to comment on the social, intellectual, and political mores of his native France. He also offers the very latest in Western thinking about the East in his depiction of his Muslim protagonists, Usbek and Rica, and touches widely on Western notions of the Orient, including its science, learning, and reason in general. Among his sources were recent French travel literature, such as Jean Chardin's *Voyages en Perse*, and Antoine Galand's translation of *Les mille et une nuits* (Healy 1999:xi). The result is not incompatible with the classical narrative.

In letter XVIII, a cleric from the Persian Holy City of Qom chides Usbek, presumably now under the influence of his host culture, for questioning established Muslim religious tradition: "You are always asking questions that have been asked of our holy Prophet a thousand times. Why do you not read the traditions of the doctors of religion?" (Montesquieu 1875:95 [my translations in all citations to this edition]). In letter XXXI, Usbek's nephew, now in Venice, reports that he has studied the art of commerce and the ways of princes, among other things Western: "I am applying myself to medicine, physics, and astronomy; I study the arts. I am, at last, lifting the clouds that covered my eyes in the land of my birth" (130).

And in letter XCVII, Usbek reports to the Persian "dervish" Hassein that the West prefers to follow reason rather than to celebrate the "divine frenzy" or otherwise to attain Oriental wisdom. This preference, he notes, has led to some remarkable discoveries: "They have cleared up chaos and explained, by a simple mechanism, the order of the divine architecture. The creator of nature has given motion to matter: nothing else is needed to produce the large range of effects that we see in the universe" (Montesquieu 1875:310). Of course, Adelard of Bath and his cohort brought back the same lesson to the West from the Muslim world six hundred years earlier.

Rica, meanwhile, recounts in letter CXXXV a visit to a Parisian library where a stranger volunteers to act as his guide. When the guide, apparently a well-meaning Frenchman keen to display his nation's cultural strengths, dismisses as unworthy of their attention the library's collection of books on "judicial astrology" and other occult subjects, Rica informs him that in the East astrological prediction plays the role reserved for algebra in the West—that is, for science: "We make use of astrology as you use algebra. To each nation its own science" (Montesquieu 1875:421).

In presenting the characters Usbek and Rica in *The Persian Letters*, Montesquieu is engaging in what Foucault calls "controlled *derivation*," in which each type and character belongs to a recognized system of generalizations (1994b:138, emphasis in original; see also Said [1978] 2003:119). According to this notion, drawn from the practice of natural science in the seventeenth century, identity is not absolute or unique but can be set out only in comparison with an Other: "There can no longer be any signs except in the analysis of representations according to identities and differences. . . . An animal or a plant is not what is indicated—or betrayed—by the stigma that is found to be imprinted upon it; it is what others are not" (Foucault 1994b:144). Montesquieu's protagonists are not Persians or Muslims so much as they are *Persia* and *Islam*. Or, put another way, they are products of the Western idea of Persia and Islam, part of a "system of representations framed by a whole set of forces that brought the Orient into Western learning, Western consciousness, and later, Western empire" (Said [1978] 2003:202–203). As such, Usbek and Rica are derivative of the Muslim East as antiscience, irrational, and imprisoned by tradition, judicial astrology, and "the divine frenzy."

Such controlled derivations—and there are plenty of examples in contemporary European travel works and other popular literary forms—provided the backdrop, then, to Napoleon's invasion of Egypt in 1798 (Lowe 1990:119). This invasion was as much an act of Orientalist imagination and Orientalist scholarship as it was an act of war, for it was the first such venture to have harnessed directly and in advance the expertise of the Orientalist as a means of colonial expansion (Said [1978] 2003:80–83). Napoleon's small army of scholars formed a crucial part of his much larger Armée d'Égypte, and it was to play an outsize role in the Egypt campaign.

These savants—historians, biologists, philologists, archaeologists—were not there to learn *from* the Muslims, but to learn *about* them; to confirm and classify this knowledge along Western lines; and to record it in the grandly named *Description de l'Égypte*, which eventually filled twenty-three large volumes. Napoleon's scholars were central to the colonial project and worked closely with the military authorities to achieve French colonial aims. Writing in the work's preface, Jean-Baptiste-Joseph Fourier noted that their aim was to advance civilization in a land that "has transmitted its knowledge to so many nations, [but] is today plunged into barbarism" (quoted in Said [1978] 2003:85).

But just what was the source of that "barbarism"? In an influential lecture delivered toward the end of his career, "L'Islamisme et la science," the

French philologist Ernest Renan argues that Islam itself is the problem. And he attributes the decline of that scientific tradition to the orthodox Muslim theologians' counterattack around 1200, once internal heresy in the form of the Ismailis and external threat in the shape of the Crusaders were safely suppressed: "Islam is something harmful to human reason" (1883:19).

In keeping with the spirit of his times, Renan was not content simply to assert this claim; he had, he assured his many students and readers, the science to back it up. For Renan, this "science" went under the rubric of his beloved philology, which he defined as follows: "Philology is the *exact science* of mental objects. It is to the sciences of humanity what physics and chemistry are to the philosophic sciences of bodies" (1890:149; translated and quoted in Said [1978] 2003:132–133). Following on the heels of the German scholars of Indo-European languages, Renan applied the evolving techniques of comparative linguistics and cultural anthropology to the Semitic tongues. It was but a small step from "the history of language to history-through-language" (Rashed 1994:337).

Thus Renan concludes in his *Histoire générale et système comparé des langues sémitiques* that the Semitic tongues are not really suitable for abstract thought and certainly are not on a plane with Aryan—that is, Indo-European languages—in this regard:

> The unity and simplicity which characterize the Semitic race are found in the Semitic languages themselves. Abstraction is unknown to them and metaphysics is impossible. As a language is a necessary mould for the intellectual activities of a people, an idiom almost bereft of syntax, without variety of construction, deprived of conjunctions that establish such delicate relations between members of thought, that depict objects by their external qualities, must be eminently suited to the eloquent inspiration of visual thinkers and the image of fugitive impressions, but must reject any philosophy, any intellectual inspiration. . . . We may say that Aryan languages compared with Semitic languages are the languages of abstraction and metaphysics compared with those of realism and sensitivity. (1858:18; translated and quoted in Rashed 1994:337n.4)

Fortified by the findings of science, such as the philology espoused by Renan and his contemporaries, the system of controlled derivations that had already established the Muslim as irrational, superstitious, and ultimately unsuited to science or philosophy gained a lasting handhold on the Western imagination. Even when later historians began to jettison Renan's brand of crude cultural anthropology, they retained much of the same fundamental orientation that had flowed from his work, chiefly the inability or unwillingness to consider a significant role for the Arabs and Muslims in the creation of Western science (Rashed 1994:338–339).

Where a tradition of science and philosophy within an Arab or Muslim cultural milieu is acknowledged, it is invariably circumscribed neatly within the boundaries of a Golden Age. Only the parameters of such an age are left open to debate, and so defining and then explaining them have become the central tasks of Western historians of Islamic science. Here, the decisive factor is invariably one of the core tenets of the anti-Islam discourse: Islam's hostility to rational thought and exclusive reliance on a religious orthodoxy that is inimical to scientific endeavor.

Nowhere is this tenet more in evidence than in the work of Ignaz Goldziher, whose seminal essay "The Attitude of the Old Islamic Orthodoxy Toward the 'Ancient Sciences'" provides a direct link between the Orientalist traditions of the late nineteenth and early twentieth centuries with the classical narrative still popular among many of today's scholars. Published in German in 1916 and translated into English in 1981, this essay has been called the single most influential study of its kind (Makdisi 1981a; Gutas 1998:166; Iqbal 2002:138–139). It provides the theoretical superstructure for the later work of prominent Western scholars, including Bernard Lewis (1976, 2002), A. C. Crombie (1979), David Lindberg (1992), Toby Huff ([1993] 2003), and Edward Grant (1996), among others.

Goldziher recapitulates the Western history of tensions between religion and science by framing any opposition within the Muslim world to Aristotelian science and philosophy as the work of an Islamic "orthodoxy." Thus he concludes: "Quite clearly, it was primarily Aristotelian metaphysics that was rejected by orthodoxy. The principles and results of this metaphysical system were believed to be fundamentally opposed to the doctrines of Islam" (1981:192). In other words, science succumbed to the internal logic of Islam, which is by its nature antirationalist, obscurantist, and inhospitable to innovation of any kind. Other explanations for the decline of the Islamic scientific tradition—economic malaise, geopolitical weakness, foreign invasion, climate change, plague and other outbreaks of disease, the collapse of vital irrigation systems, even the onset of imperial decadence—are rarely, if ever, given serious consideration.

Some modern critics have found Goldziher's notion of "orthodoxy" in Islam highly problematic. Islam has no centralized authority and includes a pronounced stress on each individual's relationship to God, so it is difficult to locate an institutionalized arbiter of either the orthodox or the heretical. Nor, as Dimitri Gutas (1998) reminds us, is it possible to identify more than a few, very specific periods in Islamic history in which science did not carry on alongside its critics, many of whom appear to have had no particular religious motivation whatsoever. Moreover, Islamic astronomy attained perhaps its highest point and was the object of enormous institutional support at the very moment—in the thirteenth century—when such "orthodoxy" established its everlasting predominance, according to Goldziher and others (Gutas 1998:169–172; see also Iqbal 2002:140). Goldziher's analysis is further complicated by contemporary circumstances, which tended to shade his views and those of his colleagues in favor of Islam as practiced among the more familiar Ottomans of the nineteenth century and against that of their rivals, the Wahhabis or neo-Wahhabis of more remote and—in Westerners' eyes—more inhospitable Saudi Arabia (Makdisi 1981a:219).

Such objections, however, have done little to discredit the classical narrative of Muslim science, which rests, unmoved and unmoving, on the bedrock of the anti-Islam discourse. In fact, in *The Rise of Early Modern Science*, Huff openly invokes Goldziher's authority to support his own contention that Islam and science were ultimately incompatible: "In general, the structure of thought and sentiment in medieval Islam was such that the pursuit of the rational or ancient sciences was widely considered to be a tainted enterprise. This has been shown most systematically in the work of Ignaz Goldziher" ([1993] 2003:70). Huff further cites Goldziher's assessment that such science was seen by Muslims as ungodly.

Throughout the history of Western engagement with the question of science and philosophy from the Islamic world, various social groups and institutions have stepped forward to uphold their own particular interests. The arrival of Muslim science in the Latin West in the eleventh and twelfth centuries sparked two significant responses: its eager embrace by an emerging social elite of educated urban intellectuals, scholars, and professionals and the equally impassioned denunciation of it as black magic by more entrenched social, religious, and political interests.

Once the building blocks of Islamic science and philosophy were sufficiently mastered and naturalized, however, Europe was able to free itself from any acknowledgment of the Arab contribution. The early humanists of the fourteenth century, led by Petrarch, advanced their own careers at court, in the rising cities and towns, and in the church hierarchy by promoting a new, "reborn" European learning whose roots lay in an idealized notion of ancient Greece and Rome. Here, the discourse of Islam as fundamentally irrational proved a powerful tool of social advancement for this new generation of scholars and bureaucrats, schooled in Greek and the classical Latin of Cicero rather than in the language of the Qur'an, al-Khwarizmi, and Avicenna.

The French algebraists of the sixteenth century deployed this same discourse to denigrate Muslim scholarship as a prelude to the creation of their own history of mathematics and the ensuing enhancement of their academic and professional prestige and of their political and social influence. Nineteenth-century Europe elevated elements of this narrative—that the Muslims were irrational and thus intellectually ill suited to the rigors of metaphysics and abstract thought in general—to a "scientific" principle supporting and justifying the West's colonialization of Eastern lands.

Each of these distinct social groups successfully invoked the Western discourse of Islam along the way, reinforcing its power and institutionalizing its teachings. Neither our knowledge of the Islamic intellectual tradition nor our knowledge of ourselves and our "Western" culture is the better for it. Yet as the next two chapters show, a very similar process has shaped our views of a range of issues that seemingly divide East from West: violence, religious warfare, and the rights of women.

5

ISLAM AND VIOLENCE

They've been hating us for a long time. In a sense, they've been hating us for centuries, and it's very natural that they should.

BERNARD LEWIS

JUST AS THE West has safeguarded its exclusive authority over modern science from any serious encroachment by the Islamic tradition, so, too, has it arrogated to itself a monopoly over the legitimate uses of force in conflicts involving the Muslim world. As with modern science, the production of Western statements on the subject of violence and war is shaped profoundly by some of the central tenets of the anti-Islam discourse: that Islam is inherently violent and spread exclusively by force; that Muslims are irrational and are motivated by religious fanaticism; and—a more recent accretion that flows from these others—that Muslims are filled with jealous rage against the West, its freedoms, and its lifestyles. Here, again, the Muslim East is held up as the opposite mirror image of the Judeo-Christian West.

The result is an unchallenged discourse that affords the West the power to determine which tactics, weaponry, and targets are legitimate and which are not. This same discourse also allows the West to define its conflicts with Islam in ways that successfully mobilize support at home for the use of force while simultaneously circumscribing Muslims' actions and discounting, delegitimizing, and even eliminating altogether their motives or goals. And it has benefited successive social groups and institutions, the Islam experts, all of whom have exploited and preserved the discourse virtually unchanged from its earliest roots in Crusader Europe.

The U.S. response to the attacks of September 11, 2001, on New York and Washington, D.C., has seen the most spectacular and spectacularly successful intersection of these two discursive phenomena: Western monopoly over the legitimate use and the technologies of violence as well as Western control of the equally important definition of the enemy. The former allows the West access to its arsenal of high-tech weaponry, from unmanned drones to so-called precision munitions. It also dismisses civilian deaths as "collateral damage," while condemning the enemies' deployment of car bombs, suicide attackers, and the highly effective roadside munitions, the so-called improvised explosive devices, as lacking any legitimacy.[1]

The latter phenomenon, meanwhile, deprives Muslims of any claim to specific rational motivation, whether grounded in historical grievance, political opposition, social dissidence, or specific readings of religious tradition. President George W. Bush took pains in public to say that the war on terrorism was not a war on Islam and the Muslims. Yet, as chapter 1 demonstrates, Bush's own repeated use of the word *crusade* and the apocalyptic language embraced by his strong supporters among the Christian Right, his own senior aides' anti-Muslim statements, the scope and practice of the subsequent law enforcement and military campaigns, the political rhetoric, and the groundswell of popular anti-Islam sentiment fueled largely by the media drumbeat in support of this war—all appear to contradict that claim. Moreover, virtually the entire Islamic world and many non-Muslims as well see the war on terrorism as just such a war on Muslims.

In *Writing the War on Terrorism: Language, Politics, and Counter-Terrorism*, Richard Jackson defines this war as "both a set of institutional practices and an accompanying set of assumptions, beliefs, forms of knowledge, and political and cultural narratives. It is an entire language contained in a truly voluminous store of 'texts'" (2005:16–17). From such texts flow all the security laws and legal rulings, the patriotic symbols and slogans, the policy documents, briefing papers, and so on that compose the war effort (17–18).

As discussed in chapter 1, the war on terrorism has been presented as part of a never-ending struggle in defense of Western civilization and values against fanatical, nihilist Muslims who hate modernity, democracy, and the very notion of freedom. Politicians, the military, the new generation of security experts, pundits, commentators, and journalists have reprised the central themes of the anti-Islam discourse as they sought to set the events of September 11, 2001, into a narrative that could simultaneously address the public's demands for some sort of an explanation of the attacks and shape the state's political and military responses. This effort culminated in a popular rhetorical question, Why do they hate us?—a catchphrase that all but dictates the inevitable answer but does not in itself pose a meaningful query.

This chapter investigates the ways in which the established Western discourse of violence in Islam has fueled the war on terrorism, while at the same time coloring its rhetoric, shaping its public reception, distorting its policy choices, and determining its outcomes. I begin with an examination of popular studies and commentaries on the phenomenon of contemporary terrorism, including the best-selling works of historian Bernard Lewis and New York Times columnist Thomas L. Friedman, among others. I then look back at how the anti-Islam discourse has performed the same task in relation to other conflicts with the world of Islam, from early modern Europe's rivalry with the Ottoman Empire to the high point of Western colonialism. I endeavor throughout to address the question of which groups, parties, institutions, and other social actors rely on and benefit from this discourse of Islam and violence.

Under the influence of Catholic Church ideologues, the seizure of Muslim territory in the late eleventh century by force of Christian arms was righteous specifically because the enemy was declared outside the pale of religious and therefore human society. In the eyes of Christian Europe, the Muslims lusted after power and violence, as was self-evident from their occupation of the Holy Land, whereas the Crusaders sought only the rightful liberation of Christ's sacred resting place. For Petrarch, the defining voice of early European humanism, the Muslims posed a natural existential danger. He went on to urge preemptive Western conquest of the Near East as the only suitable response.

The rise of Ottoman power and the threat felt across Europe from the armies of the sultan, brought home by the Muslims' seizure of Belgrade from Hungarian control in 1521, saw Europe's anti-Islam discourse reinvigorated both by the fear of impending attack and by the discourse's increasing utility as an ideological weapon in the domestic, European struggle over the Reformation. In the process, the Muslim world was again reduced to an undifferentiated mass, standing only for evil, violence, tyranny, bloodlust, and general mayhem; it had no cause, only effect. Later, in Napoleon's Egypt and British India, Muslim resistance to Western colonial occupation was viewed solely in terms of religious "fanaticism" and a taste for violence, and any desire for independence, self-determination, and restoration of religious and cultural values was marginalized or simply ignored. The primary carriers of this anti-Islam discourse have benefited from its perpetuation virtually intact across the centuries.

The events of September 11, 2001, pierced the complacency that had settled on the West in the years since the fall of the Berlin Wall, just as they silenced the triumphalist note struck by Francis Fukuyama's (1992) notion that Western civilization had at last successfully negotiated "the end of history." In fact, the immediate aftermath of the attacks on the United States saw the West turn its back on what we now can recognize as little more than a brief detour through the anti-Communist Cold War. It soon reverted to its more familiar geopolitical trajectory: the millennium-long contestation with the world of Islam.

That this radical shift in political, social, and intellectual mobilization from Cold War to war on terrorism was carried out so completely, so swiftly, and so easily—virtually without any meaningful opposition or serious deliberation—bespeaks the enormous power and influence of the established anti-Islam discourse. This discourse provided quite literally an off-the-shelf response that seemed in the eyes of many to address the questions plaguing political leaders and ordinary citizens alike: *Who are these people? Why did they attack us? What do they want?* And—as posed by Bush and then echoed in the media—*Why do they hate us?*

The ready response served up by the anti-Islam discourse to an anxious and bewildered public is perhaps best illustrated by the remarkable success of a slim volume of essays by Bernard Lewis, which appeared shortly after the September 11 attacks and zoomed up the best-seller lists. As noted earlier, Lewis's *What Went Wrong? Western Impact and Middle Eastern Response* was already in production at the time of the attacks. The author, a retired Ottoman specialist with a string of more than twenty scholarly and popular works to his credit, apparently saw no need to revisit his manuscript to explain the phenomenon of al-Qaeda and the deadly attacks of September 11, 2001—a day that Lewis's patrons in the Bush administration, including the powerful vice president, Dick Cheney, say changed the world forever. Rather, Lewis simply affixed the briefest of prefaces to the work before presenting it to a marketplace suddenly thirsting for information about the new threats coming from the skies. Within weeks, there were eighty thousand copies in print, an enormous figure for a work of its type.

Naturally enough, Lewis's legions of fans in government, in the media, and among the reading public as well as the author himself saw the prepared text of *What Went Wrong?* as unerringly prophetic. Islam is inherently violent, fundamentally antimodern, unable to develop politically or economically without outside intervention, and all the while enmeshed in impotent, anti-Western rage, Lewis writes, reprising familiar themes he had long professed. "I'd rather have been proven wrong, but I wasn't," he told *USA Today* (quoted in Minzesheimer 2002).

Lewis's apparent prescience further cemented his already strong ties to the neoconservatives in and around the Bush White House, who increasingly turned to him for both policy advice and intellectual backing for the war on terrorism and its stepchild, the invasion of Iraq. Lewis advised the administrations of both George H. W. Bush and George W. Bush, and Vice President Dick Cheney honored him in an address to the World Affairs Council of Philadelphia in 2006, noting his valuable briefings at the White House.

Lewis is also a regular contributor to influential conservative publications and a sought-after voice on news programs and talk shows, leading the *New York Times* to celebrate him as a "media star" (November 3, 2002, cited in Abrahamian 2003:541). As George W. Bush's speechwriter David Frum told the *Wall Street Journal*, the administration's response flowed naturally from Lewis's proscription: "Bernard comes with a very powerful explanation for why 9/11 happened. Once you understand it, the policy presents itself afterward" (quoted in Waldman 2004). That policy, which the same newspaper dubbed the "Lewis Doctrine," called on the United States to intercede forcibly to bring forth what the Muslim Arabs were incapable of achieving on their own: a recognizable—that is, Western-style—democracy. With Lewis and like-minded academic Fouad Ajami leading the way, neoconservatives already itching for an attack on Baghdad could now paint their project as a necessary exercise in democratic nation building.

But was Lewis "right" after all? Or was he simply following in the long line of Western Islam experts who had preceded him, such as Petrus Alfonsi, Petrarch, and Montesquieu, each of whom turned to the established narrative of Islam and the West as a way to benefit himself, his social cohort, and his allies? In other words, was Lewis, too, simply overwhelmed by the anti-Islam discourse to the extent that his "answers" preceded any question he or his powerful political patrons were likely to pose? A close reading of his popular works—books, newspaper op-ed articles, and interviews—suggests that this is precisely the case, for what Lewis presents as analysis of Islam in *What Went Wrong?* and related writings takes little or no account of the actual Muslim world or of the Muslim actors themselves. As we have come to expect, Islam qua Islam is ignored once again. "The book was already in page proof on September 11. But anyone who followed the Middle East could see which way things were going," Lewis (2001a) told a television interviewer. There was, then, no need to address the actual phenomenon of al-Qaeda, the specific rise of Osama bin Laden, previous American support for his anti-Soviet campaign in Afghanistan, the appeal of bin Ladenism, or related issues in order to diagnose and explain "what went wrong."

As Edward Said has shown in his writings on Orientalism, one of the over-riding characteristics of such scholarship is the complete disregard for what Muslims actually say and do in favor of what the Islam expert says that they say and do—and mean: "It should be noted that Orientalist learning itself was premised on the silence of the native, who was to be represented by an Occidental expert speaking *ex cathedra* on the native's behalf, presenting that unfortunate creature as an undeveloped, deficient, and uncivilized being who couldn't represent himself" (2002:71). Referring directly to Lewis's *What Went Wrong?* Said notes: "Announcing portentously that Muslims have 'for a long time' been asking 'what went wrong?' he [Lewis] then proceeds to tell us what they say and mean, rarely citing a single name, episode, or period except in the most general way" (72). Rather, Lewis's words appear to leap directly from the pages written by Pope Urban II's wartime ideologues and their successors.

Lewis makes this connection for himself. Receiving an award in 2007 from the American Enterprise Institute, bastion of Washington's neoconserva-tives, Lewis received a standing ovation for portraying the Crusades as "a late, limited and unsuccessful imitation of the *jihad* that spread Islam across much of the globe" ("Bernard Lewis Applauds the Crusades" 2007). In the same address, he condemned today's Muslim migration to Europe as an attack on the West and cited what he called the Muslims' natural advantages over their adversaries in "ideological fervor" and "demography"—the latter claim presumably a reference to relatively high birth rates in Muslim communi-ties. Lewis's argument here recalls his defense in 2001 of President Bush's comparison of his own war on terrorism to a crusade, a comparison that Lewis labeled "unfortunate, but excusable" (2001b). He went on to denounce, without irony, Osama bin Laden's own use of the same terminology.

So what lies at the heart of Lewis's view of Islam and the Muslims? What exactly did "go wrong"? Several distinct strands are repeated continually throughout his works, perhaps most prominently what he presents as the essential failure of the Muslim lands to modernize at the pace and in the direction dictated by the West and the anger, hatred, and resentment this failure has produced in the Muslim soul. Underpinning this view is a total-izing narrative of the world of Islam as a single civilizational bloc always at or near a state of all-out religious warfare with the West, a condition Lewis confidently traces back to the earliest days of Islam itself and in particular to the Muslim practice and understanding of *jihad*. The outlines of this argu-ment, presented in early form in "The Roots of Muslim Rage" (1990), mark Lewis—not Samuel Huntington—as the true father of the "clash of civiliza-tions" thesis so eagerly absorbed into the public discourse after the al-Qaeda attacks on New York and Washington (Said 2002:71; Abrahamian 2003:541).

In promoting *What Went Wrong?* in the aftermath of the al-Qaeda attacks, Lewis was more explicit in positioning the Islamic world as the antithesis of everything "Western":

> They've been hating us for a long time. In a sense, they've been hating us for centuries, and it's very natural that they should. You have this millennial rivalry between two world religions, and now, from their point of view, the wrong one seems to be winning. And more generally, I mean, you can't be rich, strong, successful and loved, particularly by those who are not rich, not strong and not successful. So the hatred is something almost axiomatic.
>
> The question which we should be asking is why do they neither fear nor respect us? (2001a)

For Lewis, this "axiomatic" hatred takes center stage, and there can be no other possible explanation for any anti-Western sentiment among Muslims except Islam's cardinal impulse toward armed, global expansionism and its chronic losing hand in the "millennial rivalry" with the West. Other possible sources—such as rejection of Western notions of modernity, resistance to colonial domination, opposition to global capitalism, reaction to Western interference in the affairs of Muslim societies, and so on—are never examined. Nor does he allow for consideration of a specific, Islamic ethic and worldview that has no interest in following blindly along the Western path. To return to Michel Foucault's exceedingly useful phrase, none of these possible sources of rejection is "within the true"; all are, instead, among the many things that *cannot* be said about Islam and thus are swept aside by the West's anti-Islam discourse. What is left, then, is an inevitable clash of civilizations, of which the war on terrorism is but a dangerous and alarming symptom.

The central discursive formation at work here is the organic link created between violence carried out by Muslims—any Muslims, anywhere—and the requirements of their faith as identified with the religious concept of *jihad* and the oft-associated notion of the *shahid* (martyr).[2] In fact, the prevailing Western discourse of violence in Islam can be seen clearly in the Orientalist tradition of textual scholarship surrounding these terms, of which Lewis is perhaps the most prominent and effective contemporary practitioner. This is particularly the case with the word *jihad*, which has entered the popular Western vocabulary as "holy war," not least on Lewis's (1988:72–73) authority.

Today, this term has been wholly naturalized and taken on a life of its own in the Western imagination. In their best-selling book *The Age of Sacred Terror* (2002), former Clinton administration counterterrorism officials Daniel Benjamin and Steven Simon do not even include *jihad* in the otherwise detailed glossary that appears at the back of the text, apparently on the assumption that everyone shares their definition of its meaning. Thus there is nothing between *jahiliyya* and "Ka'ba"—a vivid illustration of just how effectively such a complex, multivalent concept as *jihad* has been denatured and then assimilated into the Western vocabulary of the war on terrorism. In their account of the bombing of the U.S. embassy in Nairobi, the authors simply refer to the attack as "a jihad mission" (2002:29), presenting *jihad* as an accepted term whose uniform meaning and significance are understood and shared by all readers—and by all Muslim believers as well.

That contemporary militant Muslim groups often embrace a similar understanding of *jihad* is an indication that they, like the Western experts, have found the same discourse of Islam and violence a useful source of social, political, and religious mobilization. In this vein, the Western discourses of Islam and science and of Islam and women have periodically found favor to varying degrees within elements of Muslim societies.[3]

Given the power of the anti-Islam discourse, it is not surprising that glossary entries presented by Benjamin and Simon offer an inconsistent mix of classical and contemporary understandings of Islam, selectively deployed to bolster their argument about the central place of violence in the faith. For example, their definition of *dar al-harb* reinforces their notion of an endlessly expansionist Islam: "the realm *not yet* under Islamic law" (2002:447, emphasis added). In fact, the history of the concept of *dar al-harb*—literally, the "abode of war," but essentially referring to the non-Muslim world—suggests that it evolved with Islamic thinkers' recognition that a permanent state of actual warfare between the *dar al-Islam* and the *dar al-harb* was untenable and doomed to failure. This recognition was soon followed by that of another such abode, non-Muslim states with which the Muslims have treaties, the *dar al-ʾahd* (Mottahedeh and al-Sayyid 2001:28–29).

None of these terms can be found in the Qurʾan or the Prophet's sunna, and they were instead shaped by geopolitical realities of later times. Classical jurists ultimately abandoned them because they could not be applied successfully to the real world (Afsaruddin 2008:118–119). In contrast, Benjamin and Simon's definition of the militant Zionist group Gush Emunim makes no mention of the movement's well-known history of assassinations and car bombings against Palestinians or of its failed plot to blow up the Dome of the Rock (Sprinzak 1987). They simply identify Gush Emunim as "an Israeli settler movement founded in 1974" (Benjamin and Simon 2002:447).

In an extensive endnote, the two authors cite the authority of Bernard Lewis, backed by what they call "modern scholarly consensus," in support of their contention that the Muslim understanding of *jihad* has consistently imposed a religious obligation to carry out armed struggle against non-Muslims. And they dismiss all other religious understandings of the concept, including the "greater *jihad*," the individual believer's internal struggle to overcome his base human nature and be a better Muslim—a concept that encompasses personal development, education, acts of charity, and other good works:

The last century has seen a trend toward the interpretation of the so-called greater jihad as the more genuine form of Islamic struggle. The terminology comes from a hadith of disputed reliability in which Muhammad is reported to have said, upon returning from battle, that he has now returned from the lesser jihad to the greater, spiritual, jihad. Until recently, however, *Muslim scholars were unanimous* in insisting on the priority jihad had as warfare against the unbeliever. Bernard Lewis made this case most famously, but *modern scholarly consensus* on the matter is summed up by the new edition of the *Encyclopedia Islamica*. (2002:55n.2, emphasis added)

Although Benjamin and Simon literally relegate their understanding of *jihad* to the back of the book, this understanding and the "scholarly consensus" it represents put on full display the anti-Islam discourse that underpins *The Age of Sacred Terror* as well as Lewis's *What Went Wrong?* and many other such works. Foremost, in the great Orientalist tradition perfected in the nineteenth century, this discourse produces statements about the Muslims' beliefs and practices—thus we are told of the unanimity of "Muslim scholars"—without actually naming them and without presenting any Muslim voices. Second, it walls off other possible interpretations, such as the greater or spiritual *jihad*, by dismissing them as outside "the true" even as it hints at their very existence. Third, it purports to offer a scientific narrative based on a definitive reading of Muslim texts that may or may not reflect what Muslims say or do in real life. And it presents violent action carried out by Muslims as a natural and necessary outgrowth of their faith, thereby depriving them of motivations that may be rooted in worldly matters, including competing Western actions, ideas, or interests.

These approaches can be seen all the more clearly by examining the article, cited by Benjamin and Simon, on *jihad* in the *Encyclopedia of Islam* (Tyan 1991), a standard Western reference work edited by Bernard Lewis, among others. They also cite an essay on *jihad* by Douglas E. Streusand (1997), which in turn invokes the Lewis approach to understanding the term. Thus the circle is completed. In the encyclopedia's entry for *djihad*, Émile Tyan writes that the notion "stems from the fundamental principle of the universality of Islam: this religion, along with temporal power which it implies, ought to embrace the whole universe, if necessary by force" (1991:538). As a result, armed *jihad* is an obligation for all Muslims at all times, and any peace with non-Muslims is by nature transitory and may be revoked without notice whenever circumstances better favor success. "Certain writers," Tyan notes, in particular among the Shiʿites, explain *jihad* in terms of internal, spiritual struggle or set very strict limits on use of armed aggression, but such circumscription, we are told, is inconsistent with both "general doctrine and historical tradition" (538).

Tyan dismisses as mere apologetics those interpretations of *jihad* that do not conform to his model of perpetual warfare:

> Finally, there is at the present time a thesis, *of a wholly apologetic charac-*
> *ter*, according to which Islam relies for its expansion exclusively upon
> persuasion and other peaceful means, and the [*jihad*] is only authorized
> in cases of "self defense" and of "support owed to a defenseless ally
> or brother." Disregarding entirely the previous doctrine and historical
> tradition, as well as the texts of the Qurʾan and the sunna on the basis
> of which it was formulated, but claiming, even so, to remain within the
> bounds of strict orthodoxy, this thesis takes into account only those
> early texts which state the contrary. (1991:539, emphasis added)

He similarly mentions only briefly the rich etymology of the term *jihad*, with its Arabic root *j-h-d* and its linguistic relationship to *ijtihad*, the practice in Islamic law of independent reasoning applied to religious sources. One who carries out *ijtihad* is known as a *mujtahid*, from the same *j-h-d* root. However, this link between the intellectual and religious activity of *ijtihad* and the related understanding of *jihad* is largely ignored in favor of an exclusively militaristic reading.

Other possible readings and other possible interpretations beyond this "modern scholarly consensus"—a more perfect example of metonymy applied to the anti-Islam narrative is hard to imagine—of both the religious ideal and the actual practice of *jihad* have been pushed beyond the boundaries of "the true" by the discourse of violence in Islam. Impelled by Foucault's stratagem of reversal, we might well ask, What if the key strands in this discourse were set aside or otherwise negated? Specifically, what if Islam were *not* inherently violent, spread only by force, maintained by coercion, and driven by hatred for the non-Muslim West?

Asking these questions opens up a number of important new pathways for an understanding of *jihad* and of Muslims' actions and behaviors in general. For one, it removes the facile dismissal of that "wholly apologetic" reading, by the Shiʿite jurists among many others, of *jihad* as internal, personal struggle, as self-defense, or as legitimate aid to an ally or fellow Muslim under attack. Second, it allows us to explore seriously the variable context of the Islamic understanding over time of *jihad*, its legitimate scope, targets, and aims. And it holds up to scrutiny the notion, advanced so forcefully by Lewis and other purveyors of this "modern scholarly consensus," that historically there has been only one single interpretation of the term—a religious obligation of aggressive warfare against all non-Muslims.

Such explorations have been the focus of some recent scholarship on the problem (e.g., Hashmi 1996; Mottahedeh and al-Sayyid 2001; Afsaruddin 2006a, 2008:108–120; Bonner 2006), much of it in direct response to the foregrounding of the notion of *jihad* in the public discourse of Islam and violence after the al-Qaeda terrorist attacks. Each of these studies reveals in different ways the complex and ever-shifting understanding among Muslims of the religious concept of *jihad* as well as the relationship between this understanding and the social, political, and religious context of the times. Challenging the "modern scholarly consensus" that *jihad* ever had only one, consistent meaning—that of aggressive warfare against all non-Muslims—Roy Mottahedeh and Ridwan al-Sayyid write: "In fact, differences about the status and nature of *jihad* are a marked feature of early Islamic law, and details about the conduct of *jihad* continue to reflect historical circumstance throughout the history of Islamic law in the Middle East" (2001:23).

These differences concern the legitimacy of aggressive war altogether; the nature of legitimate targets of any such aggression (that is, only Arab polytheists or those people who do not follow a book of scripture or non-Muslims in general); the necessary religious authority to declare and lead a *jihad*; its rules and mode of conduct; and so on. Also at issue is exegetical theory, including the disputed notion of abrogation (*naskh*), by which some jurists consider some verses in the Qurʾan to have superseded others that appear, at least to limited human understanding, to offer contradictory guidance.

The most important examples of *naskh* for this discussion lie with the Qurʾan's so-called sword verses, which sanction slaying "idolaters" after the sacred truce months have elapsed (9:5), and attacking those "People of the Book" who ignore the sacred teachings and flout God's will (9:29). Some Muslim jurists in the centuries after Muhammad's death in 632 steadily advanced this militaristic understanding of *jihad* and argued for the abrogation of more conciliatory verses, including those that emphasize peaceful coexistence with enemies and the right to make treaties with non-Muslims as well as the more explicit verse "There is no compulsion in religion" (2:256).

Asma Afsaruddin, a scholar of early Islam, finds that many prominent Muslim legal thinkers never accepted the abrogation of this verse. Among those who did not were Muhammad Jarir al-Tabari (d. 923) and Ibn Kathir

(d. 1373). Ibn Taymiyya (d. 1328), mentor to Ibn Kathir and a figure often invoked as the spiritual father of the strict Wahhabi movement predominating to this day in Saudi Arabia, saw *jihad* as a defensive endeavor to be waged only against those unbelievers who were hostile toward the Muslims. Muhammad ibn Idris al-Shafiʾi (767–820), founder of one of the four major schools of Sunni law, condoned offensive *jihad*, but he specifically limited it to only the Muslims' struggle against pagan Arabs (Afsaruddin 2006a:22–23).

The Qurʾan, the fundamental text in Islam and the only one that is divine, has little to say on the subject of *jihad*, particularly as it relates to fighting and warfare.[4] And it offers even less in the way of a comprehensive doctrine of war (Bonner 2006:22). In general, the word *jihad* appears in the Qurʾan with the meaning "striving" or "effort," and it frequently precedes the phrase "in the path of God" (*fi sabil allah*). By contrast, the holy text specifically uses other Arabic words to denote fighting, killing, or armed combat (*qital*) or war in general (*harb*) (Bonner 2006:22; Afsaruddin 2008:109). In all, words containing the Arabic root *j-h-d*, denoting "effort" or "striving," appear forty-one times in the Qurʾan, with just ten of them referring to the conduct of warfare— all uses that also stress devotion to God, self-sacrifice, and righteous conduct (Heck 2004:97–98; Bonner 2006:22).

Thus fully formed, absolutist notions of *jihad* such as that invoked in the anti-Islam discourse cannot necessarily claim sanction in the only infallible text in Islam. Instead, these and competing interpretations appear to have evolved in an organic fashion in the centuries following the revelation in response to changed and changing social and political circumstance. The association between the Qurʾanic *jihad* and a fully formed and "complex doctrine and set of practices relating to the conduct of war . . . seems to have taken place sometime after the revelation and collection of the Qurʾan itself," writes Michael Bonner. "It is important to remember, however, that the concept of *jihad* was not, in the Qurʾan, primarily or mainly about fighting and warfare. The 'internal,' 'spiritual' [greater] *jihad* can thus claim to be every bit as old as its 'external,' 'fighting' counterpart" (2006:22).

Historical, social, and political context also plays a large role in the understanding and application of *jihad* throughout history. This role can be seen in both the shifting approaches to *jihad* in the legal literature and the changing political and social circumstances that have necessarily influenced this understanding. Max Weber reminds us in *The Sociology of Religion* of the distinction between the vocation of a prophet and that of later priestly classes, who then regulate "the content of prophecy or the sacred traditions by supplying them with a casuistical, rationalistic framework of analysis, and by adapting them to the customs of life and thought of their own class and of the laity whom they controlled" (1965:69).

The same process is reflected in the changing landscape of *jihad*. Thus classical scholars in the Arabian heartland of the Hijaz (where the Holy Cities of Mecca and Medina are located), well away from the Muslims' direct political and military competition with Christian Byzantium, tended to place relatively little emphasis on *jihad*, whereas Syrian jurists along the borderlands supported obligatory warfare against their non-Muslim neighbors and political and economic rivals in Constantinople. Hijazi views were also colored by their abiding doubts about the legitimacy of the Umayyads in Damascus, who as rulers of the Islamic Empire would lead any *jihad* (Mottahedeh and al-Sayyid 2001:26–27; Afsaruddin 2008:116). In all cases, later understandings of *jihad* appear to have enjoyed something of an independent existence, separate and distinct, from the revelation to Muhammad. In terms of our own analytical question "Cui bono?" we can recognize the process whereby successive groups, classes, and institutions—including Islam experts such as best-selling authors Daniel Benjamin, a prominent Washington figure confirmed in 2009 as the State Department's coordinator for counterterrorism, and Steven Simon—have benefited directly from advancing their own notions of *jihad*.

Here, again, we are not concerned so much with establishing the "truth value" of any one particular understanding of *jihad* as we are with underscoring the presence of a single, persistent Western discursive formation of violence in Islam that remains largely immune to serious challenge on historical, linguistic, and theological bases. As discussed earlier, some recent work has begun to chip away at this "modern scholarly consensus," but it has made no real impact on the predominant discourse of violence in Islam, nor should we expect that it would do so.

Benjamin and Simon (2002:40) are not content merely to parrot the consensus reading of *jihad*; they then extrapolate this absolutist understanding as central to obligatory Muslim religious practice and fashion an entire theology of violence in which terrorist attacks like those carried out by al-Qaeda constitute "a form of sacrament" in a cosmic battle between good and evil. In this way, a seamless connection is drawn between the attacks on New York and Washington, D.C., in 2001 and the very roots of the Islamic faith, as represented by God's revelation to the Prophet Muhammad in seventh-century Arabia.

Thus the authors' brief narrative of the al-Qaeda attacks is prefaced by excerpts from the Qur'an in which God outlines the fiery end that awaits the unbeliever, who is too proud, too arrogant, or too skeptical to receive the sacred teachings sent down for his own salvation:

> I will surely cast him into the Fire. Would that you knew what the Fire is like! It leaves nothing, it spares no one; it burns the skins of men. It is guarded by nineteen keepers.

> We have appointed none but the angels to guard the Fire, and made their number a subject for dispute among the unbelievers, so that those to whom the Scriptures were given may be convinced and the true believers strengthened in their faith. (quoted in Benjamin and Simon 2002:33)[5]

This imagery was, perhaps, simply too much to resist, given the fiery end of the Twin Towers in New York and the deadly blaze at the Pentagon. What else might have motivated the selection of lines from this famous sura, generally known as "The Cloaked One," as an epigraph to murderous terrorist attacks? The language at work here—condemning unbelievers to hellfire—would not at all be out of place in the Christian tradition. To cite just one well-known example, Dante's *Divine Comedy* (canto 28:30–31) recounts in detail the hideous torments of Muhammad in hell, his body split asunder so that his entrails hang out—an image that may reflect the Western discourse that casts Muhammad not as a prophet, but as a Christian schismatic. Nor would it be wholly unfamiliar to the followers of other religious traditions that offer true redemption only to those who accept and follow a specific creed and describe torments for those who fail to do so.

But Benjamin and Simon's reliance on "The Cloaked One" is problematic in other ways as well. Sura 74 is among the earliest revelations[6] and calls on a terrified Muhammad, who has been covered in a cloak by his loving wife Khadija after his shock encounter with the Angel Gabriel, to toss aside his protective wrap and preach the Word of God to his fellow man: "O thou enveloped in the cloak, Arise and warn" (74:1–2). We have here the very outset of Muhammad's sacred vocation, one that places him within the general pre-Islamic Arabian tradition of spiritual "warners" and in the specific line of the Abrahamic prophets recorded in earlier Jewish and Christian scriptures.

God then assures Muhammad that only those who fail to heed the holy teachings need worry at the End of Time: "For when the trumpet shall sound, surely that day will be a day of anguish, not of ease, for disbelievers" (74:8–10). Subsequent lines make it clear that "those to whom the Scriptures have been given and believers" (74:31)—that is, the pious People of the Book—will be spared such a fate in the afterlife. These lines are in keeping with Muhammad's own understanding of his prophetic mission, which is to restore for good the true essence of past revelation that had been corrupted or neglected by Jewish and Christian practice.

Impelled by the discourse of violence in Islam, Benjamin and Simon present the spiritual warning conveyed in "The Cloaked One" as a fitting introduction to mass murder. Likewise, this logic induces them to see the al-Qaeda attacks strictly as necessary acts of religious devotion and—as we have come to expect from the anti-Islam discourse—allows for no other possible factors or explanations: "The motivation for the attack was neither political calculation, strategic advantage, nor wanton bloodlust. It was to humiliate and slaughter those who defied the hegemony of God; it was to please Him by reasserting His primacy. It was an act of cosmic war. What appears to be senseless violence actually makes a great deal of sense to the terrorists and their sympathizers, for whom this mass killing was an act of redemption" (2002:40).

This Muslim theology of violence, larded with other central elements of the anti-Islam discourse, runs throughout the commentaries of Thomas Friedman, whose power and influence as the foreign-affairs columnist for the leading U.S. newspaper the *New York Times* dwarfs those of the authors of *What Went Wrong?* and *The Age of Sacred Terror*. Friedman's columns reach hundreds of thousands of newspaper readers every week, including most of the American elite, and many millions more around the world on the Internet. In the spring of 2002, he won a Pulitzer Prize for distinguished commentary. The awards committee cited Friedman's "clarity of vision, based on extensive reporting, in commenting on the worldwide impact of the terrorist threat" in the aftermath of the al-Qaeda attacks on New York and Washington, D.C.[7] Friedman's columns were also collated into a best-selling book, *Longitudes and Attitudes: Exploring the World After September 11* (2002), which features on its cover a detail from an Italian mannerist painting of the Battle of Lepanto, when the naval forces of European Christendom decisively defeated the

Muslim Ottomans in 1571 in what is traditionally regarded as a turning point in the balance of power between the Islamic East and the Christian West.

Writing from Jerusalem in his first published commentary on the events of September 11, 2001, Friedman invokes the powerful imagery of the last great shooting war between rival global worldviews: "Does my country really understand that this is World War III? And if this attack was the Pearl Harbor of World War III, it means there is a long, long war ahead" (2002:45). The attacks, he writes on September 13, were the work of "super-empowered angry men and women *out there*," who pervert Western science for their own, evil ends: "What makes them super-empowered . . . is their genius at using the networked world, the Internet and *the very high technology they hate*, to attack us. Think about it: They turned our most advanced civilian planes into human-directed, precision-guided cruise missiles—a diabolical melding of their fanaticism and our technology. Jihad Online" (46, emphasis added). He then continues his military theme by recalling the U.S. Marine Corps motto in his final call to arms: "It won't be easy. It will require our best strategists, our most creative diplomats and our bravest soldiers. Semper Fi" (48). Friedman's columns often draw on this discourse of military might, leaving no doubt about how he frames the problem of al-Qaeda and terrorism by Muslim groups in general. A December 9, 2001, essay concludes: "Mr. President, where do we enlist?" (87).

Friedman briefly appears to step outside the prevailing discourse and calls the attacks "an amazing technological feat" despite the antitechnology bias that he attributes to the perpetrators' religious beliefs. In the end, of course, this tribute to the Muslim hijackers' skill and planning cannot be allowed to stand, and he immediately introduces an unnamed "Israeli military official" to sound a skeptical note that all the attackers did was manage to fly planes that were already in the air: " 'It's not that difficult to learn how to fly a plane once it's up in the air,' [the official] said. 'And remember, they never had to learn how to land' " (2002:48).

For Friedman, the lesson is clear: wed to an antipathy for science, reason, and the modern world grounded in their religion, members of al-Qaeda and their ilk—in contrast to the suddenly embattled West—know only how to fight and destroy. This theme is more developed in a column of October 2, 2001: "The terrorists can hijack Boeing planes, but in the spiritless, monolithic societies they want to build, they could never produce them. The terrorists can exploit the U.S.-made Internet, but in their suffocated world of one God, one truth, one way, one leader, they could never invent it" (2002:46).

It is worth juxtaposing Friedman's reference to "one God"—the very definition of monotheism shared by Muslims, Christians, and Jews—to Pope Gregory VII's one thousand years earlier.

Three days later, on October 5, 2001, Friedman lashes out at any suggestion
that the hijackers and their network had anything but apocalyptic designs:

> One can only be amazed at the ease with which some people abroad
> and at campus teach-ins now tell us what motivated the terrorists.
> Guess what? The terrorists didn't leave an explanatory note. Because
> their deed was their note: We want to destroy America, starting with
> its military and financial centers. Which part of that sentence don't
> people understand?
>
>   Have you ever seen Osama bin Laden say "I just want to see a smaller
> Israel in its pre-1967 borders," or "I have no problem with America, it
> just needs to have a lower cultural and military profile in the Muslim
> world"? These terrorists aren't out for a new kind of coexistence with
> us. They are out for our non-existence. (2002:67)

In March 2002, Friedman again maintains that the hijackers and their supporters and masters were devoid of all political demands (2002:211; cited in
Abrahamian 2003:531–532).

In fact, Osama bin Laden and the leadership of al-Qaeda had made it
clear much earlier what they were seeking, first in the so-called fatwa of
1996, "Declaration of War Against the Americans Occupying the Land of
the Two Holy Places" (bin Laden 1996), and again in a shorter document
in 1998, "Declaration of the World Islamic Front for *Jihad* Against the Jews
and the Crusaders" (bin Laden, al-Zawahiri, and others 1998).[8] Among their
demands were the withdrawal of American military forces from Muslim
lands, particularly from Saudi Arabia, home to the Kaʾba, the holiest site
in Islam; an end to Western support for Israel and its repression of the Palestinians; a halt to violence against Muslim communities worldwide, from
India and Central Asia to the Balkans; and an end to U.S. support for corrupt
and repressive regimes in Islamic countries, especially bin Laden's native
Saudi Arabia.

The later "fatwa" includes a declaration of war to enforce these
demands: "The ruling to kill the Americans and their allies—civilians
and military—is an individual duty for every Muslim who can do it in any

country in which it is possible to do it, in order to liberate the al-Aqsa Mosque [Jerusalem] and the holy mosque [Mecca] from their grip, and in order for their armies to move out of all the lands of Islam, defeated and unable to threaten any Muslim" (bin Laden, al-Zawahiri, and others 1998). Moreover, the 2001 hijackers left behind their own letter or "testament," which was soon in the hands of the Federal Bureau of Investigation (Abrahamian 2003:531–532).

The al-Qaeda attacks of September 11 caught the Western world by surprise, although members of the intelligence community had uncovered plenty of advance warnings, and bin Laden himself had spelled out the threat to American military and civilian targets should his demands be ignored. But there was, of course, no such corresponding gap in time or failure to be heard for the anti-Islam discourse. As we have seen, Bernard Lewis, Daniel Benjamin and Steven Simon, Thomas Friedman, and countless other Islam experts stepped forward to advance the dominant discursive formation of violence in Islam. In doing so, these experts furthered their policy objectives toward the Muslim world; ensured their own centrality to the Western foreign-policy debate; enriched themselves through book sales, lecture fees, and think tank, academic, and political appointments; and provided invaluable support to their allies in government and industry.

Media companies likewise rushed to embrace the same discourse, now wrapped up neatly in the "clash of civilizations" thesis advanced first by Lewis and more explicitly by Huntington. The New York Times created its special daily section devoted to the attacks, "A Nation Challenged." Opinions and viewpoints beyond this framework were declared outside "the true" and were notably absent from the airways, the news pages, and the Internet. Intellectual debate was also choked off. The Muslim intellectual Tariq Ramadan, a Swiss national and well-known European thinker, was barred from entering the United States and taking up a prestigious teaching post at Notre Dame University for "security reasons," and several prominent non-Muslim academics who strayed too far outside the discourse were denied promotions and tenure or even ousted from the academy.[9]

One need only recall the almost universal vilification of the late Susan Sontag for writing in the New Yorker two weeks after the al-Qaeda attacks that the events had to be seen in the context of America's long role in the Muslim world and the opposition and anger that such a role had engendered in many quarters:

The disconnect between last Tuesday's monstrous dose of reality and the self-righteous drivel and outright deceptions being peddled by public figures and TV commentators is startling, depressing. The voices licensed to follow the event seem to have joined together in a campaign to infantilize the public. Where is the acknowledgement that this was not a "cowardly" attack on "civilization" or "liberty" or "humanity" or "the free world" but an attack on the world's self-proclaimed super-power, undertaken as a consequence of specific American alliances and actions? (2001)

Concludes one scholarly study of the American media response: "A cursory glance at the U.S. media after September 11 leaves no doubt as to Huntington's triumph. The media framed the whole crisis within the context of Islam, of cultural conflicts, and of Western civilization threatened by the Other" (Abrahamian 2003:531). Television "talking heads," security experts, journalists, and academics were not the only social beneficiaries of the discourse of violence in Islam. The immediate militarization of America's response to al-Qaeda, a policy that grew organically out of the underlying anti-Islam discourse, created a bonanza for the military–industrial complex, with lucrative procurement and service contracts, research-and-development investments, and so on; for the security apparatus, with its expanded powers, larger budget, and growing cadres, and the corresponding clampdown on civil liberties; and for the politicians who led the charge. Yet none of that would have been possible without the firm grounding of the "text" of September 11 in a thousand-year narrative, only this time costumed as an inevitable civilizational clash between Islam and the West.

As we have seen, the Western discourse of Islam dates to the First Crusade and was at first perpetuated chiefly by the Catholic Church's reformist elite, personified in the figure of Pope Urban II, and by its allies among the ruling houses of Europe. It also received the backing of charismatic preachers such as Peter the Hermit, who rallied public support among the masses for the crusading enterprise, and of adventurers and minor nobles alike who saw in it a pathway to riches, land, and even hereditary titles in territories conquered in the name of Christian holy war. Yet none of these direct beneficiaries of the discursive formation had had anything but the most cursory acquaintance—if that—with the world of Islam and the Muslims.

Seen from a distant Europe and reflected in the chronicles of the First Crusade, almost all of which were recorded well after the event, the Christian victories over the Muslim armies offered proof that God had foreordained the success of the Crusade in general and the capture of Jerusalem in particular. The Holy City was likewise widely assumed in Latin circles to have been historically Christian, with Muslim suzerainty an anomalous, short-lived, and clearly reversible state of affairs. As a result, the Crusaders arrived as an army of liberation to restore God's order to the geopolitical map of the Near East. This characterization gave the campaign a preeminent and permanent place in the sacred history of Christendom, something to which none of the later Crusades could ever aspire. As Norman Daniel has stated,

> The First Crusade was one of the principal events in the history of European consciousness. This is obvious from the number of second-hand accounts of it that were written; and there has never been a time when Europe has not, in one way or another, remembered the First Crusade. Accounts of later crusades are ordinary histories and travels; the first was the response to a clerical idea which satisfied a wider—and more powerful—emotional need. . . . What began as a common enthusiasm broke up immediately into its constituent parts, and yet a certain common attitude, which was pan-European, remained. (1975:113)

Also contributing to the breakup of this "common enthusiasm" was the relentless logic of facts on the ground. At the end of the eleventh century, the creation of the Crusader states, comprising the Kingdom of Jerusalem and its vassal states Edessa, Tripoli, and Antioch, added a new dimension to the region's complex political and religious landscape. The rulers of this Latin East soon saw that their own fate was bound up with the fates of the Muslims, Christian Arabs, and Jews who populated the region; there would be no significant reinfusion of European Christians to help colonize the new Crusader states. The Crusader movement—and, later, Europe as well—found itself increasingly enmeshed in the cultural, political, military, and economic life of the Muslim world in ways that would have horrified men such as Peter the Hermit and Pope Urban II, who died just days before the news of Jerusalem's capture reached Rome.

As with countless invaders before them, the Crusaders soon discovered that the act of conquest leaves its mark on the besiegers as well as the besieged. There would be numerous campaigns to come—even the mystery of the so-called Children's Crusade of 1212, which, according to Christian legend, ended in mass enslavement at Muslim hands—but the idea of crusading would never really return to Urban II's vision. The adaptable Normans took on the best aspects of Arab life even as they expelled Muslim rulers from the eastern Mediterranean, creating sumptuous courts whose learning and culture began to rival those of the great caliphs and sultans. Meanwhile, the symbolic value of Jerusalem as a place worth fighting and dying for began to fade—if only gradually—in the face of new economic, political, and cultural realities.

Chief among these realities was the spectacular growth of East–West trade. The Catholic Church clearly recognized the danger that this trade posed to the survival of its anti-Muslim agenda, and it sought to strangle commerce with the infidel, particularly in such strategic goods as wood for shipbuilding, iron, arms, and even foodstuffs (Daniel 1960:137). Yet money from this new trade with the East began to flow into the merchant coffers of southern Europe. Genoa dominated commerce with North Africa and the Black Sea region, and Venice maintained a lock on trade with Egypt and Syria (Atiya 1962:171).

Along with shipments of oil, textiles, and precious metals came new ideas, technologies, and systems of thought. Our modern Arabic numerals were popularized in the West thanks to contracts and other trade documents drawn up between Muslim merchants and their Italian counterparts. Trade terminology in numerous European languages still bears the mark of Arabic and Persian commercial usage. Seaborne commerce required navigational aids such as sophisticated maps, charts, and instruments—all areas where the medieval Muslims excelled. One measure of these expanding economic ties was the appearance of Muslim gold in European treasuries as far away as England. The minting of gold coins, halted in ninth-century Europe for lack of bullion, resumed in the Italian city-states four centuries later after supplies from the East were secured (Abulafia 1994:10).

Changes in the nature of the Crusades were also striking. Later campaigns, which continued off and on for centuries, were either designed to claim territory already retaken by the Muslims or else perverted by political ambition or greed, such as the sack of Christian Constantinople in 1204 at the instigation of the merchants of Venice. The initial disarray among the Muslims that had coincided with the first arrival of the Crusaders soon began to dissipate, and within forty-five years they began to push back the Christian advances, a process eventually crowned by Saladin's triumphant entry into Jerusalem in 1187 at the head of a unified force from Egypt and Syria.

The glories of the Latin East were gone forever, but the discursive formation that had made the First Crusade possible continued unabated and largely unchanged by the growing interaction and evolving dynamic between East and West. In Europe's early modern period, the central elements of this discourse—the notions of Islam as violent, corrupt, deceitful, tyrannical, and perverse—were soon turned inward as Europe struggled with the social, religious, and political dislocations ushered in by the Reformation. The discourse of Islam, then, provided a ready-made template for new generations of ideologues and experts to take down from its shelf and apply to a Christian Europe now divided along sectarian lines. Even without the intimate and bloody interactions that once characterized the Crusades, Islam was to remain a permanent fixture of the European imagination.

Two literary forms of the early modern era illustrate the breadth and scope of this discursive formation, even as they presided over a subtle shift in focus from the Muslim Other to the European Self. The first consisted of the so-called *Türkenbüchlein*, popular German pamphlets of the early sixteenth century that invoked the threat of Turkish invasion in support of demands for Christian repentance and reform (Bohnstedt 1968:3). The second comprised works of romance, long the preeminent literary form by which Christendom had imagined its relationships and conflicts with the outside world (Robinson 2007:2).

The most famous *Türkenbüchlein* are undoubtedly three works by Martin Luther, but many of his lesser-known contemporaries on both sides of the new Christian divide tried their hand at the genre. The earliest such work dates to the spring of 1522, shortly after the fall of Belgrade to the Ottoman armies, with the phenomenon having largely run its course within two decades (Bohnstedt 1968:3). All took the existential threat to Christendom posed by the Turkish armies in nearby eastern Europe for granted, and the Ottoman sultan, Suleiman the Magnificent, was generally depicted as a "hereditary foe of all Christians." Massacres, torture, the murder of the unborn in the mother's womb, and other abominations were ascribed to "the Turk," now synonymous with "Saracen," "Persian," and "Mahometan" (Bohnstedt 1968:18–19).

Yet the same texts quickly turned their fire on ideological enemies within the Christian camp, whether Lutheran or Catholic. Many identified the Turks as a scourge sent by God either to punish the Lutheran heresies or to force reform on a wayward and erring Roman Church, as the case may be. A children's hymn, written by Luther and used well into the nineteenth century, when any Turkish threat must have been at most a distant memory, links the pope and the sultan in eternal infamy: "Keep us true to thy Word, O Lord, and preserve us from murder by the Pope and the Turk, who would topple Jesus Christ, thy Son, from thy throne" (quoted in Bohnstedt 1968:24n.25). In a similar vein, the first English translator of the Qur'an, Alexander Ross, dismisses Oliver Cromwell as an English-speaking "Mahomet" (Robinson 2007:172).

Luther's early polemics with the church seemed to suggest that he saw the Turk as the lesser of the two evils and that a fight against the Muslims would only serve to prolong church corruption. He soon clarified his stance and produced numerous anti-Turkish pamphlets and sermons, most prominently *On War Against the Turk* (Forell 1945:257–259; Robinson 2007:43–44). As part of the ideological battle with Islam, Luther was also instrumental in securing the publication of the Qur'an, in Robert of Ketton's polemical Latin paraphrase, over the initial objections of the authorities in Basel (Kritzeck 1964:201; Tolan 2002:xix). In a letter to the city council, Luther writes: "To honor Christ, to do good for Christians, to harm the Turks, to vex the devil, set this book free and don't withhold it" (quoted in Clark 1984:11).

Just as the *Türkenbüchlein* naturalized the anti-Islam discourse and adapted it to the religious controversies of contemporary Europe, so did early modern literary romance seek to make sense of a changed and changing world in which Islam and the Muslims were now a permanent fixture, an agreed reference point, against which to measure other threats and other enemies. Among the key texts is Edmund Spenser's *Faerie Queene* (published in two parts in 1590 and 1596), which presents Philip II in the figure of the "Souldan," the Muslim sultan, and thus casts Protestant England's military struggle with Catholic Spain as a holy war (Robinson 2007:36–38). But other works from the early modern period similarly introduce the Western notion of the Muslim into what are essentially internal European struggles with changing religious, economic, and political realities—a category that could accommodate Shakespeare's explorations of alterity in *The Merchant of Venice*, *Othello*, and *The Tempest*.

The early modern European writers, influenced by the Ottomans' rising power and by their own limited understanding of the Muslim world, increasingly displaced "Saracen" or "Moor" in favor of the catch-all "Turk." According to Benedict S. Robinson, such interchangeable usage forced the rich collection of Muslim cultures and histories into a uniquely Western fantasy of the Islamic world. "In a sense," he writes, "Europe has always refused to treat Islam as a religion at all, preferring to inscribe it into theories of racial, political, and cultural difference, and thereby refusing to acknowledge Islam's claim to universality while at the same time insisting that it is always the same, across vast reaches of time and space" (2007:5).

For these early modern interpreters and experts, there was no Islam qua Islam, only an Islam that met their own social and institutional demands. Each side in the European struggle over the Reformation sought to tar the other by rhetorical association with the violent and dangerous "Turk." And each side invoked, understood, and accepted this discourse in identical terms. In this way, the anti-Islam discourse saw itself further entrenched and its traditional content further solidified in Western social, political, and intellectual life—even as it became increasingly divorced from the Muslims themselves.

Similar demands can be seen, albeit in a very different era and context, in another, seemingly cataclysmic threat to the West: the Indian rebellion of 1857, which, at least in the eyes of the British, threatened to overwhelm their once-unquestioned rule over the subcontinent and even to shake the foundations of the empire itself. On the face of it, the insurrection began when mounting discontent among the Indian recruits who made up the overwhelming majority of the British-led armed forces exploded at Meerut on May 10, 1857, over fears of ritual pollution from the introduction of new Enfield rifles and their greased cartridges. The rifle featured a bored barrel that greatly increased its accuracy and range over those of existing weapons, but the design required that grease be applied to the ball in order to coax it into place. Rumors of uncertain origin soon spread that the grease on the new paper cartridges had originated from the fat of cows, deeply offensive to Hindus, and that of pigs, forbidden by Islam. The alarmed troops mutinied, turned on their officers, killed them and some of their families, and then raced toward the old imperial capital, Delhi.

The intervening 150 years have seen the growth of a rich and varied histo-riographical tradition surrounding the causes and context of the revolt. Was the rebellion a glorified mutiny provoked by indifferent British leadership of the restive native armies, as many contemporary critics argued? Or was it, perhaps, the result of a vast religious and political intrigue, as the colo-nial administration maintained? Some later assessments have found, among other interpretations, an outbreak of leaderless peasant revolts in the face of mounting economic distress (Stokes 1978, 1986); a restoration campaign on behalf of the fallen Muslim Mughal Empire (Buckler 1972); an anticolonial resistance movement fueled by radical changes in land ownership (Mukher-jee 2002); an expression of fundamental alterations in social, cultural, and sexual relationships between colonizers and colonized (Sharpe 1993; Paxton 1999; Park 2000); and a "fictive event" of epochal impact on Victorian and post-Victorian consciousness that decisively outweighed its objective his-torical import (Herbert 2008:3).

At the time of the rebellion itself, though, Anglo-Indian officials had no doubt: it was nothing less than a "Mahommedan conspiracy," fueled by Mus-lim fanaticism and lust for religious warfare, which managed to suborn the traditionally placid Hindus to make common cause against the Christian interlopers. At the center of this conspiracy, said the victorious British, sat the aged Muhammad Bahadur Shah II, formally the latest in a long line of Mughal emperors but in reality little more than a British pensioner with a domain limited to the confines of the high walls at Delhi's famed Red Fort palace.

Summing up the government's case against the man now in the dock, listed with bureaucratic understatement simply as the "ex-King of Delhi" in contemporary documents, chief prosecutor Major F. J. Harriott told the grandly named European Military Commission:

> The known restless spirit of Mahommedan fanaticism has been the first aggressor, the vindictive intolerance of that peculiar faith has been struggling for mastery, seditious conspiracy has been its means, the prisoner [Bahadur Shah] its active accomplice, and every possible crime its frightful result. . . .
>
> Thus the bitter zeal of Mahommedanism meets us everywhere. It is conspicuous in the papers, flagrant in the petitions, and perfectly demonic in its actions. There seems, indeed, scarce any exemption from its contagious touch. (U.K. House of Commons 1859:152)

Harriott, the deputy judge advocate general, had already led the success-ful prosecution of members of the king's court and much of his male kin, many of whom were hanged for rebellion against British rule. A number of others had already been executed summarily in the immediate aftermath of the British assault on the Red Fort. Much to the chagrin of Harriott and other senior colonial officials, Bahadur Shah would not face a similar fate, for the British officer who cornered the former king on the outskirts of Delhi had promised him that his life would be spared in exchange for his peaceful surrender.

Any disappointment that Harriott may have felt over the promise to spare the king's life, which the Anglo-Indian establishment loudly decried as "unau-thorized" but nonetheless decided to honor, was more than compensated for by the zeal the prosecutor unleashed in describing the Muslim conspiracy. Nevertheless, it is clear that Harriott's address to the military court was not merely his personal assessment of the events of 1857, but the collective opin-ion of British colonial officialdom after a lengthy investigation into the rebel-lion conducted by local resident agents, linguists and translators, intelligence officers, and so on. "Our investigation has involved inquiry over a period of sev-eral months, when rebellion was rampant in this city; and I trust we have suc-ceeded in tracing, with considerable minuteness, many of the different events as they evolved themselves," Harriott told the military tribunal. "I, of course, allude to the causes, either remote or immediate, which gave rise to a revolt unparalleled in the annals of history" (U.K. House of Commons 1859:133–134).

For Harriott and his teams of colonial investigators and intelligence bureaucrats, what they universally referred to as "the mutiny" began as a minor disturbance in the Bengal Native Army and was then cunningly manipulated by Indian Muslims, backed by an international Islamic revan-chist movement that grouped together such disparate forces—and mutually distrustful rivals—as the Shi'ites of Persia, the Ottoman Turks, and the mili-tant Sunni followers of Muhammad ibn Abd al-Wahhab. At its center sat the figure of Bahadur Shah, whose native cunning, scheming temperament, and bloodthirsty nature belied his eighty-two years, his gentle countenance, his love of calligraphy, and his skillful composition of Sufi poetry. This view was, in short, the dominant discourse shared by the ruling Anglo-Indian elite and taken up enthusiastically by the public at large back home in England and elsewhere in the West. Its echoes can be heard in the discursive formation that comprises today's war on terrorism.

Inflamed by the news media and the popular literary journals, the British public rallied in support of an aggressive, even bloodthirsty stance against the defeated rebels. Relying on wild gossip, fear mongering, and rampant rumor, especially reports—inaccurate, as it happens—of widespread sexual abuse of English women before they were killed by their native captors, the Victorian press created an "imagined India," a dark place that could be forcibly subdued and ruled but never wholly trusted, reformed, or uplifted (Brantlinger 1988:200; Park 2000:87–89).

Pulp novels set in the times of the rebellion and fusing violence and sex with exotic Indian locales soon emerged as a popular and remarkably enduring literary form. By one count, at least fifty such works were published before 1900, with another thirty or more appearing before World War II (Brantlinger 1988:199). The popular journals of the day were not to be outdone. They quickly jettisoned any discussion of errant colonial administrators and incompetent military leaders who may have contributed to the rebellion and asserted that an iron fist was the only way to tame "Asiatic barbarism" and "fanaticism."

Thus the *Illustrated London News*, under Charles Dickens's personal direction, presented the conflict in clear tones of racial and religious essentialism: "Bengal Sepahees,[10] who, from good and valiant soldiers, have, through the instrumentality of wild fanaticism and their own worse passions ... become converted ... into miscreant thieves and murderers" (August 8, 1857:186; quoted in L. Peters 2000:116). One month later, the journal introduced its readers to the king of the north Indian state of Adwadh, a "true Mahommedan type—bloodthirsty, vindictive, selfish and dissolute, and unrelenting" (September 12, 1857:257; quoted in L. Peters 2000:117). Such villains were juxtaposed to the figure of the valiant Englishman, hopelessly outnumbered but ultimately victorious and now avenging the lost honor of his countrywomen through bloody but wholly necessary reprisals. As such, this figure was transformed in the public imagination from the helpless victim of Indian violence to the powerful, righteous defender of Victorian womanhood and the British way of life (Park 2000:87–88).

Dickens's *Illustrated London News* had no time for half-measures, and it endorsed the proposed razing of Delhi in the name of British security, an idea that the military authorities eventually dropped. "No cry ... of cruelty that may arise from the ultra-humanitarians, 'who live at home in ease,' will prevent or retard consummation," the journal thundered (September 12, 1857; quoted in L. Peters 2000:121). Nor were such views restricted to a British Empire facing down the threat of insurrection. The American writer Oliver

Wendell Holmes used the pages of the new *Atlantic Monthly* to endorse British vengeance and urge the "deletion" of the Mughal capital from the face of the earth: "The India mail brings stories of women and children outraged and murdered; the royal stronghold is in the hands of the babe-killers. England takes down the Map of the World, which she has girdled with empire, and makes a correction thus: [DELHI] *Dele*. The civilized world says, Amen" (1894:96; quoted in Stokes 1986:92).

There were, to be sure, some discordant voices at the time. Most famous among them was that of Benjamin Disraeli, who used a long address to the House of Commons to identify "an accumulation of adequate causes" of the rebellion, which included disruption of India's social and economic order, general heavy-handedness by the colonial authorities, increased interference in local dynastic politics, and growing isolation and alienation of the British military and colonial administrators from the people, languages, and cultures of the subcontinent. Karl Marx, writing in the *New York Daily Tribune*, viewed the affair as nascent nationalist rebellion (both discussed in Brantlinger 1988:202).

John William Kaye (1864–1880), the early historian of the rebellion, saw the causes of the revolt in problems and challenges facing Indian civil society as a whole, a view with which his colleague G. B. Malleson (1857:63) generally concurred (Kaye and Malleson 1897–1898; see also Stokes 1986:5). Others, including William Howard Russell, a prominent correspondent for the *Times* of London, questioned whether the British even had the right to try Bahadur Shah. After all, the East India Company, which ruled much of the region, was formally still his vassal and agent, and so the legal theory that he could be in rebellion and guilty of treason against the company and against England was tenuous at best (Russell 1860, 2:60–61; Dalrymple 2006:399–400).

But there was no stopping the official diagnosis of a vast Muslim conspiracy, and Harriott offered the court a wealth of evidence and documentation to support this view. The prosecution presented witness statements against the king—often from Christian converts, Hindu courtiers, and those who had remained close to the British—and official orders and proclamations said to bear Bahadur Shah's imperial seal. Yet the heart of the case against the last of the Mughals was essentially rhetorical, patched together from familiar elements of the anti-Islam discourse, without which Harriott's official version of the Indian rebellion would have collapsed under its own shoddy legal construction and sheer logical absurdity.

Among the evidence presented against the defendant, Harriott reminded the court in his summation, was an order from the king at the outset of the disturbances that his royal guards take full control of weapons, powder, and ammunition stored in the magazine. This order might seem like a wise precaution in times of political instability and social unrest, when angry native soldiers were swarming over the precincts of the Red Fort and demanding that the aging king lead their cause against the British. But in Harriott's hands it became prima facie evidence of well-planned criminal conspiracy, underpinned by Bahadur Shah and his fellow Muslims' inherent cognitive shortcomings and lack of rational judgment and forethought: "We thus see with what alertness and dispatch this most important object, the seizure of the magazine, was attempted. Is it, however, to be believed that such was the ready, immediate, and, as it were, impulsive decision of the king, or of those who formed the court? To attribute to them anything of this nature would be to give them credit for a coolness of calculation, combined with a quickness of apprehension, such as pertains only to the more gifted of mankind" (U.K. House of Commons 1859:138).

Harriott also took aim at the notion that there could have been any rational grounds for rebellion against British colonial domination—as we have seen, a familiar rhetorical device that serves to underscore the Muslims' religious fanaticism, irrational and reflexive, as the only true cause and to deprive them of any real voice. The affair of the greased cartridges was but a pretext; after all, any sepoy truly offended by the idea of coming in contact with animal fat could simply have resigned from the army and spared his religious sensibilities. Nor was the mounting Christian missionary zeal among many officers and colonial administrators to blame. "It seems beyond the bounds of reason to imagine that these men were drawn into acts of such revolting atrocity by any grievance real or imagined. . . . I believe, indeed, that the facts elicited on this point may be ranged appropriately under the head of 'Mahommedan conspiracy,' this chief object of which seems to have been the spread of disaffection and distrust of British rule, and . . . to prepare all the people for change and insurrection" (U.K. House of Commons 1859:135, 147). This conspiracy had to have originated with the king as titular head of the Muslim community and with his court.

But Bahadur Shah was not working alone, Harriott asserted. Rather, he sat at the center of an international Muslim plot, backed by the Shiʿites of Persia and their Sunni rivals, the Ottoman Turks, and abetted by religious fanatics whipped up by itinerant Muslim preachers and other clerical leaders. The prosecution case on the former score rested on anonymous announcements and placards, supported by widespread newspaper reports, that popped up in Delhi falsely heralding the imminent arrival of the Persian armies, backed by the Turks and perhaps even by England's rivals the Russians and the French, to shore up the rebellion: "Are we then to suppose in all this that there was no connection between the palace and the press? Were all these concurrences fortuitous? . . . Are the circumstances appealing to Mahommedan pride, to their superstitious bigotry, to their lust for religious war, and to their hatred for the English, dwelt upon with a less perfect knowledge of their peculiar inherences?" (U.K. House of Commons 1859:150).

Finally, Harriott turned to the Muslims' penchant for violence, a quality inherent to their faith. In doing so, he suddenly made half the population of Delhi, much of northern India, and the overwhelming majority of the rebellious Bengal Army—that is, the Hindus—somehow disappear completely from the scene and essentially absolved them of any meaningful role in the revolt.[11] Harriott reminded the military court that one government witness, Jat Mall, among a number of Hindus to testify against the king, had reported no enthusiasm for the rebellion among "respectable" Hindus, whereas "the Mahommedans as a body were all pleased at the overthrow of the British Government" (U.K. House of Commons 1859:146).

In fact, the prosecutor's investigation concluded that the Hindu population had been essentially forced to go along with their militant Muslim neighbors in revolting against India's colonial masters:

It is a most significant fact on these proceedings, that though we come upon traces of Mussulman intrigue wherever our investigation has carried us, yet not one paper has been found to show that the Hindus, as a body, had been conspiring against us, or that their Brahmins and priests had been preaching a crusade against Christians. In their case, there has been no king to set up, no religion to be propagated by the sword. . . .

Hinduism, I may say, is nowhere either reflected or represented; it if be brought forward at all, it is only in subservience to its ever-aggressive neighbor. The arguments in reference to a Mahommedan conspiracy are now closed. (U.K. House of Commons 1859:148–149, 153)

It took the five-member European Military Commission only a matter of minutes to reach a unanimous verdict of guilty on all counts against Bahadur Shah, ratifying the government's grand vision that a large Muslim conspiracy, fueled by sectarian hatred and the violence of the faith, lay behind the worst native unrest to strike at the heart of the great British Empire. Had it not been for the promise of the officer who had arranged his surrender, the last of the Mughals would certainly have hanged. Instead, he was transported to Rangoon, where he died in captivity in 1862 at age eighty-seven.

On the face of it, the government case for a "Mahommedan conspiracy" looks unpromising at best. In the first place, the British themselves, since the late eighteenth century, had deliberately set out to create the very Bengal Army later to be at the center of the rebellion as a virtual Hindu institution, dominated by high-caste Hindu peasants and farmers: Rajputs, the traditional warriors of northern India, and the priestly class of Brahmins or their military wing, the Bhumimars (David 2003:20; Dalrymple 2006:126). In British eyes, this approach conferred a number of important benefits, not the least of which was the heavy reliance on the very agrarian class that had served as the traditional backbone of their own armed forces back home. Further, members of the higher castes were seen as physically bigger and stronger than representatives of lower social groups. And high caste was presumed to carry with it greater loyalty to the British cause while also providing the colonial masters with greater social and political legitimacy within Indian society (Alavi 1995:39; David 2003:19–20).

The deliberate recruitment of high-status Hindus was accompanied by a number of measures that tended to reinforce caste distinctions and to play to the religious and social sensitivities of the Rajputs and Brahmins, a process that Seema Alavi has called the "sankritization" of the armed forces (1995:76). These measures included the agreement, later rescinded, not to deploy these sepoys across the "black water"—that is, across the sea, in violation of caste rules. Even more important was the elaborate attention paid to the requirements of caste dietary laws, efforts that often exceeded what the recruit might have been able to demand back in his native village (Alavi 1995:76). The net effect was the creation of considerable esprit de corps in the Bengal Army regiments, grounded in a heightened awareness of Hindu caste and the notion of being part of an Indian military elite.

By 1815, upper-caste Hindus represented around 80 percent of the infantry in the Bengal Army. This proportion declined to around 65 percent by 1842 as the British began to incorporate more middle Hindu castes as well as Muslims and other groups, and it was further reduced somewhat in succeeding years. Yet all the mutinous regiments were virtually dominated by high-caste Hindus, with Muslims typically composing just 20 percent or so of recruits—on a par with "middling" Hindu castes and much less than the percentage of the Rajputs and Brahmins taken together (David 2003:22–24). Bengal Army regiments with a majority of upper-caste Hindus overwhelmingly sided with the mutiny, whereas those in which Muslims predominated, such as the eighteen regiments of Bengal Irregular Cavalry and the Bengal Artillery, were far less involved in the rebellion, if at all (David 2003:25–26).

Second, there was the matter of packaging Bahadur Shah as the active genius behind a vast Muslim military and sectarian plot that cut across northern India's complex politics, reached into Persia and Constantinople, and even extended to England's Western rivals, the courts of Paris and Moscow. By the time hundreds of armed sepoy rebels, fresh from the mutiny at Meerut and the slaughter of British officers, administrators, women, and children, burst into the Red Fort in May 1857 and demanded that the king lead their rebellion against the British, he was eighty-two years old and had little of the energy, let alone the practical experience, that such an undertaking would have required. Rather, the last of the Mughals was, among other accomplishments, a major Sufi poet and a great connoisseur of the arts, but he evinced none of the political acumen, military prowess, or sweeping vision of his famed ancestors, Genghis Khan and Timur.

This incongruity was not lost on Russell, the *Times* correspondent. Escorted to see the royal prisoner after the recapture of Delhi, Russell could not help wondering: "Was he, indeed, one who had conceived that vast plan of restoring a great empire, who had fomented the most gigantic mutiny in the history of the world? . . . His eyes had the dull, filmy look of very old age" (1860, 1:60; quoted in Dalrymple 2006:8).

Even Harriott, the prosecutor, had allowed that Bahadur Shah might have been swept up by the logic of Muslim militancy, although this in no way mitigated his own guilt: "Insignificant and contemptible as to any outward show of power, it would appear that this possessor of mere nominal royalty has ever been looked upon by Mahommedan fanaticism as the head and culminating star of its faith" (U.K. House of Commons 1859:134). For his part, Bahadur Shah maintained his innocence and told the court, in a three-page written submission that represented his entire defense, that he had been the rebels' virtual prisoner: "What confidence could I place in troops who had murdered their own masters? In the same way that they murdered them, so they made me a prisoner, and tyrannized over me, keeping me on in order to make use of my name as a sanction for their acts" (133).

Other elements of the plot were equally problematic. Much was made in British colonial circles and in the press of the role of volunteer detachments of militant Muslim devotees, led by their *maulavis* (learned preachers) and committed to a *jihad* against the British. There were certainly significant elements in and around Delhi who had long rejected the Mughal court's historic engagement with Sufism and its syncretic, heterodox approach to religion and society. Yet there remain significant doubts surrounding both the actual number and the military utility of these religious volunteers, untrained and poorly armed as they were, in the face of the disciplined British units and their still-loyal native forces. Standard accounts of the day put the defenders of Delhi confronting the British assault at around thirty thousand (Roberts 1897:13), and General James Hope Grant's private journals report another seventy thousand volunteers in support, "most Mahommedans . . . armed to the teeth and capable of fighting even more desperately than the sepoys" (1873:86–87).

More recent scholarship, relying in part on accounts from Delhi residents and other Indian witnesses, has put the number closer to seven thousand to ten thousand, roughly on a par with a British-led attacking force backed by powerful artillery units that made the final conquest of Delhi "relatively easy" (Stokes 1986:94). Even some contemporaneous British documents seem to cast doubt on the theory of a revolt fueled by widespread Muslim zeal. The so-called Descriptive Rolls, a most-wanted list of four hundred or so prominent rebels assembled by the colonial administration, included the names and other details of relatively few religious leaders (Chick 1974:163; Llewellyn-Jones 2007:43).

Moreover, there is considerable evidence that Bahadur Shah resolutely refused to play the card of religious war, despite the militant *maulavis'* demands and the appearance of anonymous proclamations of *jihad* in Delhi's main mosque. A courtier's diary, published well after the events, recounts the king's anger at attempts to stoke sectarian passions. "This day the standard of the Holy War was raised by the Mahommedans in the [main] Jumma Masjid," recorded Mainodin Hassan Khan, the Delhi police chief, on May 19, 1857.

"The King was very angry and remonstrated, because such a display of fanaticism would only tend to exasperate the Hindus." Khan noted in the next day's entry that Bahadur Shah successfully ordered the removal of the green standard of holy war on the grounds that "such a *jihad* was quite impossible and such an idea an act of extreme folly, for the majority of the [native] soldiers were Hindus" (quoted in Metcalfe 1898:98).

The successful prosecution of Bahadur Shah as the central figure in a vast Muslim conspiracy shows once again the explanatory benefit of the anti-Muslim discourse. Here, it virtually dictated both the ways the British colonial regime apprehended the Indian rebellion—the regime's own immediate practical and policy responses to the crisis—and the public's willingness to accept these responses as fitting, natural, and just. Harriott's prosecution dovetailed neatly with the Western narrative of Islam as violent and fanatical, and the discourse of Islam and violence was clearly at work in preventing alternative approaches or explanations from receiving serious consideration.

As we have seen, a discourse's power to dictate what *cannot* be said is among its most important features. In the case of the Indian rebellion, the anti-Islam discourse made it simply not possible for the general public to wonder, as did a few isolated voices, how it was that an overwhelmingly Hindu army had so easily become the tools of revanchist Muslim militants under the leadership of an aged and infirm "shadow" emperor who spent his days composing mystical verse in Urdu, Persian, and Punjabi and practicing his exquisite calligraphy inside a fort that constituted the whole of his domain.

Not surprisingly, the same discourse was also in keeping with the self-interest of India's colonial and military establishment, in particular its leading administrators and its top experts on intelligence, security, and religious affairs. For the military and political leaders of British India, the notion of a Muslim conspiracy at the heart of the events of 1857 effectively inoculated them against any whiff of incompetence or malfeasance for not having perceived the danger of rebellion and for having allowed the unrest in the first place. Advancing and perpetuating the anti-Islam discourse supported the interests of the entire colonial enterprise by marginalizing any possible legitimate grievances—such as foreign domination or British-fostered disruptions in the local economy or growing fears of Christian evangelism—that may have mobilized the rebels. This discourse likewise benefited a generation of Islam experts and Orientalist scholars who drew heavily on it and their experiences in India.

Foremost among these scholars was the enigmatic William Muir, who stood at the nexus of intelligence, scholarship, and the media—a powerful position that prefigures the role of today's star terrorism experts at the center of the contemporary Islam discourse. Muir received a battlefield promotion during the earliest days of the uprising to head the British intelligence effort, a task he carried out with dedication and zeal. Colonial officials "had wisely organized an Intelligence department, of which William Muir had the chief direction. . . . [A]nd no man could have done the work better than Muir," concluded John Kaye (1864–1880, 3:406). Like many other intelligence officers of the day, Muir was a scholar of Islam and the author of a number of books and religious pamphlets on the subject. He also apparently led a secret life during the rebellion, filing news reports for the *Times* under the pen name "Judex" (P. Taylor 1996).

Muir's own intelligence findings, the reports of his spies and other informants, and his correspondence with leading military men, colonial figures, and resident agents across the areas affected by the uprising were compiled into an invaluable collection, *Records of the Intelligence Department of the Government of the North-West Provinces of India During the Mutiny of 1857* (1902).[12] This collection offers important evidence of just how the prevailing discourse of Islam shaped the British perception and understanding of events unfolding around them and then determined their responses.

What is equally striking here is how this discourse also manages to crowd out or marginalize other interpretations—competing texts—that threatened to contradict or challenge it. The pervasive power of this "crowding" effect can be seen in the early historiography of the war. Some of the first accounts of the affair, including the initial investigation by Kaye, saw the rebellion as an expression of deep discontent across Indian society and blamed the military and colonial administration for ignoring what was in essence a national insurrection. But subsequent colonial histories, including a later reworking of Kaye's classic study by an editor, tended to give more and more weight to the notion of a Muslim conspiracy (Stokes 1986:4–8).

Muir's own intelligence reports and correspondence are dotted with references to Muslim fanaticism. Alluding to the cartridge affair in a June 2, 1857, letter to his brother, Muir notes: "It is the very nature of the Mahometan faith to seize upon such an incident as a religious principle, impelling the more devoted or fanatical to an attempt for re-establishing the ascendancy of Islam" (1902, 1:35). Four months later in another letter to the same brother, Muir explains the rebels' success at Aligarh: "All the ancient feelings of warring for the faith, reminding one of the days of the first Caliphs, were resuscitated" (46).

Sent from his base in Agra, which held out successfully against the rebels, Muir's October 6, 1857, intelligence note reads: "You will remember that a week or ten days ago the Mohammedan fanatics of this district, joined by some bad characters, ejected our adherent, Rajah Gobind Singh, who with . . . a few others, were [sic] holding [Aligarh] for us" (1902, 1:174). He describes nearby Akrabad as "a nest of fanaticism and disaffection" (175).

Muir's spies and colleagues saw the rebellion in very much the same light as the intelligence chief. One source's brief note of July 16, 1857, reports that a town outside Aligarh was bent on Muslim holy war: "Coel is in disorder. The fanatical lower Mussulmans . . . raising the cry of 'Deen—Deen' [faith—faith]. No traveler safe" (Muir 1902, 2:6). And Muir's primary informant on Indian Muslim affairs was not a Muslim at all, but the pious Hindu Chaube Ghuanshaym Das, brother of a loyalist notable. Like Muir and other colonial officials, both brothers saw the uprising exclusively as an exercise in restoring Islam to predominance in the region (Bayly 1996:326). E. A. Reade, a senior administrator at Agra, meanwhile, found that "mussulmanophobia" swept the town in the first two months of the rebellion (cited in Bayly 1996:324). Although trapped inside their fort and virtually cut off from all sources of information, the British of Agra knew without question who was to blame for the insurrection and ensuing mayhem.

The same discursive formation at work here is evident in Muir's own learned studies of Islam, reflecting the seamless union of security analysis and Orientalist scholarship that we have seen in the works of Bernard Lewis, Steven Simon, and Richard Benjamin. Among his scholarly titles are *The Life of Mahomet* (1858–1861); *The Caliphate, Its Rise, Decline, and Fall: From Original Sources* (1892); and *The Coran: Its Composition and Teaching, and the Testimony It Bears to the Holy Scriptures* (1896). Muir is also the author of *The Rise and Decline of Islam* (1883), which reveals striking parallels between his understanding of Islam and his earlier intelligence work during the Indian rebellion.

Reprising the themes of the Western discourse of Islam in general, Muir constructs an Islam that inevitably founders without the backing of military force and the promise of unlimited sexual gratification to its male followers. "The progress of Islam was slow until Mahomet cast aside the precepts of toleration, and adopted an aggressive, militant policy. Then it became rapid," he writes in a one-page preface to *The Rise and Decline of Islam*. "As the first spread of Islam was due to the sword, so when the sword was sheathed Islam ceased to spread" (1883:27).

Muir acknowledges that Islam's teachings contain some philosophical truths, but he has no doubt that without armed force and material inducements, including men's access to multiple sexual partners, it would never have progressed beyond the confines of Arabia and become a world faith: "The weapons of its warfare were 'carnal,' material and earthly; and by them it conquered. . . . The license allowed by the Coran between the sexes—at least in favor of the male sex—is so wide, that for such as have the means and desire to take advantage of it, there need be no limit whatever to sexual indulgence" (1883:20, 31).

He then seeks to scandalize his readers with lurid tales of sexual license among the Muslims of "modern times." They include an account of some unnamed "Malays of Penang" who had up to twenty wives by the age of thirty-five; a report from Edward William Lane's canonical Orientalist text *An Account of the Manners and Customs of the Modern Egyptians* (2003) of men who take a new wife every month; and a tale of a forty-five-year-old Arab who divorced and married so often that he had had fifty wives in all (Muir 1883:33). Although both of these themes, the Muslim as inherently violent and the Muslim as sexual deviant, clearly come straight from the Crusades-era discourse of Islam, Muir himself draws a straight line between his own thinking and that of the medieval polemicists whose legacy he had inherited. In fact, Muir openly invokes the "author" of a famous medieval anti-Muslim text of uncertain provenance for many of the ideas presented in *The Rise and Decline of Islam*: "Such are the reflections of one who lived at a Mahometan Court, and who, moreover—flourishing as he did a thousand years ago—was sufficiently near the early spread of Islam to be able to contrast what he saw, and heard, and read, of the causes of its success with those of the Gospels, and had the courage to confess the same" (28).

This reference is to no less than the author of the *Apology of al-Kindi*, which purports to represent a ninth-century Christian's adversarial dialogue with a Muslim friend who seeks the former's conversion to Islam. Little is known about the actual origins of the text, although it is almost certainly not—as Muir confidently asserts—from inside the Abbasid court of Caliph al-Mamun, who died in 833. Rather, it represents one example in an established genre of pseudo-epistles tailored to fit the times and context of theological debate. The *Apology* was most likely written in Arabic by a Nestorian Christian, with some borrowings from what appear to be tenth-century texts. Even the author's name gives away its generic quality; the text itself identifies him only as "al-Kindi," and a later work calls him "'Abd al-Masih al-Kindi," a clear reference to Jesus Christ (Isa al-Masih) and invoking his role as Christian champion (Daniel 1960:6; Tolan 2002:60–63; Burman 2007:77). The same text was used by Peter the Venerable, the abbot of Cluny, in the twelfth century in the preparation of his own attacks on Islam, the *Summa totius haeresis Saracenorum* and the *Contra sectam sine haeresim Saracenorum* (Kritzeck 1956:178–179).

The discourse of Muslims as inherently violent, treacherous, and fanatical determined British actions and policy responses throughout the Indian crisis. And it paved the way for the widespread notion of the sexual abuse of English women and girls before their murder at the hands of their Indian captors. At the outset of the uprising, this discourse also impelled colonial administrators to purge the rolls of many skilled Muslim civil servants, depriving the system of much-needed talent and valuable sources of information, understanding, and institutional memory.

In an entry dated July 20, 1857, Muir acknowledges the heavy British reliance on Muslims—Hindu civil servants were then comparatively rare—for "information and advice." But, he laments, they were simply no longer reliable: "However excellent and trustworthy these men under other circumstances might have been, they were now placed in a peculiarly trying position from the religious and Mahometan element at this time dominant in the Mutineer movement." He goes on to praise his superiors' "judicious" decision to rely mainly on the Hindus, "whom alone we can, at this juncture, as a body depend upon" (1902, 1:12–13).

Just as the use of the anti-Islam discourse by George W. Bush and others set the stage for today's war on terrorism and virtually ensured that any Western reaction would be confined solely to military and security responses, so the same narrative guaranteed the bloodthirsty repression of the Indian uprising by the victorious British. By stripping out other possible causes and eliminating competing texts, the prevailing view of violent Muslim conspiracy closed off all avenues—such as economic or social reform, religious tolerance, recognition of local political and economic tradition, and so on—that might have been used to redefine relations between British ruler and Indian ruled. Instead, the embedded notion of Islam as essentially violent and implacably so left the conquerors of Delhi with only one option—brute force to exterminate the threat.

Giddy British forces and their loyal native soldiers raided whole city quarters, slaughtered their civilian populations, and plundered their goods. Not even those whose support for the colonial masters had never flagged, such as some of the big merchant families and the local nobility, were spared. One British "gentleman" recalled in letters to the British and Indian press the prevailing sentiment that saw the native populace not as human beings, but as "fiends, or, at best, wild beasts deserving only the death of dogs" (quoted in Martin 1861:449). In such circumstances, he continued, mercy was not on offer: "All the city people found within the walls when our troops entered were bayoneted on the spot; and the number was considerable, as you may suppose when I tell you that some forty or fifty persons were often found hiding in one house. They were not mutineers, but residents of the city, who trusted to our well-known mild rule for pardon. I am glad to say that they were to be disappointed" (449; see also Dalrymple 2006:336–337).

With the insurrection increasingly under control in the autumn of 1857 and Delhi now firmly once again in the hands of the British military, this discourse continued to exercise its influence on both colonial policy and the official assessments of just what exactly had gone wrong in the first place. The British immediately set about reorganizing the colonial civil service, with an eye to far greater reliance on Hindus. This narrative likewise shaped the question of what to do with the conquered capital and its huge civilian population, which effectively had been expelled to the countryside by British forces and was in dire need of adequate shelter, food, and water and subject to attack by roaming bands of local tribesmen.

Senior civil authorities, such as William Muir and C. B. Saunders, the commissioner at Delhi, remonstrated with the military commanders to relax their grip on the vacant capital and to recognize a distinction between the

Muslim enemy and more trustworthy Hindus among a refugee population of around 150,000 people. In a letter dated October 12, 1857, more than three weeks after the recapture of the city, Muir approvingly quotes Saunders as having pressed his case on behalf of the Hindus: "I have been anxious to induce them [the armed forces], at any rate, to permit the respectable Hindu merchant families, *bunyas* [entrepreneurs], and trades people generally, to return to their occupations, but hitherto with little success. I conceive that there really is no good ground for excluding the above, as no danger need be anticipated from allowing them to re-enter the town and return to their avocations. The case is different with a very large proportion of the Mahommedan population who have taken so prominent and violent a part against us" (1902, 1:190).

For his part, Muir argues that the extreme hardships faced by the expelled populace risked fueling further rebellion and that exceptions must be made, at least for non-Muslims: "Among the Hindu portion, at any rate of the one hundred and fifty-three thousand inhabitants, there must be numerous and large classes which one would have thought might have been easily distinguishable as not disaffected and as safely to be readmitted" (1902, 2:92). Muir reacts elsewhere to an intelligence report that the Hindus of Bareilly had fared badly in the rebellion, suffering financial losses and insults to their caste standing: "These facts should open the eyes of the Hindus to the real object of the rebellion, and show them what they have to expect from their Mahommedan fellow-countrymen" (178).

As with Harriott's prosecution of Bahadur Shah, the intelligence officers and political administrators of British India could not escape the anti-Islam discourse, even when confronted with evidence that seemed to challenge this accepted central narrative. Thus the information compiled in the *Records of the Intelligence Department* can result ultimately in only one reading of the raw intelligence from spies, informants, the local Indian press, and other sources.

In the midst of the crisis, Lord Charles Canning, the governor-general, directed Muir to investigate the alleged rape and sexual abuse of English women and girls held in captivity by the rebels and subsequently murdered. The result is thirteen pages of memoranda, reports, surveys, letters, and so on, collected under the heading "Memo. on Treatment of European Females" (Muir 1902, 1:367–379). Muir's investigation leads him to conclude that there was in fact no pattern of sexual abuse, although individual incidents may have occurred. Rather, the awe with which the Indians viewed their colonial masters, even as they sought to overthrow and kill them, "operated to chill and repress the idea of any familiar approach," and the "cold and heartless bloodthirstiness" directed against the English remained "at the farthest remove from the lust of desire" (369). Despite the conclusions of this top-level investigation, tales of rape and other sexual abuse of female prisoners became both a staple of the political speech of the day and a recurring theme in the copious literary output back home inspired by the rebellion. Given the established anti-Muslim discourse, it was unthinkable *not* to think that such outrages had not taken place in the land of the "Oriental" harem. And so no one did not think it.

On January 8, 1858, Muir similarly notes that a police investigation undertaken by a Major Williams into the earliest days of the uprising at Meerut had made substantial progress in unraveling the causes of the rebellion: "Major Williams is getting on marvelously with his Meerut police investigation, and will have a mass of evidence as to the origin of the Mutiny which will not fit easily with the popular notion of a long preconceived plot" (1902, 1:338). Four days later, Muir summarizes Williams's preliminary findings that the insurrection was largely the work of "a disorganized mob" with no real discernible objectives or goals (342).

But by now the case against Bahadur Shah and his international Muslim conspiracy—what Muir blandly calls the "popular notion"—was the official, agreed text of the Indian mutiny, and the case against Bahadur Shah was about to go to court, sealing the acceptance of this version of the events of 1857 as a vast Muslim conspiracy and of all that has flowed from this version ever since. There were simply too many institutional interests to allow any reassessment of the discourse of Islam and violence in light of what might actually have happened on the ground.

As we have seen throughout this study, other Western social groups and institutions in other times and other settings have repeatedly benefited from this same discourse of Islam and violence. Medieval Europe's considerable mobilization of men, money, and matériel for the First Crusade would have been impossible without a powerful narrative that cast the Muslim as the violent, death-dealing Other, intent on the destruction of Christendom and the enslavement of its people. In the hands of eleventh-century reformers and ideologues—Europe's first Islam experts—this discourse advanced a program of radical restructuring of church–state relations, opened the prospects to Latin Christendom's eastward expansion, aided the purging of dissident theological voices, and enhanced the overall social standing of the established religious hierarchy.

The early modern period saw Europe effectively resigned to the continued presence of a large Muslim empire on its eastern flank. Yet lively trade, growing diplomatic contact, and even the odd treaty between the Ottoman court and the emerging European nation-states did little to break down or modify the established notions of Islam and violence. Unable for a considerable time to contemplate anything except uneasy coexistence with the West's powerful neighbor, competing European diplomatic and religious factions instead invoked the discourse in their own internal rhetorical struggles. Thus Protestant England could denounce the ruler of Catholic rival Spain as the new "Souldan," or sultan, and both Luther and his enemies in the church called down the Muslim scourge on one another. These voices helped solidify the meaning and content of the discourse of Islam and violence in European consciousness and further separated it from any independent reality of the Muslims themselves.

For the senior colonial administrators and military leaders in India, Muslim fanaticism and predilection for violence provided the most useful and convenient explanation for the rebellion of 1857, one that diverted unwanted attention from the colonialists' own possible malfeasance. For the growing cohort of evangelical Christians in the colonial ranks, the discourse of Islam and violence justified and bolstered the importance of their expanding mission. For India's Anglicized, non-Muslim elites, it reinforced their own reliability and value to the ruling British. For publishers and authors, it produced an entire new literary genre of sensationalist tales of the abuse and even rape of Christian women and girls at the hands of their Muslim captors.

The same discourse freed the Victorian man to carry out bloody reprisals against the rebels and to avenge the flower of English womanhood, and the politicians and the public at large found in the discursive formation of Islam and violence invaluable support for the continued British presence in India and for England's armed civilizing mandate. At the same time, the discourse obscured any rational motivations or legitimate grievances on the part of the rebels, such as demands for an end to the British colonial presence, a halt to Western disruptions of local social and economic relations, or a cessation of Christian evangelism among the Hindu and Muslim populations.

Today, the discourse of violence in Islam securely underpins the war on terrorism. It colors the war's rhetoric and provides a supporting political and academic language with its own internal logic, as seen in the popular use of such terms as *jihad, crusade, martyrdom,* and *Islamofascism.* This discourse, as it did after the Indian rebellion 150 years ago, shapes official and public understanding of events, spells out policy responses, and determines their outcomes. It dismisses or eliminates altogether the enemy's own goals, motivations, and objectives, making negotiated settlement or other nonviolent resolution all but impossible. And it has served well a new generation of terrorism analysts, military leaders, politicians, and corporate and media interests and allowed them to advance their own agendas within a powerful and established framework that effectively remains immune to serious challenge or revision.

6

ISLAM AND WOMEN

What the [Orientalist] postcard proposes as the truth is but a substitute for *something that does not exist.*

MALEK ALLOULA, *THE COLONIAL HAREM*

TAKEN TOGETHER, THE discursive formations discussed in chapters 4 and 5 have deprived the Muslims of any claim on modern science—that is, on the essence of modernity itself—and severely circumscribed their ability to defend themselves by force if necessary. The same narratives have left the Muslim world vulnerable to demands for radical social reforms along Western lines as the pathway to material, political, and economic success. Nowhere is this more the case than in the relations between Muslim men and women. In fact, much of the Western discourse of Islam over the past two hundred years can be seen as a discourse of what the Victorians commonly referred to as women's "degradation" within the tyranny of the Muslim family, which in turn stood for the despotism, violence, and backwardness of Muslim society as a whole.

This chapter traces the emergence of this discourse of Islam and women from within the greater anti-Islam narrative, commencing with the Enlightenment and progressing to the war on terrorism. And it shows how the Enlightenment thinkers and their successors as Islam experts—from the classical Orientalist scholars, politicians, and travel writers of the nineteenth century to today's specialists and media commentators—have deployed and perpetuated the discourse of Islam and women by successfully harnessing the established narrative to advance their own social, political, and economic interests.

Since the eighteenth century, the harem has been the most frequently invoked symbol of this degradation and despotism. As Billie Melman has argued, this notion of the harem came to encompass the entire Western critique of state and society in Islam: "From the earliest encounters between Christians and Muslims till the present, the harem as the locus of an exotic and abnormal sexuality fascinated Westerners. It came to be regarded as a microcosmic Middle East, apotheosizing the two characteristics perceived as essentially Oriental: sensuality and violence. . . . From the Enlightenment onwards, the harem came to be not merely a psychosexual symbol, but a metaphor for injustice in civil society and the state and arbitrary government" (1992:60).

By the early twentieth century, the institution of veiling had for the most part supplanted the harem as the focal point of Western attention, a position it still holds. However, the underlying dynamics of the discourse of Islam and women remain unchanged. The end result has been a "sexualization" of the general Western view of Islam and the Muslims, one in which the totality of Muslim beliefs and practices and even the entire Islamic civilization are frequently reduced to Western perceptions and assessment of the male-female dynamic.

Witness the obsession with the veil—its use or disuse, its size and color, its degree of transparency, and so on—as a barometer of social progress and overall well-being within Islamic societies, to such a degree that it has become a commonplace of Western mass-media coverage, social activism, and political discussion alike. The contemporary debate over the wearing of the veil among France's large Muslim population, to present just one example for now, mirrors a similar debate in colonial Egypt under British rule.

The influence of Montesquieu on the early institutionalization of this process cannot be overlooked. According to Norman Daniel, "The most important work in this category was Montesquieu's *Lettres persanes*. He used the whole accumulated apparatus of oriental legends to illustrate a variety of themes which have the central point of freedom. The political satire is clear, but it is not the most important element. It is the notion that women should be free that inspires this book. . . . Montesquieu conceived the family life in Islam as servitude. The image of the harem was of orgiastic license within, and the dead hand of jealousy without" (1966:22).

The French novelist and thinker, for example, ignores relatively sophisticated contemporary accounts of actual Muslim beliefs and practices regarding women and sexuality—including works found in his own personal library—in favor of an imagined Orient that both conforms to the accepted discourse and simultaneously serves his own polemical purposes. The later Victorian traveler—the voyeur par excellence—likewise arrived in the Muslim world with a firmly fixed idea of Oriental society—cruel, sensual, languorous, and thus ripe for the picking, or at least for reeducation. No degree of personal experience or observation could dispel what Leila Ahmed has called the "illusory familiarity" of the Orient (1978:85).

When the Orient failed to meet expectations or, worse, was simply off-limits or otherwise unattainable, as was generally the case with the precincts of the harem or the face of the veiled woman, it was simply conjured up from the existing discourse, and this conjured image was accepted as an accurate representation of Eastern ways. In the Victorian mind, the degradation of Muslim women had to be addressed through an end to veiling and other practices that retarded social, political, and economic development and prevented the adoption of Western ways and the integration of Muslims into the worldwide capitalist order.

Today, this argument can be heard loud and clear across the Western political spectrum, where the armed invasion of Muslim lands and the projected remaking of Muslim societies and their economies are routinely cast in terms of the liberation of the veiled woman and an end to Muslim backwardness. No wonder, then, that Bernard Lewis, one of the intellectual architects of the war on terrorism, has called the status of women "probably the most profound single difference between the two civilizations" (2002:67).

As we have already seen, the Muslim empires' economic, military, and political power and influence throughout Europe's early modern period was simply too great to dismiss them or wish them away. The Muslims, it seemed, were destined to remain a permanent fixture on the periphery of the Western world, to be deplored and combated as existential enemies or to be engaged in trade or to be called on as allies or otherwise accommodated—or perhaps all three simultaneously as circumstances might require.

The confluence of two powerful trends began to change all that: signs of erosion in the Muslims' traditional economic and military supremacy and the European Enlightenment, which began to grapple with profound questions of man's relationship with the relatively new phenomenon of the nation-state. Here, then, were both *opportunity* in the form of perceived and actual Muslim weakness and *motive* in the form of the Muslims' already-established alterity against which to measure, judge, and then advocate Western "progress." Not surprisingly, the usual suspects were drawn from the West's latest social cohort of Islam experts—in this case, the *philosophes* of the Age of Enlightenment.

On the military front, the late seventeenth century witnessed serial setbacks in Europe for the once-unassailable Ottoman Empire: the failed campaigns against Vienna, followed by the loss of Hungary and the humbling Treaty of Carlowitz. Meanwhile, the Mughal Empire began its slow decline with the death of the accomplished Aurangzeb in 1707, and the fall of the Safavid dynasty in Iran in 1722 completed a new and unfamiliar Western picture of disarray and decline in the Muslim lands.

These developments also conferred enormous benefits on the rising social class of Enlightenment artists and intellectuals, who began to invoke examples of failed Muslim government as they sought to validate their own visions of proper social and political organization at home. Thus the *philosophes* of the Enlightenment reached into the established anti-Islam discourse to advance their own agenda, principally an assault on the dangers of unchecked rule, typically decried as "despotism." For such leading figures as Montesquieu and Voltaire, the failings of Islamic society were rooted ultimately in bad governance. The more classically inclined Edward Gibbon blamed the Muslims for ignoring the spiritual uplift available in Greek and Roman works on morals and politics (Saunders 1963:703).

Even before the Enlightenment, Europeans had begun to view the Ottoman Empire less as a legitimate political entity than as a bastion of tyranny, ruled solely by fear and characterized by a mixture of blind obedience and fatalist acceptance on the part of its enslaved subjects (Valensi 1993:2–5, 31–45; Kaiser 2000:9–10). In this scheme, Islam's religious imperatives were seen as reinforcing despotism by demanding unquestioned and thus unreasoned obedience to the ruler. Where, for example, the power of the French kings may have been *absolute*, that of the eastern sultans was *arbitrary*—a quality, the French apologists tell us, that defies the dictates of reason and makes a mockery of the essential institution of private property (Venturi 1963:134; Kaiser 2000:16). Institutions that might appear similar from the outside, such as the unrestrained rule of the French monarchs and that of their Ottoman contemporaries, were nonetheless differentiated by the Otherness of Islam.

In contrast to what traditional notions of the history of ideas suggest, growing familiarity with the world of the Muslims throughout this period did little or nothing to create anything like a real paradigm shift—or Gaston Bachelard's "discontinuities"—in the Western idea of Islam. Far from it: the anti-Islam discourse functioned as effectively as ever to restrict the increasing volume of reports from European travelers, diplomats, merchants, and even captive sailors to that which remained "within the true" to the Western imagination.

Take the case of Joseph Pitts, a poor lad from Exeter who went to sea only to be seized by North African pirates and sold into slavery before finally making his way home fifteen years later. Pitts published a well-received narrative of his ordeal and observations of Muslim society in 1704 under the title *A True and Faithful Account of the Religion and Manners of the Mohammedans*. Pitts's standing as a direct witness to Muslim life—eased greatly, we are told, by his involuntary conversion to Islam under extreme physical duress—conferred on his work enormous influence and authority in its day, and it enjoyed numerous reprintings as late as 1774 (al-Azmeh 1996:162).

Yet *A True and Faithful Account* instills little confidence that it is in fact just such an account. It offers little beyond the staples of the old, familiar discourse: Islam as a hodgepodge of recycled legends, bastardized Christianity, and Jewish imports; Muhammad as an imposter and debauchee; and the Muslims as a perverse, unholy lot who greatly prefer sodomy to the "Natural Use of the Woman" (quoted in al-Azmeh 1996:124, capitals in original). Pitts's narrative was artfully crafted to meet the demands of his publisher and the expectations of his readers (Daniel 1966:14).

Lady Mary Wortley Montagu also left behind eyewitness accounts of social life in the Ottoman Empire, compiled between 1716 and 1718, when her husband was briefly the British ambassador to the Ottoman court. Montagu's collected letters, first published in 1763, one year after her death, were to become what one modern scholar calls a "canonical text" on life in the East (Melman 1992:2), and she does attempt at times to explain and clarify the true place of women in the elite Ottoman social circles in which she traveled.

In a letter dated April 1, 1717, from Adrianople, the summer capital of the Ottoman court, she takes aim at the prevailing European notion that the famed Turkish baths, like the harem itself, was the place of unbridled sexuality. As she joined the naked women in the baths, reclining on sumptuous sofas and surrounded by their slaves, "there was not the least wanton smile or immodest gesture among them" (Montagu 1893:356). She also reports that Muslim women enjoyed property rights well in excess of those of their Western counterparts, and she goes on to suggest the many advantages to a women's privacy that came with wearing the veil. Earlier, in November 1716, Alexander Pope had invoked the image of the harem as the locus of jealousy, sexual frustration, and licentiousness to tease Lady Montagu in a letter of his own about the dangers to her virtue as she traveled eastward: "I shall look upon you no longer as a Christian when you pass . . . to the Land of Jealousy, where unhappy women converse with none but Eunuchs, and where the very Cucumbers are brought to them Cutt" (1956:368).[1]

Despite her astute observations of Muslim life, Montagu cannot always help but slip into the predominant Western narrative of Islam, one that threatens the organic link between her own personal experience, on the one hand, and moral and political evaluation and judgment, on the other. Thus she endorses the imagery and representations popularized throughout Europe in the widely successful and fanciful editions of *One Thousand and One Nights*, also known as *Arabian Tales* or the *Arabian Nights' Entertainment* (Daniel 1966:21). In a letter dated March 10, 1718, to her confidante the Countess Mara detailing her visit to the wondrous palace of the Ottoman sultana, Montagu assures her interlocutor that, with a few obvious exceptions, everything Europe has heard about the East is true: "Now, do I fancy that you imagine I have entertained you, all this while, with a relation that has, at least, received many embellishments from my hand? This is but too like (say you) the *Arabian Tales*: these embroidered napkins! and a jewel as large as a turkey's egg!—You forget, dear sister, *those very tales were written by an author of this country, and* (excepting the enchantments) *are a real representation of the manners here*" (1893:347, emphasis added).

One hundred and twenty years after the first appearance in French of *One Thousand and One Nights*, another recognized authority on life among the Muslims, the British Arabist and ethnographer Edward William Lane, concurred with Lady Montagu's assessment: "There is one work, however, which represents most admirable pictures of the manners and customs of the Arabs, and particularly of those of the Egyptians; it is *The Thousand and One Nights*, or *Arabian Nights' Entertainments*." He goes on to add, "If the English reader had possessed a close translation of it with sufficient illustrative notes, I might almost have spared myself the labor of the present undertaking" (2003:xxiv n.1).[2] In the case of Lane and, to a lesser extent, that of Lady Montagu, the firsthand accounts of the Muslim world now being amassed in Western travelogues, memoirs, letters, and other similar statements tended to reinforce the existing discourse by adding to it the authority of direct, personal experience. The true subject of these works was once again not Islam itself, but the Islam of the Western discursive imagination.

This acute sense of Muslim alterity reverberated throughout the Enlightenment and beyond. It provided new generations of Islam experts—Montesquieu, Voltaire, and later Johann Gottfried Herder and G. W. F. Hegel, to name just a prominent few—with a baseline or marker against which to assess, evaluate, and judge Western social, political, and intellectual life. The ensuing comparisons between East and West invariably dismissed the former and privileged the latter, especially as the need to explain the decline of the once formidable Muslim enemy increasingly intruded on Western consciousness.

Hegel says in *Lectures on the Philosophy of History*, published after his death in 1831, that the Muslim, for all his undoubted energy and enthusiasm, is in essence a fanatic, incapable of creating anything of a lasting or permanent nature. He has, in short, no real history and thus no possible interest or ability to fashion civil society: "With all the passionate energy he shows, the Mahometan is really indifferent to this social fabric and rushes on in the ceaseless whirl of fortune." The great Muslim dynasties and empires, concludes Hegel, "did nothing but degenerate; the individuals that composed them simply vanished" (1861:372). For Hegel and his fellow Enlightenment thinkers, Islam was now "a deficient order of things, an order of deficient things" (al-Azmeh 1996:168). In this way, it stood in direct contrast to Western plenitude and even perfection—or, more specifically, to the idea of Western perfectibility.

This notion of Muslim deficiency, coupled with growing Muslim geopolitical weakness vis-à-vis the West, set the stage for the lasting critique of the Islamic world—its society, practices, and mores—that remains in effect today. It also charted a future course to address this society's obvious failings, by force if necessary. In other words, the Islamic world's documented shortcomings were susceptible to rectification at Western hands. Here, then, lie the intellectual and moral foundations for the European colonial enterprise that was looming just over the horizon and that first began to take shape with Napoleon before reaching its full flower with the wholesale Western occupation of Muslim lands.

But first such ideas had to manifest themselves in terms of the existing anti-Islam discourse, whose familiar themes—those pairs of opposites distinguishing Christian from Muslim—date back to the Middle Ages. And they had to be given consistent expression by succeeding cohorts of Islam experts, all of whom have benefited from the perpetuation of the predominant narrative they received from earlier generations. Writing in *Islams and Modernities*, Aziz al-Azmeh notes this progression through varying historical eras:

> The discourse involved is one of contrasts, very much like the primitive logic that underlay medieval and early modern conceptions. Alongside the continuing contrast of good with evil, orthodoxy with heresy, moral probity with libertinism and sodomy, the Enlightenment scheme of things required the presence of other players in this game, which it could call its own. These were reason, freedom, and perfectibility, the three inclusive categories of the present epoch. Along with this, the birth of modern Orientalist scholarship in the Enlightenment was accompanied by the secularization of the profession. Clerics gave way to traders, dilettantes, gentlemen of leisure, and to consuls. In the course of the nineteenth and twentieth centuries, journalists took the place of dilettantes, salaried academics that of gentlemen of leisure, while colonialists and sundry spies joined the ranks of all categories. (1996:130)

The nexus of the established anti-Islam narrative and the *philosophes'* concern with governance, the dangers of despotism, and the place of reason in the relationship between human society and the nation-state found salient expression in the Western discourse of women and sexuality in Islam. For Montesquieu and his colleagues, the Muslim family unit as represented in such popular works as *One Thousand and One Nights*, with its seclusion of women and the titillating institutions of the harem and the veil, provided the basic building block of Eastern despotism.

Here we can discern the recognizable outlines of the traditional discourse of Islam and women, dating back at least to the West's first serious, organized encounter with the idea of Islam, led by Peter the Venerable in the mid-twelfth century, and running through it ever since. As we saw in chapter 3, Peter, the powerful abbot of Cluny, devoted much of two polemical collections, the *Summa totius haeresis Saracenorum* and the *Contra sectam sine haeresim Saracenorum*, to an assault on Muslim morality and sexual behavior, a theme already introduced to the Latin world by an earlier Islam expert, Petrus Alfonsi.

For Peter and his fellow clerics, Islam was a false faith, imposed by force and maintained by the promise of unlimited sexual license for its male followers. And Islam's sanction of an active sex life between husband and wife—specifically sura 2, verse 223, of the Qur'an, which calls on husbands to enjoy their wives "as you will"—scandalized the abbot and his aides, who took this verse as an open invitation to sodomy.[3] A letter from one of his translators assured Peter the Venerable that such practice was both accepted and widespread among the Muslims: "The chapter about using wives dishonorably which is also there should not scandalize you in any way, for it really is in the Qur'an and, as I have heard for certain in Spain . . . all of the Saracens do this freely, as if by Muhammad's command" (quoted in Kritzeck 1964:56).

Even those in the medieval West who openly admired the Muslims for their intellectual prowess—for example, Roger Bacon—balked at their supposed sexual excess. The thirteenth-century philosopher, an ardent student of learned Arab texts, writes in his *Opus majus*: "With Mahomet, many sins are allowed, as is evident in the Qur'an, and no perfection of life is observed since they are absorbed in sensual pleasures because of their polygamy" (1927:814). Others were even less charitable. Guibert de Nogent, the Crusades chronicler, says that Muhammad offered his followers a "new license of promiscuous intercourse," and the fourteenth-century canon lawyer Guido Terrena declares the Muslims ready practitioners of "every shame of carnal intercourse," including incest and bestiality (both quoted in Daniel 1960:169).

For the thinkers of the Enlightenment, as for their colonialist and modern-day successors, the same notion of the Muslims' sexual perversity and their associated maltreatment of women were continuing sources of both horror and fascination. Only now a new secular gloss was applied to the old theological framework. Islam's inherent violence and reliance on force made room for an interrelated image of cruelty and despotism, and its intrinsic wantonness began to accommodate a romantic eroticism that the West found both forbidden and irresistible (Daniel 1966:23). And the entire question of women in Islam—a question that could not be posed in the West in any meaningful way until then—soon came to represent an intricate maze of Western attitudes, ideas, opinions, and proscriptions about the deficiencies of Muslim life and of Islam itself. As with other central elements of the grand narrative of Islam, what the Muslims actually did or actually thought about the subject was, as it still is today, largely irrelevant.

The newly discovered "deficiencies" of the Muslim world—its unexpected weakness and surprising impermanence, its lack of history, and its exclusive reliance on passion rather than on intellect—required an explanation from the *philosophes* of the eighteenth century. At the same time, these thinkers, artists, and political theorists were engaged in their own project to introduce such notions as reason, freedom, and the perfectibility of man into the affairs of state and society, an implicit slap at the rigid and autocratic order of their own day. This overlap in interests led to the creation of an effective Western critique of Islam and Muslim societies that flowed from the existing anti-Islam discourse while simultaneously carving out social and political space for these new Enlightenment ideas and programs. In other words, it was to the direct benefit of the *philosophes* to perpetuate and strengthen the predominant discourse rather than to challenge or question it, even in the face of new evidence, additional information, and further learning.

At the center of this Enlightenment critique was the figure of the Oriental despot and his mirror image, the master of the Oriental harem, or seraglio, who held the destiny of his women, children, and servants completely in his hands, just as the sultan controlled the life and death of each one of his subjects. Nowhere was the juxtaposition of these two universes, the private and the public spheres of Muslim life, as deliberate or as effective as in Montesquieu's *Persian Letters*, particularly in the highly eroticized inner tale of life in the seraglio, which Usbek, one of the novel's two central figures, leaves behind in Isfahan.

During Usbek's lengthy travels abroad, mostly in Paris, the weakness of his position as absentee master slowly reveals the untenable position of all despots: Usbek can only stand alone and helpless as his wives eventually revolt, culminating in the collapse of the entire system and the suicide of his favorite, Roxane. In all, the tragic story of Usbek's harem occupies just one-quarter of Montesquieu's imagined correspondence, yet its intended preeminence is highlighted by the way it frames the entire work and serves as both introduction and conclusion (Vartanian 1969:23).

The political lampoon aimed at the growing authoritarianism of France's ruling Bourbons is clear, as is the implicit warning that the repression of self-fulfillment that is part and parcel of despotic rule inevitably leads to revolt, violence, and ultimately ruin (Vartanian 1969; Shanley and Stillman 1982). But *The Persian Letters* and its tale of the seraglio can also be read for what it tells us about the power and persistence of the anti-Islam discourse, the way it flows so seamlessly through the entire Western experience, and how each new generation draws so effortlessly on succeeding generations' shared imagery, ideas, and conceptions—that is, the discursive statements— concerning Islam and the Muslims.

Montesquieu's *Persian Letters*, with its account of two Persian men far from home, also raises the question of identity, a topic much discussed in early-eighteenth-century Europe, when the arrival of exotic foreign texts such as *One Thousand and One Nights* and of equally exotic, alien objects and artifacts fed a mania for classification and taxonomy (Pucci 1990:148). In one well-known passage, Rica, the second of the two main characters, tires of being stared at and examined on the street and exchanges his Persian garb for Parisian fashion so as not to disturb "the calm of a great city." Suddenly, he is a nobody, abjectly ignored and woefully anonymous. Rica's attempts to rekindle interest by dropping hints that he is in fact Persian prompt only disbelief from all sides: "Ah! Ah! The gentleman is a Persian? What an extraordinary thing! How can one be a Persian?" (Montesquieu 1875:129 [my translations in all citations to this edition]).

This anecdote prompted the modern French philosopher Louis Althusser to ask in an essay on Montesquieu's theory of government: "If the Persian does not exist, where does a French *gentilhomme*, born under Louis XIV, get the *idea* of him?" (1972:75). The answer, of course, lies in the Western discourse of Islam and in its stepchild, the relatively new European discipline of Arabic and Islamic studies. Thus Montesquieu expropriates those statements about Islam that both fit the needs of his political philosophy and remain "within the true" of the broader discourse but discards all others.

By Montesquieu's day, educated Europeans had access to a number of relatively reliable accounts of Muslim beliefs and practices that sought to correct some of the West's deeply held images of the faith. Nevertheless, many of these scholars proved unable to break out of the established discourse in any significant way. Edward Pococke, the prominent Arabist at Oxford who died in 1691, challenged a number of popular Western fables—for example, that the Prophet had artfully used trained doves to contrive certain miracles to impress his followers—but he retained the West's fascination with the exotica of the Muslim Orient as well as the deep-set hostility toward Muhammad as a hypocrite and false prophet (Netton 1990:28–29).

George Sale, whose English translation of the Qur'an appeared in 1734 and whose sympathy for his subject matter angered many—Gibbon, for example, once dismissed him as "half a Musulman"—refuted the ideas then common in the West that Muslims believed women had no souls and thus could not go to heaven and that Islam was in fact a form of idolatry (Netton 1990:30–32). Yet in the preface to his translation, Sale refers to Muhammad as a "criminal" and attributes the success of a patently false faith to its reliance on force and violence: "It is certainly one of the most convincing proofs that Muhammadism was no other than a human invention, that it owed its progress and establishment almost entirely to the sword" (quoted in Netton 1990:33).

Prominent French work in the field at the time included Adrian Reland's *La religion des Mahométans* (1721), which accurately presents the meaning of Islam as submission to God, and Henri de Boulainvilliers's *Vie de Mahomed* (1730), which emphasizes Muhammad's consistent commitment to monotheism. Montesquieu even had a copy of *La religion des Mahométans* in his personal library (Gunny 1978:152n.4), and he got to know Boulainvilliers in Paris after completing his law studies in Bordeaux (Richter 1977:13–14).

Despite these direct connections to Reland and Boulainvilliers, Montesquieu ignores their work and that of other like-minded writers and instead constructs the political and social satire of *The Persian Letters* on an idea of Islam that never strays outside the boundaries of the established discourse. Among his preferred sources is the seventeenth-century French translation of the Qur'an by André Du Ryer, who uses his preface to warn his readers: "This book is a long colloquium of God, Angels, and Mahomet which this false Prophet has rather clumsily contrived. . . . It will amaze you that these absurdities have infected the greater part of the world" (1649:4; quoted in Gunny 1978:152). Du Ryer does manage to explain accurately some of the teachings of Islam, such as the belief that men and women alike may find a home in paradise, but Montesquieu ignores these explanations (Gunny 1978:154). In letter XXIV, for example, Rica notes: "For since women are of a creation inferior to ours, and since our prophets tell us that they cannot enter heaven, why should they struggle to read a book intended only to teach them the route to paradise?" (Montesquieu 1875:112). Letters LXVII and CXLI repeat the same notion.

Of course, Montesquieu is interested in much more than a few points of Islamic theology. He is, rather, determined to fashion his salutary tale of despotism and its inevitable human toll by invoking a stylized and a highly eroticized depiction of Muslim life. In one letter, we are told that one of the courtesans has had sex with fifty male slaves during a single night, and elsewhere Usbek bemoans the difficulties facing a Muslim man who must satisfy so many wives and concubines. In letter CXIV, a dejected Usbek complains to a confidant: "We lapse into this state of failure due to the great number of women, who exhaust us more than satisfy us" (Montesquieu 1875:359). That the Qur'an (4:3) states explicitly that a man must take only one wife unless he can treat up to three others equitably and fairly is beside the point. So is the fact that French scholars of Montesquieu's time were well aware that contemporary practice in Persia involved only monogamous marriage (Gunny 1978:161–162).

In one of its most explicit passages, *The Persian Letters* recounts how Usbek was once called on to resolve a quarrel among the women of the seraglio as to which one is the most beautiful and desirable. One concubine, still savoring her triumph, later recalls in breathless detail how Usbek directed the women to disrobe and to strip away their priceless ornaments and remove their elaborate makeup: "Long we saw you wander from enchantment to enchantment. . . . You cast your curious gaze to the most secret places; you had us take a thousand different poses; always new commands and always new compliance" (Montesquieu 1875:59).

Here, as in every aspect of the women's lives, Usbek is the determinant force, with only the mediating offices of his eunuchs, who keep outsiders from the harem and bar the inhabitants from leaving without an escort and their master's consent. For Montesquieu and his readers, the parallels with the despotic state would have been unmistakable (Vartanian 1969; Shanley and Stillman 1982). And he returned to this theme explicitly in his treatise on political theory, *Ésprit des lois*, twenty-seven years later: under despotism, "everything is reduced to reconciling political and civil government with domestic government, the officers of the state with those of the seraglio" (quoted in Shanley and Stillman 1982:67). To underscore this notion, *The Persian Letters* includes a message from the chief eunuch in which he declares, "I find myself in the seraglio as if in a little empire, and my ambition, the only passion that remains to me, is somewhat satisfied" (Montesquieu 1875:72). In this way, the structure of Montesquieu's seraglio mirrors that of the despotic state: Usbek is both husband and despot; his eunuchs enforce his will, as do ministers or other state functionaries; and the wives suffer without recourse in the same way as the despot's subjects (Shanley and Stillman 1982:67).

Of course, it all ends badly. The pretense maintained in the early correspondence between Paris and Persia that the seraglio is held together by love and mutual benefit fades over time to reveal Montesquieu's central point—that despotism must ultimately rely on fear and that such a system is necessarily fleeting, as is Muslim "history" in general; it crushes the human spirit and is doomed to destruction and failure. In the end, the women rebel, and Usbek's favorite, Roxane, subverts the eunuchs' authority, takes a lover, and then commits suicide. With the poison already in her veins, she addresses a last letter—the novel's final entry—to Usbek: "Yes, I tricked you; I seduced your eunuchs . . . and made your dreadful seraglio into a place of delights and pleasures. . . . I have lived in servitude, but I have always been free. I reformed your laws by those of nature, and my spirit has always held fast to independence" (Montesquieu 1875:489).

It might be tempting to dismiss Montesquieu's decision to set his parable of governmental malfeasance and its crippling effects on the human spirit in the exotic locale of a Persian harem as little more than a device to entertain his European readers and an attempt to minimize confrontation with the French authorities. And certainly these factors may have played a role; the author also took the precaution of having the book printed in the Netherlands, under the name of a fictitious German publisher, and then smuggling the finished volumes into France in early 1721, where the work became an instant sensation and enjoyed a long success (Healy 1999:vii). Yet, as we have seen, *The Persian Letters* binds up the emerging discourse of women in Islam together with the deeper historical narrative in some profound ways.

In the first place, there is Montesquieu's selective use of the material available and the jettisoning of anything outside the confines of the prevailing Western discourse of Islam. Second, we have the association of tyranny with the peripheral lands, those outside the pale of the civilized, Western world. For Montesquieu and his legions of readers, as Althusser notes, "The location of despotic regimes already suggests their excess. Despotism is the government of extreme lands" (1972:72). Further, Muslim life is transient; it lacks Hegelian "firmness" and is characterized by both violence and sensuality, even if the latter proves on closer inspection to be largely hollow.

Most important of all, Montesquieu was both advancing his own interests and Enlightenment ideals and playing on what Aram Vartanian has called Western "affinities with the inefficiency and self-destructiveness of Oriental tyranny" (1969:33). In this way, Montesquieu helped establish in the Western canon an essentialist link between the social and political deficiencies of Islam and the Muslims, on the one hand, and the relations between the sexes, on the other. In the nineteenth century, the golden age of Orientalism and its offspring, the colonial domination of the Muslims, would raise this tendency to an art form.

Legions of Western merchants, adventurers, artists, scholars, and diplomats began to pour into the Middle East in the nineteenth and early twentieth centuries in greater and greater numbers, and general awareness of Islam and the Muslims increased throughout Europe. However, the level of actual knowledge of the faith, its practitioners, and Islamic civilization in general continued to languish. As a result, this significant widening of contacts between East and West had no appreciable effect on the predominant discourse of Muslim society as captured in the narrative of women in Islam. Only now the emphasis began to shift from what Muslims were said to believe to what they were said actually to do (Daniel 1966:22–23).

In effect, popular ethnography took the place of popular theology. The West's gaze, emboldened by changes in its favor in the balance of power, shifted from religious rivalry and existential conflict to political and social contestation. Muslim women and sexuality, epitomized in the Western imagination by the harem and the veil, became a central focal point of the anti-Islam discourse. Increased access to the world of Islam did not necessarily lead to an increase in the store of Western knowledge or understanding of Muslim life. Overwhelmed by the established anti-Muslim narrative, European travelers—as with Montesquieu in the comfort of his library—saw what they expected to see and found what they expected or needed to find.

They increasingly did so by bringing the idea of the Orient with them when they traveled, for the nineteenth century was the heyday of ethnographic exhibits, the museum and its collections of Eastern exotica, the arboretum and the zoo with its alien wonders, and the great world expositions in London, Paris, and other European capitals. Here, the tendency toward classification and taxonomy of the eighteenth-century Enlightenment took on the added power of visualization and representation. Curators, organizers, and promoters spared no effort to present a real Oriental experience for legions of visitors to these living exhibits, even importing Egyptian donkeys and their handlers and replicating exact Cairo street scenes, right down to the peeling and dirty paint (Mitchell 1991:1–7).

The facades of mosques, Egyptian coffeehouses, and other tableaux were constructed in meticulous detail, all part of an effort to render the essence of the East as something that could be imagined, managed, and controlled—and eventually brought into the Western economic, political, and social order. This move toward public representation of the East, like the anti-Islam discourse from which it was born, created a reality that was more real to the Western visitor than anything he or she might actually experience among the Muslims.

European artists, photographers, and theater designers who had never seen the Middle East all too often first created their own representations of the Muslim Orient at home and then set out on their travels in search of confirmation. Four years before his own visit to Egypt, the young Gustave Flaubert presented his readers with the scene from the top of the Great Pyramid after an arduous climb under blistering sunshine: "But lift your head. Look! Look! And you will see cities with domes of gold and minarets of porcelain, palaces of lava built on plinths of alabaster, marble-rimmed pools where sultanas bathe their bodies at the hour when the moon makes bluer the shadows of the groves and more limpid the silvery water of the fountains. Open your eyes! Open your eyes!" (1996:48).

Many were disappointed or, at best, decidedly unimpressed by their experiences on the ground. Gérard de Nerval, whose *Voyage en Orient* became a classic work, once confided to a friend that the Oriental cafés back home in Paris were more authentic than those of the Orient itself, and he conducted much of his research in a French-run library in Cairo rather than mingle with the Egyptians or see their lands firsthand (Mitchell 1991:29–31). Indeed, he relied heavily on Edward Lane's *Account of the Manners and Customs of the Modern Egyptians*, even expropriating whole pages as his own. This intermingling of texts—to put the most favorable gloss on the practice of what would today be seen as outright plagiarism—was characteristic of the seeming confusion in the minds of Orientalist travel writers and artists between what they saw and what they read, between the real and the imagined (de Groot 2000:46). In fact, the former had no primacy over the latter and was often subordinate to it.

In a sympathetic account of Nerval as artist, Edward Said identifies an overwhelming impermanence and sense of loss that leaves the writer helpless to pursue his original aim: "How else can we explain in the *Voyage*, a work of so original and individual a mind, the lazy use of large swathes of Lane, incorporated without a murmur by Nerval as *his* descriptions of the Orient? It is as if having failed both in his search for a stable Oriental reality and in his intent to give systematic order to his re-presentation of the Orient, Nerval was employing the borrowed authority of a canonized Orientalist text" ([1978] 2003:184). On a more prosaic level, the American Herman Melville also came to grief in Cairo, finding it unmanageable due to a lack of order elsewhere provided by city maps, reliable street names, or any discernable, logical layout (Mitchell 1991:32–33).

This demand to represent the Muslim world in line with accepted and comprehensible categories permeated Orientalist scholarship and dictated a preference for the analysis of texts or, more precisely, of selected fragments of texts over lived experience or personal observation (Said [1978] 2003:93–99). Trends in scholarly methodology, particularly in philology, touched off a search for biblical history and for textual correspondence and parallels between Christian and Jewish scripture and the Qurʾan, reinvigorating the familiar medieval notion that Muhammad had slapped together the text from earlier teachings and then passed it off as the Word of God (Daniel 1966:29). The philologists avoided the hardships of an eastward journey; the text contained all they needed to know, so there was no point in seeing for themselves.

On those occasions when personal observation or experience on the part of the travel writer, the memoirist, or the diplomat was somehow seen to be in conflict with textual evidence, the Orientalist discourse ensured that the latter prevailed. In other words, Islam cannot be what the Muslims say or do or even what they say they mean, but only what a handful of texts—selected and then interpreted and canonized by the Western Orientalist—tells us it is and is not. This phenomenon is, of course, a classic example of what Michel Foucault means by discourse.

Orientalist representation was closely tied to the earlier Enlightenment notion of Islamic civilization as timeless, dead, and without history. The

Western imagination stepped forward everywhere to fill the void that was Islam. Only then could it be properly represented and in due course conquered, subdued, and colonized. It is important here to emphasize one of Said's cardinal arguments about Orientalism: that it preceded and put in place the necessary conditions for the Western colonial project and was not created after the fact. Said ([1978] 2003:39, 139–148) dates the birth of classical Orientalism to the work of Ernest Renan in the 1840s, whereas the period of great Western colonial expansion began in the 1870s and ended with World War II.

When it came to the women of the Muslim world, the vacuum created by the notion of an Islam without history was all the more glaring and provocative, for women, in particular those of the urban middle and upper classes, were commonly veiled and often secluded and thus inaccessible to the nineteenth-century European gaze. This "hidden" quality struck a nerve in the Western mind that went beyond common attitudes toward non-Western women elsewhere in the world and focused particular attention on the harem, presenting what was in effect an institution of the lavish Ottoman court as symptomatic of Muslim family life in general (Mabro 1991:6).

This practice of seclusion elicited two powerful strategies, both aimed at revealing the previously unseen: to draw on the storehouse of the Western imagination to fill in the blanks left by the inaccessibility of the Muslim woman, and later to break down the walls of the harem and literally unveil the women of Islam. Both responses drew on the anti-Islam discourse to produce an enormous number of Western statements about Islam and the Muslims, first in the form of Orientalist art and literature and then, beginning with outright colonial rule, in the shape of policies, reforms, and White Papers aimed at ending the degradation of Muslim women as part of the general modernization of the Middle East.

The supreme emblem of the former impulse was undoubtedly the odalisque, captured in idealized, erotic detail by such artists as Jean-Auguste-Dominique Ingres (1780–1867) and Eugène Delacroix (1798–1863). These painters and their many like-minded colleagues presented the West with an intimate portrait of Muslim female sexuality characterized by passive repose, overt submission, and sumptuous surroundings punctuated by symbolic reminders of captivity, restraint, or outright slavery. The nakedness of the odalisque—the word *odalisque* itself is a corruption of the Turkish term for a chambermaid, from *oda* (room)—is often accentuated by the presence of the fully dressed figure of an accompanying slave girl, a eunuch, or even her master. Scenes in the women's *hammam* (baths) were particular favorites, giving full rein to the popular Western idea that the seclusion of Muslim women inevitably led to unbridled passions and "unnatural" practices. Interestingly, there was little interest in depicting the men's baths or life in the *salamlik*, or quarters for men and guests, both of which would have been accessible to the hordes of male visitors from abroad.

Ingres, Delacroix, and their fellow Orientalist painters would never see the inside of a harem or a Turkish bath full of reclining, half-naked women and their servants and guards. Nor could they count on a variety of dispassionate Western accounts about harem life or about Muslim women in general; almost all those that purported to reveal the truth about the harem were based on pure invention and hearsay. Delacroix's first representations of Ottoman odalisques were made some five years before his first trip to the Muslim world, which took him to Algeria and Morocco and not to Ottoman Turkey (de Groot 2000:47n.24).

The few firsthand reports that trickled out from a handful of Western women travelers were ignored. Thus Lady Montagu's account of the proper behavior of the women observed during her own visit to the *hammam*—"not the least wanton smile or immodest gesture among them"—fell on deaf ears. Ingres himself had copied this descriptive passage from a French translation of Lady Montagu's letters (Fernea 1981:330; Ahmed 1982:525), yet his famous *Le bain turc*, painted in 1862 and now in the Louvre, offers up a frank display of homosexual eroticism among the women bathers.

Those artists and intellectuals who actively sought out the Orient through personal travel and direct experience often fared little better than the studio-bound painters of the odalisques and the *hammam*. Nerval's reliance on the work of another to document his own experiences has already been discussed, but even those who managed to produce their own accounts and observations failed to penetrate the harem, ogle the bathers, or otherwise lift the veil from Muslim womanhood.

Instead, like Flaubert, they were left to construct their own Orient from the material at hand, in this case from the prostitutes and dancing girls with whom they could interact. Flaubert's pen transforms the dancer and courtesan Kuchuk Hanem into Oriental Woman writ large, even as it casts the East as the locus of sexual fantasy and sexual freedom and, by extension, as an antidote to Western strictures on both. Flaubert was apparently unmoved by the irony surrounding his brief but intense dalliance with Kuchuk Hanem. Several months earlier, he had complained to a friend that there were no dancing girls or "good brothels" to be found in Cairo, and so he had to travel all the way to Upper Egypt in search of the Oriental woman he craved (1996:83). In fact, an edict by the Egyptian ruler Muhammad Ali Pasha had banned brothels from the Egyptian capital as part of his program of Westernization.

Flaubert's Orient was, of course, all an illusion, but such illusions turned out to be wonderfully enticing and long lasting. They were also highly marketable. His Egyptian adventure, which he undertook in 1849 at the age of twenty-seven, was to provide a lifetime of material for a substantial literary career. An entire apparatus to manufacture and maintain the eroticized imagery of the Middle East was soon in place, bolstered by the relatively new art of photography, with its promise of greater realism and even authenticity. Flaubert's traveling partner was the French photographer Maxime Du Camp. According to the Académie des inscriptions et belles-lettres, which helped finance Du Camp's travels, he would be equipped with the latest in photographic apparatus. "Thanks to the aid of this modern traveling companion, efficient, rapid, and always scrupulously exact, the result of M. Du Camp's journey may well be quite special in character and extremely important" (Flaubert 1996:23).

Yet this photographic authenticity, too, was illusory, for the photographer, like the traveler, the painter, and the writer before him, was largely excluded from his intended subject and could do little more than mirror or even re-create earlier images in the new medium. Industrious European photographers set up local studios where they could gather appropriate props, hire prostitutes as models, and then stage the harem scenes that their audiences back in the West sought and demanded (Alloula 1986:4; Bullock 2002:14–16). The finished photograph, often in the form of the erotic postcard, thus furnished "proof" that this imagined Orient was real and even provided the raw material for later paintings and other images (Graham-Brown 1988:39–40).

The West's overt sexualization of the Muslim East emerged from the broader anti-Islam discourse of the Enlightenment *philosophes*, who introduced human sexuality in its different forms and institutions into intellectual and artistic debate. The result of this new openness, however, was to reinvigorate the traditional notions of women and sex in Islam—now represented by the fantasy of the veil and in particular the harem, with its teeming, captive population of lascivious and thus dangerous females (Melman

1992:71). Any promise that the sensuality of the Muslims, with their institutions of polygamy and the harem, may have held out for the *philosophes*
as a model of sexual liberation was dashed by the accompanying Western
discursive notions of despotism and violence and the resultant degradation
of women (Porter 1990:118).[4]

Growing traffic from West to East from the early nineteenth century
onward saw the Muslim Orient, now weakened both militarily and economically, transformed from the locus of political rivalry and existential threat
to one of passion, sexuality, and somnolence as captured in the image of the
reclining odalisque and the erotic postcard or as "documented" by writers
such as Nerval and Flaubert. These statements effectively reduced social
and, by extension, political life in Islam to the Western understanding of the
harem, the *hammam*, and the veil, and they left no space for any independent
activity or interpretation outside the overriding discourse.

As a result, the harem—from the Turkish word *haremlik*, denoting either
the women of a household or the space reserved for them, in contrast to the
men's *salamlik*—could not simply retain its original meaning as the women's
wing of a palace or grand residence. It had to be the locus of violence, wantonness, and free-for-all sexuality. The women of the harem could not simply
be mothers or household managers or partners to their husbands, let alone
social and economic actors in their own right—as described, for example, by
the Egyptian feminist Huda Sharawi (1987) in her memoir of harem life in the
late nineteenth and early twentieth centuries (see also el-Guindi 1999:26)—
but only languorous odalisques devoted solely to pleasure.[5]

In this way, western Europe, increasingly devoted to its own ideal of
monogamous marriage and the emerging division of labor between the
public world of men and the private, domestic sphere of women, advanced
its own interests by deploying the anti-Islam discourse in order to exorcise
the dangers of alternative social arrangements that might challenge its own
(Ahmed 1978:151; Mabro 1991:9). The traditional narrative of sexual perversity in Islam acted as a bulwark of the emerging idea of Western womanhood
as nurturing, sexually passive, and economically dependent. The anthropologist Jane Collier writes, "Images of oppressed Islamic women, who could
neither marry for love nor develop intimate relations with polygamous husbands, must have played a crucial role in constructing images of Western
women as consenting to their disempowerment within increasingly priva-
tized and confining homes" (1995:407; quoted in Oliver 2007:57).

At the same time, this discourse now cast the once-threatening Muslim world as a place of weakness, impermanence, and violence and passions that overwhelmed the precincts of reason, discipline, and order. The Muslim East was in need of a radical refashioning of its social and political structures, in a way that only Western guidance and ultimately Western domination could provide. Here, as with our own era, the general public was not in a position to challenge or question this idea of Islam offered up by the experts. Yet the entire edifice was a house of cards—literally. "What the [Orientalist] postcard proposes as the truth," writes Malek Alloula in his study of this medium, "is but a substitute *for something that does not exist*" (1986:129n.10, emphasis in original).

By the second half of the nineteenth century, the Middle East had become increasingly enmeshed in the financial and political life of the West. This was particularly true of Egypt, a growing economic power in its own right and now at the center of the profound changes sweeping the Muslim world. Its ambitious leader, Muhammad Ali Pasha, had already placed the production of agricultural staples, primarily cotton and wheat, under the state's direct control and then sold them profitably in the European markets in order to finance his modernization effort and reduce his dependence on his formal suzerain, the Ottoman sultan. These policies had the added advantage of undermining the traditional class of Mamluk tax farmers, with its ties to the Turkish–Circassian elite. Muhammad Ali accompanied the changes with a far-reaching campaign to build factories capable of feeding his growing war machine and of producing textiles and other goods for export in direct competition with England, France, and other European economies (Owen 2002:64–76).

But a series of setbacks, including a temporary collapse in the price of cotton and the unrelenting hostility of the Western powers, doomed this bid for economic autonomy and eventually forced the Egyptian state into the arms of its European bankers. Muhammad Ali's less able successors found themselves deeply indebted to Western creditors, who drew in their governments to support demands for repayment. The European powers also shared an interest in managing the decline of the Ottoman Empire, which retained at least nominal control of the Middle East. They preferred to prop it up so as not to allow their rivals to profit from any collapse, which meant placing limits on Egypt's ambitions for greater autonomy or even independence from the Ottoman sultan.

Increased financial pressures on Egypt's coffers to service the enormous debt placed a growing tax burden on the lower and middle classes, and general mismanagement of the economy angered the rural notables. The result was the revolt led by Urabi Pasha, an Egyptian army officer, against both the ruling Egyptian Khedive and ever-growing European influence, particularly in the state's financial affairs. The British, alarmed by the threat to their financial interests and determined to maintain effective control over the recently opened Suez Canal, the shortest route to the colonial riches of India, bombarded the rebels at the port of Alexandria on July 11, 1882. Two months later, a British force defeated Urabi Pasha at the battle of Tal al-Kabir and occupied the country for what was repeatedly declared to be a temporary conservatorship leading to the swift return of Egyptian sovereignty. In the end, the British stayed until 1954.

The occupation put the world's greatest colonial power in charge of the world's most influential Muslim nation. It also transformed the issue of women, already a major element of the Western discourse of Islam, into the fulcrum around which East–West relations have turned ever since. Only now this discourse was harnessed to raw, coercive power that would permit the West to move from only imagining what lay behind the veil and inside the shuttered walls of the harem, as in classical Orientalist art and travel writing, to destroying these institutions altogether in the name of progress: "Veiling—to *Western* eyes the most visible marker of the differentness and inferiority of Islamic societies—became the symbol now of both the oppression of women . . . and the backwardness of Islam, and it became the open target of the colonial attack and the spearhead of the assault on Muslim societies" (Ahmed 1992:151–152).

Leading this attack was the imposing figure of Evelyn Baring, later Lord Cromer, who effectively ruled Egypt as British consul-general from 1883 until 1907. Baring was from the prominent British banking family of the same name, but he never served in the firm, nor did the family bank have financial interests in Egypt (Tignor 1966:57). Rather, Cromer, an experienced colonial hand and one-time fiscal overseer in Cairo, was recalled from India, where he served as financial adviser to the new viceroy, to wind down the British occupation in Egypt. He was appointed in large part due to his well-known "antijingoist" views (Tignor 1966:60), but he was also an astute enough observer of the international and colonial scenes to realize early on that a quick exit was highly unlikely. He was convinced that the changes Egypt required and that both the British public and politicians were demanding could not be carried out in anything but a gradual manner.

As a result, he threw himself into the project of ruling Egypt, all the while seeking to reassure his political backers at home that evacuation was just around the corner. If the British were truly stuck in Cairo, Cromer concluded, they had better make the best of it; besides, this outcome really was the most beneficial for all concerned. "The special aptitude shown by Englishmen in the government of Oriental races pointed to England as the most effective and beneficent instrument for the gradual introduction of European civilization into Egypt," he wrote years later in his historical account and memoir *Modern Egypt*, first published in 1908 (Baring 2000, 2:28).

A reliable son of the Victorian age, Cromer was steeped in the civilizing and modernizing mission espoused by many in the British colonial service, such as the Indian intelligence officer and Islam expert William Muir, whom Cromer cites sympathetically in *Modern Egypt* as a "high authority on Eastern affairs" (Baring 2000, 2:524). Cromer opens a section grandly titled "The Reforms" with an epigraph from Walter Bagehot's *Physics and Politics*: "In the East, we are attempting to put new wine in old bottles—to pour what we can of a civilization whose spirit is progress into the form of civilization whose spirit is fixity" (quoted on 395; for the original, see Bagehot 1881:181).

Surveying his new dominions, Cromer identified two principle obstacles— familiar elements of the anti-Islam narrative—to the construction of the kind of Egypt he desired, one that was efficient, modern, civilized, and, most of all, integrated into the Western economic and political system. The first obstacle was the lack of reason: "The mind of the Oriental, . . . like his picturesque streets, is eminently wanting in symmetry. His reasoning is of the most slipshod description" (Baring 2000, 2:146–47). As a result, Islam is inflexible and seemingly immune to history or historical development.

For confirmation, Cromer turned to Muir's *The Caliphate: Its Rise, Decline, and Fall: From Original Sources*: "Swathed in the bands of the Qur'an, the Moslem faith, unlike the Christian, is powerless to adapt itself to varying time and place, keep pace with the march of humanity, direct and purify the social life, or elevate mankind" (1892:598; quoted in Baring 2000, 2:202). It bears repeating that one of Muir's "original sources" was in fact that well-worn forgery dating from the medieval polemic against Islam, the so-called *Apology of al-Kindi*, yet another example of the persistence of the Western discourse.

The second obstacle was Islam's treatment of women, which, Cromer said, citing another Victorian authority on the East, acts as a "canker" that has infected the entire social, political, and ethical system (Baring 2000, 2:134).[6] For Cromer, Europe had benefited enormously from its Christian faith, which "elevated" woman and preserved her exalted status through the practice of monogamy, whereas Islam lagged behind due to the "degradation" of its women, as expressed in the institutions of polygamy, seclusion, and the veil (152–153).

Here, then, lay a possible key to effective and lasting reform of the Muslim world—that is, to reshaping it to resemble the West: "Change the position of women, and one of the main pillars, not only of European civilization, but at all events of the moral code based on the Christian religion, if not of Christianity itself, falls to the ground. The position of women in Egypt, and in Mohammedan countries generally, is, therefore, a fatal obstacle to the attainment of that elevation of thought and character which should accompany the introduction of European civilization, if that civilization is to produce its full measure of beneficial effect" (Baring 2000, 2:539).

Cromer marshaled two influential but very different Western constituencies behind his campaign to elevate Muslim women: Egypt's thriving community of Christian missionaries and the much smaller corps of Western feminists back home. As Leila Ahmed (1992:145–153) has shown, Cromer's invocation of the language of the new European feminism was particularly cynical, for the virtual ruler of Egypt was himself extremely hostile to the feminist cause. On his return to England, he helped found the Men's League for Opposing Women's Suffrage, and a number of his Egyptian policies, particularly on the economy and on state funding for education, including female medical training, badly undercut gains already made by women and girls under Muhammad Ali and his successors.

Nevertheless, the discourse of feminism proved effective in supporting and justifying colonial policies that attacked traditional Muslim ways and Islamic values (Mabro 1991:12; el-Guindi 1999:181–182). It positioned Western feminism as vital "handmaiden" to the colonialist enterprise, a status it sometimes retains (Ahmed 1992:155). It also gained a foothold among the small Westernized Muslim elite, fostered by the European presence in institutions of education, government, and the press. Thus Huda Sharawi, protégée of the French feminist Eugénie Le Brun, famously cast off her veil in public after returning to Egypt from a women's conference in Europe in 1923. And in 1899, Qassim Amin published his tract *On the Liberation of Women*, in which he denounced the veiling of women in terms not dissimilar to those of Lord Cromer.

These and other like-minded intellectuals focused much of their attention on the need to catch up with Europe through the adoption of Western ways and the simultaneous rejection of central aspects of Muslim culture and practice, which they saw as incompatible with the modern society they sought to construct. To be sure, not all modernizing intellectuals of the day agreed. The religious thinker Muhammad Abduh and the Muslim feminists Zaynab al-Ghazali and Malak Hifni Nassef, to cite three prominent examples, saw no need to discard their faith or its values in the quest for a revival of Islamic political, social, and economic life. For them, it was the failure to honor these values and to live the true Islam that explained the East's "backwardness."

Cromer's ties to the missionary project were more direct, and his program for women's rights in Islam struck sympathetic chords among those working in the field and others preaching back in Britain. Cromer's own sympathies clearly lay with the evangelical effort, and he spoke the language of the missionary campaign: "Monogamy fosters family life, polygamy destroys it. The monogamous Christian respects women; the teachings of his religion and the incidents of his religious worship tend to elevate them. . . . The Moslem on the other hand despises women" (Baring 2000, 2:157). In a footnote, Cromer added that Muslims could never appreciate the beauty of Wordsworth's sonnet on the Virgin—an interesting notion given Islam's veneration of Mary as the mother of a great prophet.

Cromer's approach also meshed nicely with the established discourse of Islam and women. One missionary told a meeting in London in 1888 that Muhammad had introduced the veil and justified his polygamous lifestyle as part of an effort to "extinguish women altogether" (quoted in Ahmed 1992:153). Missionaries in Cairo and across the rest of the country, convinced that women were the primary carriers of religious and ethical values, openly encouraged an end to veiling and even advocated the adoption of Western dress in general as a way to weaken the hold of Islam over Egyptian society. Christian-run schools, often the only option for local Muslim families seeking an education for their children, did the same.

The colonizing power's hostility to Islam and Islamic culture, symbolized by antipathy toward the veil, transformed a simple article of clothing[7] into the primary battleground between the forces of Westernization and those of resistance, whether religious or nationalist or—as was often the case—some combination of the two. The Western discourse saw in the figure of the veiled woman many of the root causes of the social, economic, and political ills of the Muslim world. Of equal importance, it also positioned the veil as the primary symbol of Islamic identity, rejection of Western values, and resistance to outside domination (Ahmed 1992:295–296). This characterization of the veil, in turn, thrust Muslim women into the broader contestation between West and East. From this point on, the debate on veiling and on other aspects of women in Islam has rarely been about real Muslim women themselves.

In the decades since the era of colonialism, the veil has retained its status as one of the key points of contention in the culture wars between Islam and the West, especially since the 1970s, when the vigorous reawakening of Islamic activism—part of a worldwide revival of popular religiosity—drew the battle lines anew (Abdo 2000:140–141). In Cairo, for example, it became increasingly common to see veiled teenage daughters walking side by side with their unveiled mothers, a powerful signal of generational change.

Throughout the contemporary period, Egypt's battered economy has forced more and more women to work outside the home in order to support their families. Meanwhile, men often see little choice but to leave Egypt to seek jobs overseas, mostly in the wealthy petrostates of the Persian Gulf, where they can earn large sums over the course of a three- or four-year contract before returning home to settle down. This absence of men has put urban women increasingly into the public sphere of offices, schools, and shops, and the veil provides them with the means to negotiate this terrain and still maintain privacy of both space and body (el-Guindi 1999:xvii; Abu-Lughod 2002:785).

In reaction to the Western discourse, which defines the veil as both a symbol of backward Islam and a practical obstacle to Westernization, the growing Islamic movement in Egypt and across the Muslim world promoted its adoption as a sign of resistance to foreign intrusion, on the one hand, and of religious and cultural authenticity, on the other. This campaign has been particularly successful on university campuses, from which it then spread to the broader society. The secularized elite and their Western supporters were horrified by this emerging trend. Explanations given by cabinet ministers, Western commentators, and others for the newfound popularity of the veil ranged from the ridiculous (the women were too poor or too cheap to buy shampoo or visit the hairdresser) to the outright condescending (they were seeking attention and a remedy for their humdrum existence) (Abdo 2000:150–151).

With all sides so heavily invested in the established discourse, it is no wonder that the theological nuances and sociological aspects of veiling have been lost and any prospect of deeper understanding of Islamic culture and practice has been squandered. In the first place, the scriptural foundation for the practice may be seen as ambiguous, although contemporary practice among Muslims worldwide has largely accepted the veil as a religious obligation on women past the age of puberty. However, the routine veiling of prepubescent girls, as is common in contemporary Iran, is completely without religious foundation and must instead be viewed in its proper political context.

At the center of the debate is one of the very few explicit references to the practice in the Qur'an: "And tell the believing women to lower their gaze and be modest, and to display of their adornment only that which is apparent, and to draw their veils over their bosoms, and not to reveal their adornment save to their own husbands or fathers or husbands' fathers, or their sons or their husbands' sons, or their brothers or their brothers' sons or sisters' sons, or their women, or their slaves, or male attendants who lack vigor, or children who know naught of women's nakedness" (24:31).

The holy text elsewhere directs believers who approach the Prophet's wives with any request to do so from behind a curtain: "That is purer for your hearts and for their hearts" (33:53). Do the proscriptions set out apply to all Muslim women or only to Muhammad's wives? After all, the hadith, the Prophet's recognized sayings, make a distinction between his wives and ordinary Muslim women, and sura 33 goes on to say that his wives may not follow common practice in the community and remarry after their husband's death. Jurists, theologians, and ordinary Muslims have debated this question off and on for centuries.

Also buried under the weight of the discursive formation of women in Islam are some very real differences in the approach to sex in the Christian and Muslim traditions. Unlike the Christian view, Islam does not blame women for the expulsion from the Garden of Eden, nor does it color human sexuality with an idea of original sin. Sexuality, then, is part of God's order, and enjoyment for its own sake is encouraged and rewarded, but only within a strict social order designed to regulate proper behavior (el-Guindi 1999:31; Bullock 2002:162). The Christian world, for its part, has proved unable to accommodate Muslim attitudes toward sex, beginning with what Foucault has called the "monotonous night of the Victorian bourgeoisie" (1978:3), which as it happens coincided with the great period of Western colonization of Muslim lands.

The resulting clash of these two very different approaches to human sexuality, writes Fadwa el-Guindi in *Veil: Modesty, Privacy, and Resistance*, feeds directly into a Western discourse that insists on seeing the veil and related institutions as inherently repressive and degrading to Muslim women:

> Both Islam and Christianity provide moral systems to restrain improper and disorderly behavior that threatens the sociomoral order: Christianity chose the path of desexualizing the worldly environment; Islam of regulating the social order while accepting its sexualized environment.
>
> The moral standards of Islam are designed to accommodate enjoyment of worldly life, including a sexual environment. It posed no tension between religion and sexuality. . . . In their accounts of travels, scholars and writers with a Euro-Christian background had difficulty comprehending the challenge Islam had taken upon itself in opting for the latter path. The fertile imagination that embellishes accounts of "baths and harems and veils" is woven out of an internalized culture of a desexualized society. (1999:31)

Contemporary experts and commentators rarely do better, as can be seen by following the public debate over Islam and women or by glancing at the mainstream Western media. For years now, the veil has been a staple of seemingly endless news articles, books, and documentaries, and it is captured in magazine and television images—all as shorthand for a society, a civilization, or a system that is backward, alien, immobile, and inherently antithetical to human rights and dignity. Running throughout this public discourse is the persistent binary opposition of oppression and freedom, veiled and unveiled, bad and good. Islam qua Islam is once again ignored in favor of an unquestioned Western construction.

By the autumn of 2005, the prestige and influence of the United States around the world and particularly among Muslims had plummeted to record low levels amid widely held sentiments that its war on terrorism was really a war on Islam. Surveys by the Pew Global Attitudes Project show that the centerpieces of the George W. Bush foreign policy—chiefly the wars in Iraq and Afghanistan and the war on terrorism in general—animated most of the criticism in the Islamic world and badly tarnished America's image. The surveys reveal that many feared the expanding U.S. military presence worldwide and worried that their own countries could provide the next target (Wilke 2007).

Yet Washington's response to this state of affairs was not to argue its case directly on the world stage or to attempt to present its policies in a better light—let alone to modify its approaches. Instead, the White House chose to invoke the established discourse of Islam and women in what effectively amounted to a massive propaganda campaign in the guise of "public diplomacy." And so in September 2005, Bush dispatched his most trusted aide and adviser—the Texas television reporter turned White House counselor Karen Hughes—to tour three leading Muslim countries, Egypt, Turkey, and Saudi Arabia, to press the U.S. line that its policies, including the invasions of Iraq and Afghanistan, were in the best interests of Muslim women everywhere. She would later visit Indonesia, with the world's largest population of Muslims, on a similar mission.

Hughes's tours, now carried out in her new role as undersecretary for public diplomacy and public affairs at the State Department, were the culminating moment in a multiyear public-relations campaign to link the war on terrorism to the discourse of Islam and women as a way to mobilize domestic and international support for U.S. aims. Within twenty-four hours of the terrorist attacks on New York and Washington, D.C., Bush had named Hughes to head up "wartime communications" at the White House, and she later led the campaign to position the Afghan war as a battle to liberate women under Taliban rule. "When he [Bush] called me that morning, he told me that this will be an ongoing process of educating the public," Hughes later told the *New York Times* of her discussions with the president (Bumiller 2005).

No effort was spared. Hughes was given a large budget and wide powers, stemming from her close personal ties to the president. Even Laura Bush (2001), a traditional political spouse who rarely went beyond her ceremonial White House role, was drafted into the Hughes-led effort: the First Lady made a ground-breaking radio address on November 17, 2001, to decry the past treatment of Afghan women and to proclaim their liberation by invading Western forces: "Because of our recent military gains in much of

Afghanistan, women are no longer imprisoned in their homes. They can listen to music and teach their daughters without fear of punishment. Yet the terrorists who helped rule that country now plot and plan in many countries. And they must be stopped. The fight against terrorism is also a fight for the rights and dignity of women." Similar statements were prepared for Vice President Dick Cheney, Secretary of Defense Donald Rumsfeld, Secretary of State Colin Powell, and Cherie Blair, the wife of the British prime minister, in what the newspaper called "an unusual international offensive by the Bush administration to publicize the plight of women in Afghanistan" (Bumiller 2001b).

The discourse of women and Islam was soon popping up with increasing frequency whenever the administration discussed the Afghan campaign and later its war aims in Iraq. Afghan women in exile in the United States—mostly professionals far from the field of battle—were invited to the White House to publicize the maltreatment of women back home. They were even given media training by their government handlers to better make their case to news reporters and to sidestep any unwanted questions (Bumiller 2001a). Bush peppered his public statements with regular references to "women of cover," and he used major speeches to reprise the administration's central theme: that Washington's differences with the Muslim world were at heart cultural and centered on its treatment of women. "The last time we met in this chamber, the mothers and daughters of Afghanistan were captives in their own homes, forbidden from working or going to school," he said in his 2002 State of the Union Address. "Today women are free, and are part of Afghanistan's new government" (G. Bush 2002c).

Thirty months later, the official White House Web site posted collated comments by the president going back to the 2002 State of the Union Address, under the heading, "Rights and Aspirations of the People of Afghanistan" (G. Bush 2004). Almost all the thirty-six quotations, delivered as far afield as Canberra, Australia, and Hershey, Pennsylvania, frame the Afghan war as a fight for women's rights. And in 2006, the president used the fifth anniversary of the attacks on New York and Washington, D.C., once again to cast the fight as one against "a radical Islamic empire where women are prisoners in their homes" (G. Bush 2006).

Nor did the treatment of women in Iraq, an aggressively secular state under the Baath Party headed by Saddam Hussein, escape the White House's interest. Seeking to build broad international support for a preemptive strike before Hussein could hand over weapons of mass destruction—weapons, it turns out, he never had—to terrorists, Bush told the United Nations on September 12, 2002: "If we meet out responsibilities, if we overcome this danger, we can arrive at a very different future. The people of Iraq can shake off their captivity. They can one day join a democratic Afghanistan and a democratic Palestine, inspiring reforms around the Muslim world. These nations can show by their example that honest government, and respect for women, and the great Islamic tradition of learning can triumph in the Middle East and beyond" (2005:89).

Throughout this campaign, we can clearly hear the echo of Lord Cromer and his use of the language of feminism, backed by the anti-Islam discourse. Like the Egyptian consul, George W. Bush was no feminist. Nor was his administration supportive of initiatives sought by women's groups worldwide. On his first day in office, the new president cut off all U.S. funding to international family-planning organizations that offered abortion services or even counseling (Viner 2002). A year later, he used a public proclamation to link his opposition to abortion, which remains legally protected in the United States, to the war on terrorism: both represented "a fight against evil and tyranny to preserve and protect life" (2002a; quoted in Viner 2002).

Critics have also argued that the repressive conditions for women under Taliban rule, so frequently invoked by the Bush administration and its allies, were of little interest to the West until the invasion of Afghanistan in the aftermath of the terrorist strikes on New York and Washington, D.C. In fact, negotiations between the United States and elements of the Taliban on the construction of an oil pipeline that would cross Afghan territory had been carried on for years and were well advanced (Cloud 2004; Rashid 2007). Moreover, some women's groups in Afghanistan were opposed to the invasion, seeing an immediate threat to women and children from U.S. bombs, bullets, and occupation (Cloud 2004:297; Oliver 2007:53–55). All this recalls Gayatri Chakravorty Spivak's critique of colonialist rhetoric as largely consisting of "white men saving brown women from brown men" (1988:295).

The U.S. government was able to mobilize considerable public support for two wars against overwhelmingly Muslim societies by tapping directly into the overarching Western discourse of Islam and its important subset Islam and women. This expropriation of the rhetoric of women's rights and freedoms under Islam in order to unleash deadly violence on Muslim nations shows clearly just how much the struggle for women's equality has become a discursive one rather than simply a material one (Oliver 2007:40). It is difficult to say that, on the ground, the women of Afghanistan and Iraq are materially better off after the U.S.-led invasions and the imposition of pro-Western governments. The death, destruction, and disease that invariably accompany war have certainly taken an enormous toll on Muslim men, women, and children, and the promised expansion of participation by women in public life has not been borne out, particularly in Iraq, where women today find their lives far more circumscribed than before the U.S. invasion.

Yet the totality of discursive statements, particularly in the media and the political arena, would remind us every day that things in the new Iraq and the new Afghanistan *are* better and that women there are more free and more happy—that is, they are more and more just like us. And the more like us, the better. Nowhere is this interpretation more evident than in the matter of women's clothing, especially the veil in its various forms. A photo essay titled "Kabul Unveiled" in *Time*, viewed online by tens of millions from around the world, notes the progression of images from photographs of veiled victims awaiting liberation to "photographs of feminists and other unveiled, public women [who] dominate and end the sequence" (Cloud 2004:294). Bryan S. Turner, among others, notes the importance in media representations of the exchange by Afghan women of the all-encompassing burqa for the right to go shopping, visit the hair salon, and buy makeup: "Emancipation from the discipline of the Taliban was marked by the early construction of the new Islamic identity, the consuming, post-jihadic Muslim" (2003, 1:35; see also Oliver 2007:47–57).

Likewise, foreign correspondent John Lancaster (1997) can write a breezy feature on the front page of the *Washington Post* about the brisk trade in racy lingerie in a Cairo shopping district. After interviewing shopkeepers, customers, and even a Muslim scholar at al-Azhar University, all of whom make it clear that the use of such accoutrements between married couples is acceptable and even admirable, Lancaster also cites scriptural authority for a healthy sex life between man and wife. Nevertheless, the *Washington Post* cannot stray from the established narrative: everything from the headline—"Egypt's Unveiled Industry; Sexy Lingerie a Hit in Muslim Land"—to the narrative structure of the piece turns on the Western notion that "conservative" Muslims cannot possibly enjoy sex as much as their Western counterparts.

Almost a decade later, ABC senior foreign-affairs correspondent Jonathan Karl (2005), after meeting a group of women university students, assures readers of the *Weekly Standard* that things are changing for the better in Saudi Arabia: "As I left the auditorium, I asked several students if I could email them. I was surprised by their addresses: 'sweeteyes,' 'cuteygirl85,' 'blackrose,' etc. There's something going on in Saudi Arabia."

This narrative of the veil, sexuality, and Western notions of modernity and progress reaches its height, however, whenever the subject is postrevolutionary Iran. Since the victory over the U.S.-backed shah in 1979 and the creation of the Islamic Republic, Iranian women have been required to veil in public. In the early years, dress requirements were extremely strict—no hair showing, no makeup or nail polish, no open-toe shoes, and so on—and at times brutally enforced by religious vigilantes. These practices have been relaxed significantly in recent years, and some middle-class and upper-class urban women now adopt colorful and personal expressions of the *hijab* that do little to disguise the figure or fully cover the hair.

Both the official line and public opinion toward this dress code have a complex and nuanced history (Abdo and Lyons 2003), but the Western media have universally seen and shown it as a reliable barometer of progress or lack thereof by secular civil society at the expense of the ruling religious establishment. In this schema, then, the more lipstick and hair visible to visiting foreign correspondents, the less secure the conservatives' grip on power and the better the chances of popular revolt against the Islamic system.[8]

Back from a reporting trip to the southern Iranian city of Shiraz in the spring of 2004, Nicholas Kristof, a columnist for the *New York Times*, concludes in "Those Sexy Iranians" that the transformation of the veil from shapeless, basic black to "light, tight, and sensual" marks the beginning of the end for the ruling clerics and their despotic regime. His troll through the city's shops revealed new consumer demand for robes slit up to the armpits or tied to the legs to show off the curve of the hip. "Worse, from the point of view of hard-line mullahs, young women in such clothing aren't getting 74 lashes any more—they're getting dates," he writes. Kristof then waves off objections from fashionable Iranian women who oppose Westernization—"We totally reject that," says one. "We don't want that freedom"—to assert that a style revolution profoundly threatens the Islamic Revolution. "Ayatollahs, look out," he concludes.

This transposition of the material and the discursive, of the actual and the imagined Muslim East, clouds our ability to understand cultures other than

our own, just as it hinders our ability to formulate appropriate and successful policies and responses to the inevitable conflict of interests in today's
globalized world. It also reveals the extent to which legitimate questions of
history, economics, and politics are set aside whenever it comes to Western
views of the Muslim world. Instead, questions of culture trump all. Assessing
this phenomenon after the start of the Afghan War, Lila Abu-Lughod notes:
"There was a consistent resort to the cultural, as if knowing something about
women and Islam or the meaning of a religious ritual would help one understand the tragic attack on New York's World Trade Center and the U.S. Pentagon" (2002:784).

The same confusion hopelessly entangled Karen Hughes, Bush's envoy to
the Muslim women of the world, when the powerful undersecretary of state
mistook her imagined East for the one now staring her in the face. At a meeting with professional and university women in Saudi Arabia, Hughes (2005)
was surprised to find that American notions of freedom and social participation were not necessarily shared, universal values: "We in America take our
freedom very seriously. . . . I have to tell you that—and I believe that women
should be full and equal participants in society. And I feel as an American
woman that my ability to drive is an important part of my freedom."

Members of her Saudi audience, prohibited from driving by the country's
strict social regime, were less than impressed. To these women, the educational opportunities and professional advancement they clearly enjoyed
were far more important and relevant to their lives. Nor were they impressed
by Hughes's repeated attempts to present herself as an ordinary "mom"—
a notion that struck many as odd or simply irrelevant. Similar debacles
occurred before Muslim women in both Turkey and Egypt, and even some
reporters in the traditionally sympathetic American media were withering
in their reporting of Hughes's mission. What is crucial here is not that the
worldview of any one government official should be shaped by life in subur-
ban Texas, with its driving culture and "soccer moms," but that the combined
resources of the White House—the State and Defense Departments with their
legions of consultants, public-relations advisers, Islam experts, and envoys—
could not foresee the coming train wreck.

Instead, the Bush administration adopted and perpetuated the established
discourse of Islam and women for the benefit of specific Western interests—
in this case, the military occupation and political and economic domination
of Muslim societies. By casting the wars in Afghanistan and Iraq as wars

for the liberation of Muslim women from the veil and other social restrictions, the administration both invoked this discourse and advanced it in new directions. At the same time, Bush and his fellow social conservatives were able to obscure their own opposition to women's advancement at home by contrasting the freedoms of Western women with those of women suffering under Islam.

7

WHAT'S WRONG WITH US?

It is always possible that one could speak the truth in a void; one would only be in the true, however, if one obeyed the rules of some discursive "policy" which would have to be reactivated every time one spoke.

MICHEL FOUCAULT, *THE ARCHAEOLOGY OF KNOWLEDGE*

A CLOSE READING of the anti-Islam discourse from its inception, or "zero point," in the run-up to the First Crusade to its present incarnation in the war on terrorism reveals remarkable power, influence, and—most striking of all—constancy. In fact, it is the last quality that represents its most salient feature. And it is one that has so far eluded satisfactory explanation by the social sciences. After rummaging through Michel Foucault's "toolbox," I have attempted to take a fundamental first step toward addressing this problem. This step has largely involved the powerful technique of discursive archaeology, aided and abetted by particular notions of "truth" and "history" and ultimately by the strategy of reversal—that is, of asking, What if the predominant discourse were suspended or turned on itself or suddenly ceased to exist?

I have also engaged in the task of addressing Philip W. Sutton and Stephen Vertigans's call for a fresh approach to the Western understanding of Islam: "If sociologists are to avoid contributing to the caricature of Islam as a war-like religion and civilization propagated by dogmatic Muslim militants, then there is a need to work towards a much more comprehensive sociological account which focuses on the social, cultural, political and economic contexts in which Islam is embedded. In doing so, sociology may add a new dimension to wider understandings of Islam and relations between 'Islam and the West'" (2005:31–32).

Whether one prefers to speak in terms of discursive formations or of the social contexts in which Islam is embedded, the challenge remains the same: to lay the foundations for a new and more useful way of looking at Islam and the Muslims that recognizes the distortions inherent in past efforts.

Such an approach would naturally upend both the popular view and the scholarly consensus across a range of issues, ideas, and disciplines. Foremost, it would challenge one of the cardinal precepts of the Western history of ideas: the inevitable arc of historical change and progress. As we saw in chapter 3, on the formation of the anti-Islam discourse, so-called serious speech on the subject of Islam has defied this basic notion of history. Everything in the established Western canon tells us that our knowledge and understanding of Islam should form and reform in accordance with additional information and new interactions—that is, with new data amassed over succeeding centuries of trade, travel, study, warfare, and so on. Such reformation has not happened in any meaningful way, and so we must look for ways to explain the so far unexplained.

I have sought to do so by applying an analytical framework that has at its heart one central theoretical position: the very idea of Islam has been perpetuated by those Western social groups and institutions that stand to benefit from the survival, intact and unexamined, of a thousand-year-old anti-Islam discourse, often for reasons that have nothing whatsoever to do with the putative subject. This framework, then, suggested three interrelated questions, all of them the subject of sociological inquiry when applied to the discursive formation of Islam: How is this discourse formed? How does it operate? And, last, who benefits?

This approach has allowed me to set aside for the most part claims of truth-value in the Western discourse of what it is Muslims say, do, or believe and to focus primarily on *how* and *why* such statements are produced in the first place, processes that take place outside the conscious understanding of those producing them. This is precisely what Foucault means when he refers to the effort "to reveal a positive unconscious of knowledge: a level that eludes the consciousness of the scientist and yet is part of scientific discourse, instead of disputing its validity and seeking to diminish its scientific nature" (1994b:xi).

It is only by addressing the production of Western statements about Islam outside larger questions of their validity that we can begin to acquire a deeper understanding of the sociological and epistemological phenomena at work in the background. This approach also reveals the ways in which the predominant discourse distorts the Western discipline of Islam and corrodes contemporary public debate and governmental policies with regard to the Muslim world. Last and perhaps most profound, it opens the door to Foucault's principle of reversal—specifically the negation of the accepted notion that the discourse accurately reflects a specific nondiscursive reality. This reversal, in turn, can reveal fruitful areas for future research and study.

Let me examine these ideas briefly with reference to my three central thematic concerns: Islam and science, Islam and violence, and Islam and women. Chapter 4 discussed the extent to which the Western discipline of the history of science has effectively been held hostage to the discursive notion that Islam is inherently and fundamentally irrational. The achievements of Muslim science, for a time the wonder of the Western world and the widespread source of emulation among medieval Latin scholars, were quickly submerged under the weight of the broader anti-Islam discourse. The early Renaissance humanists set this process in motion at the beginning of fourteenth century by dismissing Muslim science and philosophy out of hand—and, with it, the Middle Ages in general—and by directing the West toward new, idealized notions of "classical" Greece and Rome as the proper source of values, ideas, culture, and learning.

These new secular actors, by harnessing the anti-Islam discourse in this way and by adapting it to their own benefit, successfully carved out their own routes to social, political, and economic advancement—at court, in the universities, and even in the church hierarchy—in a rapidly urbanizing Europe traditionally dominated by the clergy. In a similar vein, the French mathematicians of the sixteenth century set out to create a European pedigree for the art of algebra as a way to lift arithmetic from a mere trade to a lofty science and in this way to advance their own professional and social standing. That this task required wholesale rewriting of the history of mathematics was, of course, incidental. Today, the same discourse underpins the Western monopoly on science, technology, and the idea of modernity in general.

As seen in chapter 5, this process of distortion, introduced by the operation of the anti-Islam discourse, takes on greater immediacy and urgency when we consider matters of contemporary public policy, such as the war on terrorism and the broader relationship between Islam and the West. Here, the discursive formation of Islam and violence colors virtually every aspect of Western thinking and response. Without it, the "clash of civilizations" thesis that underpins the present war on terrorism would likely never have arisen from relative obscurity to the position of prominence it enjoys in the media, in the political arena, and among the public at large. By deploying central elements of the anti-Islam discourse, American neoconservatives and their allies in business, the media, politics, and academia have advanced their desire to remake the Muslim world in the Western image.

Among the most corrosive derivative effects of the established narrative of violence in Islam is the way in which it obscures the enemy's possible motivations and delegitimizes their tactics in the war on terrorism while valorizing the West's approach on both scores. President George W. Bush's (2001a) insistence on portraying Osama bin Laden simply as heir to the "murderous ideologies of the twentieth century" and the accompanying rise of the popular rhetorical slogan of "Islamofascism" cast the attacks of September 11, 2001, exclusively as a totalitarian threat to the West's values, culture, and way of life.

So, too, does New York Times columnist Thomas Friedman's (2002) insistence, contrary to fact, that the al-Qaeda hijackers had no concrete demands. In other words, radical Muslims can have no other goal, objective, or interest except the wholesale annihilation of the Western world as we know it and violence for violence's sake. Any rational political, social, economic, cultural, or religious grievances that might lie behind or simply help shape and channel violent antagonism toward the West must perforce be dismissed outright or else ignored altogether. This dismissal dooms any possibility of negotiated settlement to the current contestation between Western interests and those of a resurgent Islamic world and all but guarantees a militarized response into the foreseeable future.

In the same way, the prevailing discourse of Islam and women, detailed in chapter 6, dictates that the West's approaches and policy proscriptions toward Muslim societies be seen solely through the lens of its own flawed understanding of both women and gender relations in Islam. Nothing else can adequately explain the Western fascination, obsession even, with the institution of veiling and the West's general apprehension of this institution as the root and cause of the oppressive conditions faced by many women in Muslim societies. As with the discourse on violence, the prevailing Western narrative of the veil and of the associated "degradation" of women creates the notion of an inferior Muslim world in need of rescue from itself, by force if necessary, even as it validates the West's own approach to gender relations and the rights of women.

Thus Bush and his wife, Laura—neither known for feminist sentiments—so eagerly championed the rights of Afghan women as a way to mobilize public support at home for the war against the Taliban. As we have seen time and time again with the workings of this discourse, the desires and opinions of Afghan Muslim women, a considerable number of whom opposed the U.S. invasion, were of no consequence. Nor has the continued suffering of women under the leaders of the post-Taliban regime and under general wartime conditions drawn anything like the Western attention and condemnation once directed at their predecessors.

The same campaign against the veil was used in the nineteenth and early twentieth centuries to support the colonial domination of the Muslim world and to bolster evangelical campaigns aimed at subverting Islam and gaining Christian converts, while simultaneously co-opting and even neutralizing the emerging Western feminist demand for greater women's rights at home. On this issue again, as with science and war, varying Western social groups, interests, and institutions have continued to benefit from the discourse of Islam and women even as it has failed repeatedly to articulate anything like reality on the ground.

Having explicated the formation of the anti-Islam discourse and laid out a framework for understanding its operation and perpetuation across the centuries and across a broad range of intellectual, social, and political issues, I propose a new model for approaching the world of Islam—a "hidden history," as it were, of its practices, beliefs, and culture. To begin with, we must acknowledge that the established Western discourse of Islam does not—or, at the very least, does not necessarily—reflect the reality of Islam itself, what I have referred to earlier as "Islam qua Islam." Rather, this discourse is the product of a process that has embedded a particular discursive formation in Western thought. Here, then, are the roots of what Sutton and Vertigans have identified as the prevailing "caricature of Islam" (2005:31). Chapters 4, 5, and 6 established ample grounds for such an assertion, and many more examples beyond the scope of this inquiry might likewise be marshaled in support.

Next we must deliberately remove the central pillars of the thousand-year-old anti-Islam discourse and examine what remains behind. Or, to return to the question posed at the outset, we must ask, *When we open this particular window, what is it that we see that has not been seen before?* Were we to set aside these central notions—that Islam is inherently violent and spread by the sword; that Muslims are irrational, antiscience, and thus antimodern; and that they are sexually perverse and hate women—as flawed representations of the nondiscursive reality of Islam, then whole new vistas of possible relationships between East and West will begin to open up before our eyes.

From this vantage point, we can now begin to recognize the emerging outlines of the West's enormous debt to Islamic science and philosophy and the accompanying need to reexamine the way we think about the history of ideas entirely. We can start to discern the deep fault lines that run through the predominant notion of Islam as inherently violent and the way this notion distorts the West's understanding, conceals its own motives and interests, and renders appropriate and successful policy responses virtually impossible. And we can at last acknowledge that the near-total inadequacy of our understanding of gender relations in Islamic societies has obscured contemporary Islam's claims to its own, non-Western idea of modernity.

This task involves shifting the broader problem of East–West relations from the traditional view of *inter*cultural rivalry to one of *intra*cultural contest. Rather than delimit what is a boundary between East and West, we should create one large interactive space that stretches across much of the globe. In effect, this shift would mark a return to the view of the world captured in one of the most remarkable landmarks in the history of ideas: the atlas produced by the Muslim scholar Muhammad al-Idrisi in the mid-twelfth century by commission of the Christian king of Sicily, which was then multifaith—Muslim, Catholic, and Orthodox.

The effort to place Islam and the West in the same cultural space, a shared universe foretold in the lapis lazuli shades of al-Idrisi's *mappa mundi*, flows naturally from Max Weber's classic analysis of both Christianity and Islam as "Western" religions. By opening up space for the civilization of Islam in the idea of Western culture, we are suddenly faced with a compelling new model of relations between the two—one of continuous interaction of cultures locked in relations for one thousand years—in which it is hard to say where one ends and the other begins. This model, then, calls for the compilation of a new, hidden history of Islam that fills in those areas declared off limits by the anti-Islam discourse. But, first, we must radically rephrase the West's favorite polemical question—What's wrong with Islam?—to a less comfortable query: What's wrong with us?

Notes

1. Ervand Abrahamian attributes the sudden popularity of Huntington's thesis after the terrorist attacks in large measure to its ability to "analyze international relations without discussing actual politics—especially the issue of Palestine in particular and of Arab nationalism in general" (2003:534–538). As will become clear in the succeeding chapters of this volume, I see the same phenomenon more widely as a reflection of the established anti-Islam discourse under the harsh lights of post–September 11 America.

2. Given the general chaos in Iraq, the number of civilian deaths as a result of the U.S.-led invasion has proved enormously difficult to establish. The Iraq Body Count project, which relies on media accounts, nongovernmental organization reports, and limited official data, puts the figure of civilian deaths attributable to the invasion and ensuing violence at between 98,000 and 107,000 as of October 10, 2010 (available at http://www.iraqbodycount. org). Figures kept by the Associated Press are roughly the same. A statistical study in the *Lancet* (Burnham et al. 2006) put the toll much higher, with around 600,000 deaths as of June 2006, although that figure and the

methodology behind it have seen a number of challenges. The supreme power in Iraq, the U.S. military, says it does not keep records of civilian deaths.

3. For details of the campaign targeting American Muslims, including their religious charities, see David Cole (2003:19–22). Geneive Abdo (2006b) explores the more general effects on ordinary Muslims in America after the attacks on New York and Washington, D.C.

4. I have chosen quite deliberately to present the Arabic word *jihad* in italics throughout this study in recognition that it is indeed both a foreign word and a foreign concept. By contrast, the Western discourse has sought to "naturalize" the term and to reduce its meaning to a single and consistent interpretation—that of aggressive armed struggle against all non-Muslims. As discussed in chapter 5, this interpretation is but one of many meanings and understandings of *jihad*, all of which have been shaped throughout the Islamic experience by religious, social, and political context. It is thus literally untranslatable in any meaningful sense.

5. For a biting critique of Foucault on Iran, see Janet Afary and Kevin B. Anderson (2005). For a more nuanced account, see Georg Stauth (1991).

6. *NBC News* earlier broadcast some of the tapes, provided by William Arkin, the network's military analyst.

7. The charge of pedophilia stems from the tradition that says the Prophet's last wife was a child-bride, the daughter of his close friend and ally Abu Bakr—later the first of the rightly guided caliphs. Although the practice of marriage to girls was common at the time, her precise age is still subject to dispute, as is her age when the marriage was later consummated.

8. All translations from the Qur'an are taken from Marmaduke Pickthall (1930).

9. For a study of Christian theologians' construction of the "hermeneutical Jew," see Jeremy Cohen (1999).

10. For a look at Western scholars' general unwillingness to come to grips fully with the discovery of links between Copernicus and Muslim scholars' astronomical work, see George Saliba (2007).

11. Equally interesting, although perhaps more subtle and thus less visible to the general public, is the scholarly Western discourse of Islamic law. As Wael B. Hallaq (1990, 2002–2003, forthcoming) has shown, this discourse, like the discourse of Islam and science, takes as its starting point the lack of rationality and backwardness of the Muslims and, as a result, insists on searching for the roots and origins of the sophisticated corpus of Islamic law in other,

nearby cultures, chiefly Roman, Jewish, and Hellenic. Western understanding of Islamic law—like its understanding of Islam and science, Islam and violence, and Islam and women—has languished as a result.

2. FOUCAULT'S TOOLBOX

1. In his 1918 lecture at the University of Munich, later translated into English as "Science as a Vocation," Max Weber preferred the term *intellectualization* to describe this process (1958:139; cited in Swatos and Christiano 1999:212).
2. For an overview, see Teun van Dijk (1985).
3. Although this lecture was delivered in late 1970, the text here is from the appendix to the 1972 edition of *The Archaeology of Knowledge*. It is identified in the text as 1972b, whereas *Archaeology* as a whole is designated as 1972a.
4. The sura in question, the second chapter of the Qur'an, is the longest of the 114 sections of the text. Pickthall (1930) translates the verse in question as follows: "There is no compulsion in religion. The right direction is henceforth distinct from error. And he who rejects false deities and believes in Allah has grasped a firm handhold which will never break. Allah is Hearer, Knower."
5. There are, perhaps, a few signs that Foucault had a sense of these dangers, and he appears at times to hedge his bets on whether archaeology will meet his expectations in the future (Dreyfus and Rabinow 1983:99–100). In his conclusion to *The Archaeology of Knowledge*, presented as a response to an imagined critical reader, Foucault notes that he is still at the early stages of his investigations and that there are no "means of guaranteeing" that archaeology will remain both stable and autonomous: "I accept that my discourse may disappear with the figure that has borne it so far" (1972a:208).
6. One of Said's most passionate critics, Robert Irwin (2006:4), apparently overlooks these key passages when he argues that Said denies the "Orient" any objective reality of its own outside the Western discourse.

3. THE WESTERN IDEA OF ISLAM

1. The king referred to is Muʾawiya, the first true Umayyad caliph, who ruled in Damascus from 660 to 680.
2. John Tolan (2002) sees the imperatives of Catholic sacred history as the determining factor in later Western attitudes toward Islam, and he contrasts this argument in particular with the views of Norman Daniel (1984), who

suggests that literary convention, repeated endlessly but not necessarily believed, provides the central element. Throughout this work, I argue that the predominant anti-Islam discourse allows both of these phenomena—the application of sacred history and the use of literary convention—to stand unchallenged to this day.

3. The power of this stream of thought among the three major monotheist faiths can be seen in the established Muslim tradition of Daniel apocalypses, drawing on the authority if not the actual text of the Book of Daniel (Cook 2002:55–57).

4. Scholars do not universally accept John of Damascus's authorship of the chapter on Islam in *De haeresibus*. Some argue that it was borrowed from an earlier text, and others suggest that it may have been added later. However, modern opinion generally attributes the work to John. For a summary of the controversy, see John Meyendorff (1964:116–117) and Daniel Sahas (1972:60–61). A detailed bibliography on the matter can be found in Sahas (61n.2).

5. The Jews were also subject to these social restrictions, generally at the same time they were imposed against the Muslims.

6. Here, Petrus Alfonsi departs from more accepted Christian tradition, which identifies the "heretic" said to have advised Muhammad with the Nestorian figure Sergius.

4. ISLAM AND SCIENCE

1. By contrast, the public outcry against the threat of Western cultural or economic domination has been significant and often effective. Here, the work of Sayyid Qutb, in particular the manifesto *Milestones* (1981), has been influential. A rare critical voice about the broad dangers of adopting Western technology can also be found in Jalal Al-i Ahmad (1983).

2. It is worth noting the existence of a second such problematic: Chinese science. See, for example, Joseph Needham (1969). Toby Huff ([1993] 2003:240–324), whose study of Islam and science is covered in detail later in this chapter, also provides an overview of Chinese science. For critiques, see Nathan Sivin (1984) and George Saliba (1999a, 1999b).

3. Some attribute this letter to Frederick's son, Manfred. For the view that the letter was almost certainly written by Frederick, see Thomas van Cleve (1972:303n.2).

4. Bacon completed his great work at the request of Pope Clement IV and sent it to Rome in 1267.

5. Centuries earlier, the first scholars of the Abbasid Empire, too, had been drawn to Aristotle's logical works as a useful tool in their polemics regarding other faiths and opposing Muslim sects (Gutas 1998:61–63).

6. Paul Oskar Kristeller (1992:29–91) notes that Thomism, although enormously influential for centuries, did not become the church's accepted philosophical doctrine until a little more than one hundred years ago. Before that, it was one of several important tendencies in Christian thought.

7. Albertus Magnus's study of the true "roots of science" likewise singles out for praise such Arab figures as Abu al-Zarqali, Muhammad al-Battani, Tabit ibn Qura, Nur al-Din al-Bitrugi, Ahmad ibn Muhammad al-Fargani, Albumazar, and many others (Høyrup 1996:106n.9).

8. Averroës chose his title as a direct response against Abu Hamid al-Ghazali's *Incoherence of the Philosophers* (1997), a major theological work that challenges the Arab philosophers on their own terms.

9. George Makdisi (1989) argues that both scholasticism and humanism arrived in the West from the Islamic world toward the end of the eleventh century, with humanism emerging into recognizable Western form two centuries after scholasticism amid the general rise of European urban life. He thus illuminates yet another example of the failings of traditional intellectual history in the face of the anti-Islam discourse (Hallaq 2002–2003:5–6).

10. The Vatican Library under Nicholas V was the largest collection of books in Western Christendom (Rose 1975:37). The great medieval Muslim libraries, by contrast, contained hundreds of thousands of volumes, and private collections and those affiliated with religious institutions often numbered in the tens of thousands (Mackensen 1932; Bashiruddin 1967; J. Pedersen 1984:113–117).

11. Originally written in Greek around 150 C.E., the work became known throughout the medieval world under the Arabic-influenced title *Almagest*, a derivative of one of its Greek titles (J. Evans 1998:23).

12. A famous experiment carried out on the orders of Caliph al-Ma'mun around 827 had estimated 1 degree of the earth's circumference at 69.47 miles (111.8 kilometers) in today's units, not far from the accepted modern value of 69.03 miles (111.1 kilometers), a variance of around 0.62 percent

(Donini 1991:36–37). In a sense, the Arabs had faced a similar dilemma as the later Europeans. They could not agree on how to interpret the unit of measurement used by Ptolemy. Unlike the Europeans, however, they did not simply hazard a guess but devised their own experiments to determine the proper value.

5. ISLAM AND VIOLENCE

1. It is difficult not to conclude that the use of the phrase "improvised explosive devices" in the place of the perfectly serviceable words *mines* and *bombs* is somehow aimed at denigrating and dismissing what has turned out to be a highly effective weapon against Western troops in Iraq and Afghanistan. Judging by these devices' lethality, the technology has clearly moved well beyond mere improvisation.

2. I focus this argument on the appropriation of the concept of *jihad*, although many parallels may be seen in the predominant Western discourse of martyrdom in Islam. For a recent reexamination of the ideas of martyrdom in the Christian and Muslim traditions, see Brian Wicker (2006).

3. See, for example, the discussion of the veil as a symbol of Islamic resistance to Westernization in chapter 6.

4. The Prophet's sunna may be said to be divinely inspired, but it as well as the hadith collections and the later body of jurisprudence (*fiqh*) are ultimately human endeavors and decidedly not the Word of God.

5. Daniel Benjamin and Steven Simon (2002) cite the second passage as Qur'an 74:30–31, but they have, it seems, mistakenly condensed several verses before that one. Marmaduke Pickthall's translation of the relevant passage is:

> Him shall I fling unto the burning. Ah, what will convey unto thee what that burning is!
> It leaveth naught; it spareth naught. It shrivelleth the man. Above it are nineteen.
> We have appointed only angels to be wardens of the Fire,
> And their number have We made to be a stumbling-block for those who disbelieve;
> That those to whom the Scripture hath been given may have certainty,
> And that believers may increase in faith. (1930:74:26–31)

6. The canonical order of the revelations presented in the Qurʾan was established under the direction of the third caliph, ʿUthman, after Muhammad's death. This ʿUthman codex generally arranges the verses from the longest to the shortest, with the exception of the first sura, the *fatiha*, or "The Opening." By tradition, the place of revelation, Mecca for the earlier ones and Medina for the later, are noted in the text, although debate continues in scholarly circles over some of these conventions.

7. See http://www.pulitzer.org/citation/2002-Commentary.

8. The originals appeared in the London-based Arabic newspaper *al-Quds al-Arabi*. English translations are available at http://www.pbs.org/newshour/terrorism/international/fatwa_1996.html and http://www.pbs.org/newshour/terrorism/international/fatwa_1998.html.

9. Ramadan later took up a position at Oxford. In other celebrated cases, Juan Cole, a professor of Middle East history at the University of Michigan, was blocked from an appointment at Yale in 2006 after a public outcry by conservative academics, politicians, and bloggers, and the political scientist Norman G. Finkelstein was denied tenure at DePaul University in 2007 and then left the university under similar circumstances.

10. "Sepahee" is from the Persian and Urdu word *sipahi* (soldier or horseman). The most common British usage is *sepoy*, which I have used unless the reference comes in a quotation, as it does here.

11. Percival Spear (1980:194) puts the total Delhi population at the time at around 160,000, more or less evenly divided between Muslims and Hindus.

12. For the sake of clarity, I have substituted standardized, contemporary spellings for place-names used in the original.

6. ISLAM AND WOMEN

1. Pope's reference to cucumbers was a favorite Western calumny of old but uncertain provenance. Among its early popularizers was Ottaviano Bon, the Venetian ambassador to the Ottomans more than a century before Lady Montagu's day.

2. The Western text of *One Thousand and One Nights* was a compilation from an oral tradition built up over many centuries, primarily from Indian, Persian, and Egyptian sources. It did not appear in Arabic until the early nineteenth century (Melman 1992:63). Some of the source material has never been traced. See also Dwight Reynolds (2006).

3. Marmaduke Pickthall (1930) translates 2:223 as follows: "Your women are a tilth [tillage] for you (to cultivate) so go to your tilth as you will, and send (good deeds) before you for your souls, and fear Allah."

4. Roy Porter (1990:118) goes on to argue that this tension was largely set aside once the West had discovered Tahiti, with its own promise of a sexual idyll and ease of access without the obstacles erected by Islam.

5. For a study of how gender relations in eighteenth-century Egypt flew in the face of the Western discourse, see Afaf Lutfi al-Sayyid Marsot (1995).

6. The reference is from Stanley Lane-Poole, who was Edward Lane's nephew: "The degradation of women in the East is a canker that begins its destructive work in childhood, and has eaten into the whole system of Islam" (1903:43).

7. The "veil" itself is not simple, although its Western representation has been reduced to a single concept and idea. Fadwa El-Guindi (1999:6–7) argues that the Western word *veil* cannot possibly accommodate the diversity seen in the actual practice of veiling. She points out that *The Encyclopedia of Islam* identifies more than one hundred terms for dress parts, many of which are used for "veiling." Some are for men, some for women, and some for both.

8. In fact, the opposite is generally the case. Living in Tehran from 1998 to 2001, I was able to observe firsthand that social regulation on veiling, the intermingling of the sexes in public, and the use of illicit satellite dishes to receive foreign programming was generally most relaxed whenever the authorities felt most secure. Such apparent relaxation often issued from a position of strength, not weakness.

BIBLIOGRAPHY

Abdo, Geneive. 2000. *No God but God: Egypt and the Triumph of Islam.* New York: Oxford University Press.

——. 2006a. "America's Muslims Aren't as Assimilated as You Think." *Washington Post*, August 27.

——. 2006b. *Main Street and Mecca: Muslim Life in America After 9/11.* New York: Oxford University Press.

Abdo, Geneive, and Jonathan Lyons. 2003. *Answering Only to God: Faith and Freedom in Twenty-First-Century Iran.* New York: Holt.

Abootalebi, Ali Reza. 2000. *Islam and Democracy: State-Society Relations in Developing Countries, 1980-1994.* New York: Garland.

——. 2003. "Islam and Democracy." In Barry Rubin, ed., *Revolutionaries and Reformers: Contemporary Islamist Movements in the Middle East*, 155–171. Albany: State University of New York Press.

Abrahamian, Ervand. 2003. "The US Media, Huntington, and September 11." *Third World Quarterly* 24, no. 3:529–544.

Abulafia, David. 1983. "The Crown and the Economy Under Roger II and His Successors." *Dumbarton Oaks Papers* 37:1–14.

——. 1987. *Italy, Sicily, and the Mediterranean, 1100–1400*. London: Variorum Reprints.

——. 1992. *Frederick II: A Medieval Emperor*. New York: Oxford University Press.

——. 1994. "The Role of Trade in Muslim–Christian Contact During the Middle Ages." In Dionisius A. Agius and Richard Hitchcock, eds., *The Arab Influence in Medieval Europe*, 1–24. Reading, Mass.: Ithaca Press.

——, ed. 2004. *Italy in the Central Middle Ages, 1000–1300*. Oxford: Oxford University Press.

Abu-Lughod, Lila. 1998. "The Marriage of Feminism and Islamism in Egypt: Selective Repudiation as a Dynamic of Postcolonial Cultural Politics." In Lila Abu-Lughod, ed., *Remaking Women: Feminism and Modernity in the Middle East*, 243–269. Princeton, N.J.: Princeton University Press.

——. 2002. "Do Muslim Women Really Need Saving? Anthropological Reflections on Cultural Relativism and Others." *American Anthropologist* 104, no. 3:783–790.

Abu Mashar. 1994. *The Abbreviation of the "Introduction to Astrology."* Translated and edited by Charles Burnett, Keiji Yamamoto, and Michio Yano. Leiden: Brill.

——. 2000. *Abu Mashar on Historical Astrology: "The Book of Religions and Dynasties" (On the Great Conjunctions)*. 2 vols. Translated and edited by Keiji Yamamoto and Charles Burnett. Leiden: Brill.

Adamnan of Iona. 1958. *Adamnan's "De locis sanctis."* Translated and edited by Denis Meehan. Dublin: Dublin Institute for Advanced Studies.

Adelard of Bath. 1998. *Adelard of Bath, Conversations with His Nephew: "On the Same and the Different," "Questions on Natural Science," and "On Birds."* Translated and edited by Charles Burnett. Cambridge: Cambridge University Press.

Afary, Janet, and Kevin B. Anderson. 2005. *Foucault and the Iranian Revolution: Gender and the Seductions of Islamism*. Chicago: University of Chicago Press.

Afsarrudin, Asma. 2006a. "Competing Perspectives on *Jihad* and 'Martyrdom' in Early Islamic Sources." In Brian Wicker, ed., *Witness to Faith? Martyrdom in Christianity and Islam*, 15–31. Burlington, Vt.: Ashgate.

——. 2006b. "Obedience to Political Authority: An Evolutionary Concept." In M. A. Muqtedar Khan, ed., *Islamic Democratic Discourse: Theory, Debates, and Philosophical Perspectives*, 37–60. Oxford: Lexington Books.

——. 2008. *The First Muslims: History and Memory*. Oxford: One World.

Agius, Dionisius A., and Richard Hitchcock, eds. 1994. *The Arab Influence in Medieval Europe*. Reading, Mass.: Ithaca Press.

Ahmad, Nafis. 1990. *Muslims and the Science of Geography*. Dhaka, Bangladesh: Dhaka University Press.

Ahmad, Sayyid Maqbal. 1995. *A History of Arab-Islamic Geography*. Amman, Jordan: Al al-Bayt University.

Ahmed, Leila. 1978. *Edward Lane: A Study of His Life and Works and of British Ideas of the Middle East in the Nineteenth Century*. London: Longman.

——. 1982. "Western Ethnocentrism and Perceptions of the Harem." *Feminist Studies* 8, no. 3:521–534.

——. 1992. *Women and Gender in Islam: Historical Roots of a Modern Debate*. New Haven, Conn.: Yale University Press.

Ajami, Fouad. 2002. " 'The Reckoning': Iraq and the Thief of Baghdad." *New York Times*, May 19.

Alavi, Seema. 1995. *The Sepoys and the Company: Tradition and Transition in Northern India, 1770–1830*. New Delhi: Oxford University Press.

Al-i Ahmad, Jalal. 1983. *Occidentosis: A Plague from the West*. Translated by R. Campbell. Berkeley, Calif.: Mizan Press.

Allen, Charles. 2006. *God's Terrorists: The Wahabbi Cult and the Hidden Roots of Modern Jihad*. London: Little, Brown.

Allen, Michael Idomir. 1996. "Bede and Frechulf at Medieval St Gallen." In L. A. J. R. Houwen and A. A. MacDonald, eds., *Beda Venerabilis: Historian, Monk, and Northumbrian*, 61–80. Groningen, Netherlands: Forsten.

Alloula, Malek. 1986. *The Colonial Harem*. Translated by Myrna Godzich and Wlad Godzich. Minneapolis: University of Minnesota Press.

Althusser, Louis. 1972. *Politics and History: Montesquieu, Rousseau, Hegel, and Marx*. Translated by Ben Brewster. London: NLB.

Al-Andalusi. 1991. *Science in the Medieval World: Book of the Categories of Nations*. Translated and edited by Semaan I. Salem and Alok Kumar. Austin: University of Texas Press.

Anderson, Benedict. 1983. *Imagined Communities: Reflections on the Origins of Nationalism*. London: Verso.

Appelby, R. Scott. 2000. *The Ambivalence of the Sacred: Religion, Violence, and Reconciliation*. Lanham, Md.: Rowman & Littlefield.

Arditi, Jorge. 1994. "Geertz, Kuhn, and the Idea of a Cultural Paradigm." *British Journal of Sociology* 45, no. 4:597–617.

Aristotle. 1801. *Metaphysics*. Translated and edited by Thomas Taylor. London: Davis, Wilks, and Taylor.

Arkin, William M. 2003. "The Pentagon Unleashes a Holy Warrior." *Los Angeles Times*, October 16.

Arnaldez, R. 1998. *Ibn Rushd: A Rationalist in Islam*. Notre Dame, Ind.: University of Notre Dame Press.

Arnold, Thomas, and Alfred Guillaume, eds. 1931. *The Legacy of Islam*. Oxford: Clarendon Press.

Asbridge, Thomas S. 2000. *The Creation of the Principality of Antioch, 1098–1130.* Woodbridge, Eng.: Boydell Press.

——. 2004. *The First Crusade: A New History.* New York: Oxford University Press.

Atiya, Aziz S. 1962. *Crusade, Commerce, and Culture.* Bloomington: Indiana University Press.

Attiyeh, George N. 1966. *Al-Kindi: The Philosopher of the Arabs.* Rawalpindi, Pakistan: Islamic Research Institute.

——, ed. 1995. *The Book in the Islamic World: The Written Word and Communication in the Middle East.* New York: New York University Press.

Augustine. 1942. *The Confessions of St. Augustine.* Translated by F. J. Sheed. New York: Sheed & Ward.

——. 1958. *City of God.* Translated by Gerald G. Walsh, Demetrius B. Zema, Grace Monahan, and Daniel J. Honan. New York: Doubleday.

Averroës [Ibn Rushd]. 1954. *Averroes' "Tahafut al-Tahafut."* 2 vols. Translated and edited by Simon van den Bergh. Oxford: Oxford University Press.

——. 1967. *Averroes: On the Harmony of Religion and Philosophy.* Translated and edited by George F. Hourani. London: Luzac.

——. 1986. *Ibn Rushd's Metaphysics.* Translated and edited by Charles Genequand. Leiden: Brill.

Aziz, Ahmad. 1979. *A History of Islamic Sicily.* New York: Columbia University Press.

Al-Azmeh, Aziz. 1992. "Barbarians in Arab Eyes." *Past and Present* 134:3–18.

——. 1996. *Islams and Modernities.* 2d ed. London: Verso.

Bacon, Roger. 1927. *Opus majus.* Translated by Robert Belle Burke. Philadelphia: University of Pennsylvania Press.

Bagehot, Walter. 1881. *Physics and Politics; or, Thoughts on the Natural Application of the Principles of "Natural Selection" and "Inheritance" to Political Society.* 6th ed. London: Kegan Paul.

Baldwin, John W. 1982. "Masters at Paris from 1179–1215." In Robert L. Benson and Giles Constable, eds., *Renaissance and Renewal in the Twelfth Century,* 138–172. Cambridge, Mass.: Harvard University Press.

Barber, Benjamin R. 1996. *Jihad vs. McWorld.* New York: Ballantine.

Baring, Evelyn [Lord Cromer]. 2000. *Modern Egypt.* 2 vols. London: Routledge.

Bashear, Suliman. 1991. "Qibla *Musharriqa* and Early Muslim Prayer in Churches." *Muslim World* 81, nos. 3–4:267–282.

Bashiruddin, S. 1967. "The Fate of Sectarian Libraries in Medieval Islam." *Libri* 17, no. 3:149–162.

Bauman, Zygmunt. 1989. *Modernity and the Holocaust.* Ithaca, N.Y.: Cornell University Press.

——. 1998. *Globalization: The Human Consequences.* Cambridge: Polity Press.

——. 2000. *Liquid Modernity.* Cambridge: Polity Press.

——. 2006. *Liquid Fear.* Cambridge: Polity Press.

Bauman, Zygmunt, and Tim May. 2001. *Thinking Sociologically.* 2d ed. Oxford: Blackwell.

Bayly, C. A. 1996. *Empire and Information: Intelligence Gathering and Social Communication in India, 1780–1870.* Cambridge: Cambridge University Press.

Bede. 1968. *A History of the English Church and People.* Translated and edited by Leo Sherley-Price. Harmondsworth: Penguin.

——. 1999. *Bede: The Reckoning of Time.* Translated and edited by Faith Wallis. Liverpool: Liverpool University Press.

Bello, Iysa A. 1989. *The Medieval Islamic Controversy Between Philosophy and Orthodoxy.* Leiden: Brill.

Benedict XVI. 2006. "Faith, Reason, and the University: Memories and Reflections." September 12. Available at http://www.vatican.va/holy_father/benedict_xvi/speeches/2006/september/documents/hf_ben-xvi_spe_20060912_university-regensburg_en.html.

Benjamin, Daniel, and Steven Simon. 2002. *The Age of Sacred Terror.* New York: Random House.

Berger, Peter L. 1973. *The Social Reality of Religion.* Harmondsworth: Penguin.

——. 1999. "The Desecularization of the World: A Global Overview." In Peter L. Berger, ed., *The Desecularization of the World: Resurgent Religion in World Politics,* 1–18. Washington, D.C.: Ethics and Public Policy Center.

Berger, Peter L., and Thomas Luckmann. 1967. *The Social Construction of Reality: A Treatise in the Sociology of Knowledge.* New York: Anchor Books.

Berggren, J. J. 1996. "Islamic Acquisition of the Foreign Sciences: A Cultural Perspective." In F. Jamil Ragep and Sally P. Ragep, with Steven Livesey, eds., *Tradition, Transmission, Transformation,* 263–283. Leiden: Brill.

——. 2003. *Episodes in the Mathematics of Medieval Islam.* New York: Springer.

Berkowitz, Dan, and Lyombe Eko. 2007. "Blasphemy as Sacred Right/Rite: 'The Mohammed Cartoons Affair' and the Maintenance of Journalistic Ideology." *Journalism Studies* 8, no. 5:779–797.

Bernal, Martin. 1987. *Black Athena: The Afroasiatic Roots of Classical Civilization: The Fabrication of Ancient Greece, 1785–1985.* New Brunswick, N.J.: Rutgers University Press.

"Bernard Lewis Applauds the Crusades." 2007. *Wall Street Journal,* March 8.

Bernard of Clairvaux. 1953. *The Letters of St. Bernard of Clairvaux.* Translated by Bruno Scott James. London: Bruns and Oates.

Beyer, Peter. 2006. *Religions in Global Society*. London: Routledge.

Bin Laden, Osama. 1996. "Declaration of War Against the Americans Occupying the Land of the Two Holy Places." Available at http://www.pbs.org/newshour/terrorism/international/fatwa_1996.html.

Bin Laden, Osama, Ayman al-Zawahiri, and others. 1998. "Declaration of the World Islamic Front for *Jihad* Against the Jews and the Crusaders." Available at http://www.pbs.org/newshour/terrorism/international/fatwa_1998.html.

Al-Biruni. 1967. *The Determination of the Coordinates of Cities: Al-Biruni's Tahid al-Amakin*. Translated and edited by Jamil Ali. Beirut: Centennial.

Bisaha, Nancy. 2001. "Petrarch's Vision of the Muslim and Byzantine East." *Speculum* 76:284–314.

Bishko, Charles Julian. 1956. "Peter the Venerable's Journey to Spain." In Giles Constable and James Kritzeck, eds., *Petrus Venerabilis: Studies and Texts Commemorating the Eighth Centenary of His Death*, 163–175. Rome: Herder.

Blake, Ernest O., and Colin Morris. 1985. "A Hermit Goes to War: Peter and the Origins of the First Crusade." *Studies in Church History* 22:86–90.

Blanks, David R. 2002. "Islam and the West in the Age of the Pilgrim." In Michael Frassetto, ed., *The Year 1000: Religious and Social Response to the Turning of the First Millennium*, 257–271. New York: Palgrave Macmillan.

Boethius of Dacia. 1987. *On the Supreme Good, On the Eternity of the World, On Dreams*. Translated and edited by John F. Wippel. Toronto: Pontifical Institute of Mediaeval Studies.

Bohnstedt, John W. 1968. "The Infidel Scourge of God: The Turkish Menace as Seen by German Pamphleteers of the Reformation Era." *Transactions of the American Philosophical Society*, n.s., 58, no. 9:1–58.

Bonner, Michael. 2006. *Jihad in Islamic History*. Princeton, N.J.: Princeton University Press.

Bouchier, E. S. 1921. *A Short History of Antioch*. Oxford: Blackwell.

Boyer, Carl B., and Uta C. Berzbach. 1989. *A History of Mathematics*. 2d ed. New York: Wiley.

Brantlinger, Patrick. 1988. *Rule of Darkness: British Literature and Imperialism, 1830–1914*. Ithaca, N.Y.: Cornell University Press.

Buckler, F. W. 1972. "The Political Theory of the Indian Mutiny of 1857." *Transactions of the Royal Historical Society* 4, no. 5:277–290.

Bulliet, Richard W. 1979. *Conversion to Islam in the Medieval Period: An Essay in Qualitative History*. Cambridge, Mass.: Harvard University Press.

——. 1994. *Islam: The View from the Edge*. New York: Columbia University Press.

——. 2004. *The Case for Islamo-Christian Civilization*. New York: Columbia University Press.

Bullock, Katherine. 2002. *Rethinking Muslim Women and the Veil: Challenging Historical and Modern Stereotypes*. Herndon, Va.: International Institute of Islamic Thought.

Bullough, Vern L. 1996. "Medieval Scholasticism and Averroism: The Implication of the Writings of Ibn Rushd to Western Science." In Mourad Wahba and Mona Abousenna, eds., *Averroës and the Enlightenment*, 41–51. Amherst, N.Y.: Prometheus Books.

Bulmer-Thomas, Ivor. 1979. "Euclid and Medieval Architecture." *Archaeological Journal* 136:136–150.

Bumiller, Elisabeth. 2001a. "Afghan Women Trade Shadows for Washington's Limelight." *New York Times*, November 30.

——. 2001b. "First Lady to Speak About Afghan Women." *New York Times*, November 16.

——. 2005. "Bush Picks Adviser to Repair Tarnished U.S. Image Abroad." *New York Times*, March 12.

Burman, Thomas E. 2007. *Reading the Qur'an in Latin Christendom*. Philadelphia: University of Pennsylvania Press.

Burnham, Gilbert, Riyadh Lafta, Shannon Doocy, and Les Roberts. 2006. "Mortality After the 2003 Invasion of Iraq: A Cross-Sectional Cluster Sample Survey." *Lancet* 368:1421–1428.

Burnett, Charles. 1977. "A Group of Arabic–Latin Translators Working in Spain in the Mid–Twelfth Century." *Journal of the Royal Asiatic Society* 1:62–108.

——, ed. 1987. *Adelard of Bath: An English Scientist and Arabist of the Early Twelfth Century*. London: Warburg Institute.

——. 1990. "Adelard of Bath and the Arabs." In Jaqueline Hamesse and Marta Fattori, eds., *Recontres de cultures dans la philosophie médiévale*, 89–107. Louvain-la-Neuve, Belgium: Université catholique de Louvain, Institut d'études médiévales.

——. 1994. "The Translating Activity in Medieval Spain." In Salma Khadra Jayyusi, ed., *The Legacy of Muslim Spain*, 2:1036–1058. Leiden: Brill.

——. 1995a. "Adelard of Bath's Doctrine on Universals and the *Consolatio Philosophiae* of Boethius." *Didascalia* 1:1–13.

——. 1995b. "Magister Iohannes Hispalensis et Limiensis and Qusta ibn Luqa's '*De differentia spiritus et animae*': A Portuguese Contribution to the Arts Curriculum." *Mediaevalia, Textos e estudos* 7–8:221–267.

——. 1996a. *Algorismi vel helcep decentior est diligentia*: The Arithmetic of Adelard of Bath and His Circle." In Menso Folkerts, ed., *Mathematische Probleme im Mittelalter*, 221–331. Wiesbaden: Harrassowitz.

——. 1996b. *Magic and Divination in the Middle Ages: Texts and Techniques in the Islamic and Christian Worlds*. Brookfield, Vt.: Variorum.

——. 1997. *The Introduction of Arabic Learning into England*. London: British Library.

——. 2000. "Antioch as a Link Between Arabic and Latin Culture in the Twelfth and Thirteenth Centuries." In Isabelle Draelants, Anne Tihon, and Baudouin van den Abeel, eds., *Occident et Proche-Orient: Contacts scientifiques au temps des Croisades: Actes du colloque de Louvain-la-Neuve, 24 et 25 mars 1997*, 1–78. Louvain-la-Neuve, Belgium: Brepols.

Busard, Hubert L. L. 1983. *The First Latin Translation of Euclid's "Elements" Commonly Ascribed to Adelard of Bath*. Toronto: Pontifical Institute of Medieval Studies.

Busard, Hubert L. L., and Menso Folkerts. 1992. *Robert of Chester's (?) Redaction of Euclid's Elements, the So-Called Adelard II Version*. 2 vols. Basel: Birkhauser.

Bush, George W. 2001a. Address to a Joint Session of Congress and the American People. September 20. Available at http://georgewbush-whitehouse.archives. gov/news/releases/2001/09/20010920-8.html.

——. 2001b. "Remarks by the President Upon Arrival." September 16. Available at http://www.whitehouse.archives.gov/news/releases/2001/09/20010916-2 .html.

——. 2002a. "National Sanctity of Human Life Day." January 18. Available at http:// georgewbush-whitehouse.archives.gov/news/releases/2002/0120020118-10 .html.

——. 2002b. "President Rallies the Troops in Alaska." February 16. http://www. whitehouse.archives.gov/news/releases/2002/02/20020216–1.html.

——. 2002c. State of the Union Address. January 29. Available at http://georgewbush-whitehouse.archives.gov/news/releases/2002/01/20020129-11.html.

——. 2004. "Rights and Aspirations of the People of Afghanistan." July 8. Available at http://georgewbush-whitehouse.archives.gov/infocus/afghanistan/ 20040708.html.

——. 2005. "Remarks at the United Nations, 12 September 2002." In John W. Dietrich, ed., *The George W. Bush Foreign Policy Reader*, 85–89. Armonk, N.Y.: M. E. Sharpe.

——. 2006. President's Address to the Nation. September 11. Available at http:// georgewbush-whitehouse.archives.gov/news/releases/2006/09/20060911-3 .html.

Bush, Laura. 2001. Radio address. November 17. Available at http://georgewbush-whitehouse.archives.gov/news/releases/2001/11/20011117.html.

Butterworth, Charles E., and Blake Andree Kessel, eds. 1994. *The Introduction of Arabic Philosophy into Europe*. Leiden: Brill.

Cahn, Walter B. 2002. "The 'Portrait' of Muhammad in the Toledan Collection." In Elizabeth Sears and Thelma K. Thomas, eds., *Reading Medieval Images: The Art Historian and the Object*, 50–61. Ann Arbor: University of Michigan Press.

Callus, D. A. 1943. "Introduction of Aristotelian Learning to Oxford." *Proceedings of the British Academy* 29:229–281.

Cantor, Norman F. 1991. *Inventing the Middle Ages: The Lives, Works, and Ideas of the Great Medievalists of the Twentieth Century*. New York: Quill William Morrow.

Carmody, F. J. 1960. *The Astronomical Works of Thabit b. Qurra*. Berkeley: University of California Press.

Carra de Vaux, Bernard. 1931. "Astronomy and Mathematics." In Thomas Arnold and Alfred Guillaume, eds., *The Legacy of Islam*, 376–397. Oxford: Clarendon Press.

Cavanaugh, William T. 1995. "A Fire Strong Enough to Consume the House: The Wars of Religion and the Rise of the State." *Modern Theology* 11, no. 4:397–420.

Chakravarty, Gautam. 2005. *The Indian Mutiny and the British Imagination*. Cambridge: Cambridge University Press.

La Chanson d'Antioche. 1998. In Edward Peters, ed., *The First Crusade: The Chronicle of Fulcher of Chartres and Other Source Materials*, 302–306. Philadelphia: University of Pennsylvania Press.

Cheney, Dick. 2003. Interview with Vice President Dick Cheney. *Meet the Press*, NBC, March 16. Available at http://www.mtholyoke.edu/acad/intrel/bush/cheneymeetthepress.htm.

Chick, Noah Alfred. 1974. *Annals of the Indian Rebellion*. London: Knight.

Christie, Niall, and Deborah Gerish. 2003. "Parallel Preachings: Urban II and al-Sulami." *Al-Masaq* 15, no. 2:139–148.

Cifoletti, Giovanna. 1992. "Mathematics and Rhetoric: Peletier and Gosselin and the Making of the French Algebraic Tradition." Ph.D. diss., Princeton University.

——. 1996. "The Creation of the History of Algebra in the Sixteenth Century." In Catherine Goldstein, Jeremy Gray, and Jim Ritter, eds., *L'Europe mathématique: Histoires, mythes, identités*, 123–142. Paris: Fondations de la maison des sciences de l'homme.

Cimino, Richard. 2005. "No God in Common: American Evangelical Discourse on Islam After 9/11." *Review of Religious Research* 47, no. 2:162–174.

Clagett, Marshall. 1953. "The Medieval Latin Translations from the Arabic of the *Elements* of Euclid with Special Emphasis on the Versions of Adelard of Bath." *Isis* 44:16–42.

Clark, Harry. 1984. "The Publication of the Koran in Latin: A Reformation Dilemma." *Sixteenth Century Journal* 15, no. 1:3–12.

Cloud, Dana. 2004. "To Unveil the Threat of Terror: Afghan Women and the 'Clash of Civilizations' in the Imagery of the U.S. War on Terrorism." *Quarterly Journal of Speech* 90, no. 3:285–306.

Cochrane, Louise. 1994. *Adelard of Bath: The First English Scientist.* London: British Museum Press.

Cohen, Jeremy. 1999. *Living Letters of the Law: Ideas of the Jew in Medieval Europe.* Berkeley: University of California Press.

Cole, David. 2003. *Enemy Aliens: Double Standards and Constitutional Freedoms in the War on Terrorism.* New York: New Press.

Cole, Juan Ricardo. 1981. "Feminism, Class, and Islam in Turn-of-the-Century Egypt." *International Journal of Middle East Studies* 13, no. 4:387–407.

Coles, Paul. 1968. *The Ottoman Impact on Europe.* New York: Harcourt, Brace & World.

Colish, Marcia L. [1975] 2006. "Avicenna's Theory of Efficient Causation and Its Influence on Thomas Aquinas." In *Studies in Scholasticism*, pt. XVI, 1–13. Burlington, Vt.: Ashgate.

Collier, Jane. 1995. "Intertwined Histories: Islamic Law and Western Imperialism." *Law and Society Review* 28, no. 2:395–408.

Collins, Roger. 1989. *The Arab Conquest of Spain, 710–797.* Oxford: Blackwell.

Comnena, Anna. 1928. *The Alexiad of the Princess Anna Comnena.* Translated and edited by Elizabeth A. S. Dawes. London: Kegan Paul, Trench, Trübner.

Cook, David. 2002. "An Early Muslim Daniel Apocalypse." *Arabica* 49, no. 1:55–96.

Cooperson, Michael. 2000. *Classical Arabic Biography: The Heirs to the Prophets in the Age of al-Mamun.* Cambridge: Cambridge University Press.

Copenhaver, Brian P. 1978. "The Historiography of Discovery in the Renaissance: The Sources and Composition of Polydore Vergil's *De inventoribus rerum*, I–III." *Journal of the Warburg and Courtauld Institutes* 41:192–214.

Cosmas Indicopleustes. 1887. *The Christian Topography.* Translated and edited by J. W. McCrindle. London: Haklyut Society.

Council on American-Islamic Relations. 2008. *The Status of Muslim Civil Rights in the United States.* Washington, D.C.: Council on American-Islamic Relations.

Cowling, T. G. 1977. *Isaac Newton and Astrology.* Leeds: Leeds University Press.

Crisciani, Chiara. 1990. "History, Novelty, and Progress in Scholastic Medicine." *Osiris,* 2d ser., 6:118–139.

Crombie, A. C. 1971. *Robert Grosseteste and the Origins of Experimental Science, 1100–1700.* Oxford: Clarendon Press.

——. 1979. *Augustine to Galileo.* 2 vols. Cambridge, Mass.: Harvard University Press.

——. 1990. *Science, Optics, and Music in Medieval and Early Modern Thought.* London: Hambledon Press.

Crossley, John N., and Alan S. Henry. 1990. "Thus Spake al-Khwarizmi: A Translation of the Text of Cambridge University Library Ms. Ii.vi.5." *Historia Mathematica* 17:103–131.

Crowe, Michael J. 1990. *Theories of the World from Antiquity to the Copernican Revolution.* New York: Dover.

Curry, Patrick, ed. 1987. *Astrology, Science, and Society: Historical Essays.* Woodbridge, Eng.: Boydell Press.

Curtis, Edmund. 1912. *Roger of Sicily and the Normans in Lower Italy, 1016–1154.* New York: Putnam.

Dabashi, Hamid. 2009. *Post-Orientalism: Knowledge and Power in Time of Terror.* New Brunswick, N.J.: Transaction Books.

Dales, Richard C. 1984. "The Origin of the Doctrine of the Double Truth." *Viator* 15:169–179.

——. 1990. *Medieval Discussions of the Eternity of the World.* Leiden: Brill.

Dallal, Ahmad S., ed. and trans. 1995. *An Islamic Response to Greek Astronomy.* Leiden: Brill.

Dalrymple, William. 2006. *The Last Mughal: The Fall of a Dynasty.* New York: Knopf.

D'Alverny, Marie-Therese. 1947–1948. "Deux traductions latines au Coran au moyen âge." *Archives d'Histoire Doctrinale et Littéraire du Moyen Âge* 16:69–131.

——. 1982. "Translations and Translators." In Robert L. Benson and Giles Constable, eds., *Renaissance and Renewal in the Twelfth Century,* 421–462. Cambridge, Mass.: Harvard University Press.

D'Amico, John F. 1983. *Renaissance in Papal Rome: Humanists and Churchmen on the Eve of the Reformation.* Baltimore: Johns Hopkins University Press.

Daniel, Norman. 1960. *Islam and the West: The Making of an Image.* Edinburgh: Edinburgh University Press.

——. 1966. *Islam, Europe, and Empire.* Edinburgh: Edinburgh University Press.

——. 1975. *The Arabs and Medieval Europe.* London: Longman.

——. 1984. *Heroes and Saracens: A New Look at the Chansons de Geste*. Edinburgh: Edinburgh University Press.

——. 1989. "Crusade Propaganda." In Harry W. Hazard and Norman P. Zacour, eds., *A History of the Crusades*, 6:39–97. Madison: University of Wisconsin Press.

David, Saul. 2003. *The Indian Mutiny*. London: Penguin.

Davidson, Arnold I. 1986. "Archaeology, Genealogy, and Ethics." In David Couzens Hoy, ed., *Foucault: A Critical Reader*, 221–233. Oxford: Blackwell.

Davidson, Herbert A. 1992. *Alfarabi, Avicenna, and Ibn Rushd on Intellect: Their Cosmologies, Theories of the Active Intellect, and Theories of Human Intellect*. New York: Oxford University Press.

D'Avray, D. L. 1985. *The Preaching of the Friars: Sermons Diffused from Paris Before 1300*. Oxford: Clarendon Press.

De Groot, Joanna. 2000. "'Sex' and 'Race': The Construction of Language and Image in the Nineteenth Century." In Catherine Hall, ed., *Cultures of Empire: Colonizers in Britain and the Empire in the Nineteenth and Twentieth Centuries*, 37–60. New York: Routledge.

Dekker, Elly. 1995. "An Unrecorded Medieval Astrolabe Quadrant from c. 1300." *Annals of Science* 52:1–47.

Der Derian, James. 2000. "The War of Networks." *Theory & Event* 5, no. 4. Available at http://muse.jhu.edu/login?uri=/journals/theory_and_event/v005/5.4derderian.html.

——. 2002. "*In terrorem*: Before and After 9/11." In Ken Booth and Tim Dunne, eds., *Worlds in Collision: Terror and the Future of Global Order*, 101–117. New York: Palgrave Macmillan.

Dickey, Bruce. 1982. "Adelard of Bath: An Examination Based on Heretofore Unexamined Manuscripts." Ph.D. diss., University of Toronto.

Dodd, Todd. 1998. *The Life and Thought of Siger of Brabant, Twelfth-Century Parisian Philosopher*. Lewiston, N.Y.: Mellen.

Dohrn-van Rossum, Gerhard. 1996. *History of the Hour: Clocks and Modern Temporal Orders*. Translated by Thomas Dunlap. Chicago: University of Chicago Press.

Dolnikowski, Edith Wilks. 1995. *Thomas Bradwardine: A View of Time and a Vision of Eternity in 14th-Century Thought*. Leiden: Brill.

Donini, Pier Giovanni. 1991. *Arab Travelers and Geographers*. London: Immel.

Dreyfus, Hubert L., and Paul Rabinow. 1983. *Michel Foucault: Beyond Structuralism and Hermeneutics*. 2d ed. Chicago: University of Chicago Press.

——. 1986. "What Is Maturity? Habermas and Foucault on 'What Is Enlightenment?'" In David Couzens Hoy, ed., *Foucault: A Critical Reader*, 109–121. Oxford: Blackwell.

Dronke, Peter, ed. 1988. *A History of Twelfth-Century Western Philosophy*. Cambridge: Cambridge University Press.

Du Ryer, André. 1649. *L'Alcoran de Mahomet*. Paris: Chez Antoine de Sommaville.

Dunn, Kevin M., James Forrest, Ian Burnley, and Amy McDonald. 1994. "Constructing Racism in Australia." *Australian Journal of Social Issues* 39, no. 4:409–430.

Durand, Dana Bennett. 1952. *The Vienna-Klosterneuberg Map Corpus of the Fifteenth Century: A Study in the Transition from Medieval to Modern Science*. Leiden: Brill.

Durkheim, Emile. 1915. *The Elementary Forms of the Religious Life*. Translated by Joseph W. Swain. New York: Macmillan.

El Guindi, Fadwa. 1999. *Veil: Modesty, Privacy, and Resistance*. New York: Berg.

Emerton, Ephraim. 1990. "Introduction." In Gregory VII, *The Correspondence of Pope Gregory VII: Selected Letters from the Registrum*, translated by Ephraim Emerton, ix–xxxi. New York: Columbia University Press.

Engels, Frederick. 1941. *Ludwig Feuerbach and the Outcome of Classical German Philosophy*. New York: International.

Eribon, Didier. 1991. *Michel Foucault*. Translated by Betsy Wing. Cambridge, Mass.: Harvard University Press.

Esposito, John L. 1999. *The Islamic Threat: Myth or Reality?* 3rd ed. New York: Oxford University Press.

Evans, Gillian R. 1979. "Schools and Scholars: The Study of the Abacus in English Schools, ca. 980–ca. 1150." *English Historical Review* 94:71–89.

Evans, James. 1998. *The History and Practice of Ancient Astronomy*. New York: Oxford University Press.

Fahmy, Khaled. 1998. "Women, Medicine, and Power." In Lila Abu-Lughod, ed., *Remaking Women: Feminism and Modernity in the Middle East*, 35–72. Princeton, N.J.: Princeton University Press.

Fairclough, Norman. 1989. *Language and Power*. New York: Longman.

——. 1992. *Discourse and Social Change*. Cambridge: Polity Press.

——. 2003. *Analysing Discourse: Textual Analysis for Social Research*. London: Routledge.

Fairclough, Norman. and Ruth Wodak. 1998. "Critical Discourse Analysis." In Teun van Dijk, ed., *Discourse as Social Interaction*, 258–284. London: Sage.

Fakhry, Majid. 1994. *Philosophy, Dogma, and the Impact of Greek Thought in Islam*. Aldershot, Eng.: Variorum.

——. 1997. *Averroes, Aquinas, and the Rediscovery of Aristotle in Western Europe*. Washington, D.C.: Center for Muslim-Christian Understanding, Georgetown University.

——. 2001. *Averroes (Ibn Rushd): His Life, Works, and Influence*. Oxford: Oneworld.

——. 2004. *A History of Islamic Philosophy*. New York: Columbia University.

"Falwell Brands Muhammad a 'Terrorist.'" 2002. *60 Minutes*, October 6. Available at http:www.cbsnews.com/stories/2003/06/05/60minutes/main557187 .shtml?source=search_story.

Fenn, Richard K. 2006. *Dreams of Glory: The Sources of Apocalyptic Terror*. Aldershot, Eng.: Ashgate.

Ferguson, James. 1990. *The Anti-Politics Machine: "Development," Depoliticization, and Bureaucratic Power in Lesotho*. Cambridge: Cambridge University Press.

Fernea, Elizabeth. 1981. "An Early Ethnographer of Middle Eastern Women: Lady Mary Wortley Montagu (1689–1762)." *Journal of Near Eastern Studies* 40, no. 4:329–338.

Ferruolo, Stephen C. 1985. *The Origins of the University: The Schools of Paris and Their Critics, 1100–1215*. Stanford, Calif.: Stanford University Press.

Firestone, Reuven. 1999. *Jihad: The Origin of Holy War in Islam*. New York: Oxford University Press.

Flaubert, Gutave. 1996. *Flaubert in Egypt*. Translated and edited by Francis Steegmuller. New York: Penguin.

Fleischer, Ari. 2001. Press briefing. September 18. Available at http://www.whitehouse.gov/news/releases/2001/09/20010918-5.html.

Fletcher, Richard. 1992. *Moorish Spain*. New York: Holt.

Flynn, Thomas. 2005. "Foucault's Mapping of History." In Gary Gutting, ed., *The Cambridge Companion to Foucault*, 29–48. 2nd. ed. Cambridge: Cambridge University Press.

Forell, George W. 1945. "Luther and the War Against the Turks." *Church History* 14, no. 4:256–271.

Foucault, Michel. 1961. *Folie et déraison: Histoire de la folie à l'âge classique*. Paris: Libraries Plon.

——. 1972a. *The Archaeology of Knowledge*. Translated by A. M. Sheridan Smith. New York: Pantheon.

——. 1972b. "The Discourse on Language." In *The Archaeology of Knowledge*, 215–237. New York: Pantheon.

——. 1978. *The History of Sexuality: An Introduction*. Translated by Robert Hurley. New York: Pantheon.

——. 1980. *Power/Knowledge: Selected Interviews and Other Writings, 1972–1977*. New York: Pantheon.

——. 1988. *Madness and Civilization: A History of Insanity in the Age of Reason*. Translated by Richard Howard. New York: Vintage.

——. 1991. *Discipline and Punish: The Birth of the Prison*. Translated by Alan Sheridan. New York: Vintage.

——. 1994a. *The Birth of the Clinic: An Archaeology of Medical Perception*. Translated A. M. Sheridan-Smith. New York: Vintage.

——. 1994b. *The Order of Things: An Archaeology of the Human Sciences*. New York: Vintage.

——. 1994c. "Prisons et asiles dans le mécanisme du pouvoir." In *Dits et ecrits*, 2:521–525. Paris: Gallimard.

Fowler, Roger. 1991. *Language in the News: Discourse and Ideology in the Press*. New York: Routledge.

Frassetto, Michael, ed. 2002. *The Year 1000: Religious and Social Response to the Turning of the First Millennium*. New York: Palgrave Macmillan.

French, Roger, and Andrew Cunningham. 1996. *Before Science: The Invention of the Friars' Natural Philosophy*. Aldershot, Eng.: Scolar Press.

Friedman, Thomas L. 2002. *Longitudes and Attitudes: Exploring the World After September 11*. New York: Farrar, Straus and Giroux.

Fukuyama, Francis. 1992. *The End of History and the Last Man*. New York: Free Press.

Fulbert of Chartres. 1976. *The Letters and Poems of Fulbert of Chartres*. Translated by Frederick Behrends. Oxford: Clarendon Press.

Fulcher of Chartres. 1941. *Fulcher of Chartres: Chronicle of the First Crusade*. Translated by Evelyn McGinty. Philadelphia: University of Pennsylvania Press.

——. 1970. *A History of the Expedition to Jerusalem, 1095–1127*. Translated by Frances Rita Ryan. Knoxville: University of Tennessee Press.

Gabrieli, Francesco. 1969. *Arab Historians of the Crusades*. Translated by E. J. Costello. London: Routledge and Kegan Paul.

Gerbert d'Aurillac. 1959. *The Letters of Gerbert, with His Papal Privileges as Sylvester II*. Translated by Harriet Pratt Lattin. New York: Columbia University Press.

Gergez, Fawaz. 1999. *America and Political Islam: Clash of Cultures or Clash of Interests?* Cambridge: Cambridge University Press.

Gersh, Stephen. 1982. "Platonism—Neoplatonism—Aristotelianism: A Twelfth-Century Metaphysical System and Its Sources." In Robert L. Benson and Giles Constable, eds., *Renaissance and Renewal in the Twelfth Century*, 512–534. Cambridge, Mass.: Harvard University Press.

Gerth, H. H., and C. Wright Mills. 1958. "Introduction: The Man and His Work." In Max Weber, *From Max Weber: Essays in Sociology*, translated and edited by H. H. Gerth and C. Wright Mills, 3–74. New York: Oxford University Press.

Gesta francorum. 1962. Translated and edited by Rosalind Hill. Oxford: Oxford University Press.

Gesta francorum et aliorum Hierosolymytanorum. 1945. Translated by Somerset de Chair. London: Golden Cockerel Press.

Al-Ghazali, Abu Hamid. 1997. *Incoherence of the Philosophers*. Translated and edited by Michael E. Marmura. Provo, Utah: Brigham Young University Press.

Gibbon, Edward. 1910. *The Decline and Fall of the Roman Empire*. London: Dent.

Gilson, Etienne. 1938. *Reason and Revelation in the Middle Ages*. New York: Scribner.

Gimpel, Jean. 1983. *The Cathedral Builders*. Translated by Teresa Waugh. New York: Grove Press.

Gingerich, Owen. 1986. "Islamic Astronomy." *Scientific American*, April, 74–84.

Girard, René. 1977. *Culture and Violence*. Translated by Patrick Gregory. Baltimore: Johns Hopkins University Press.

——. 1996. *The Girard Reader*. New York: Crossroad Herder.

Goldman, Harvey. 1994. "From Social Theory to Sociology of Knowledge and Back: Karl Mannheim and the Sociology of Intellectual Knowledge Production." *Sociological Theory* 12, no. 3:266–278.

Goldstein, Bernard R. 1986. "The Making of Astronomy in Early Islam." *Nuncius: Annali di Storia della Scienza* 1:79–92.

Goldstein, Bernard R., and David Pingree. 1978. "The Astronomical Tables of al-Khwarizmi in a 19th-Century Egyptian Text." *Journal of the American Oriental Society* 98, no. 1:96–99.

Goldziher, Ignaz. 1981. "The Attitude of Orthodox Islam Toward the 'Ancient Sciences.'" In Merlin L. Swartz, ed. and trans., *Studies on Islam*, 185–215. New York: Oxford University Press.

Gombrich, E. H. 1995. *The Story of Art*. Englewood Cliffs, N.J.: Prentice Hall.

Goodman, L. E. 1993. "Time in Islam." In Anindita Niyogi Balslev and I. N. Mohanty, eds., *Religion and Time*, 138–162. Leiden: Brill.

Goss, Vladimir P., ed. 1986. *The Meeting of Two Worlds: Cultural Exchange Between East and West During the Period of the Crusades*. Kalamazoo: Medieval Institute Publications, Western Michigan University.

Grafton, Anthony. 1981. "Teacher, Text, and Pupil in the Renaissance Classroom." *History of Universities* 1:37–70.

Graham-Brown, Sarah. 1988. *Images of Women: The Portrayal of Women in Photography of the Middle East, 1860–1950*. New York: Columbia University Press.

Gran, Judith. 1977. "Impact of the World Market on Egyptian Women." *MERIP Reports* 58:3–7.

Grant, Edward. 1974. *A Source Book in Medieval Science*. Cambridge, Mass.: Harvard University Press.

——. 1996. *The Foundations of Modern Science in the Middle Ages.* Cambridge: Cambridge University Press.

Grant, James Hope. 1873. *Incidents in the Sepoy War, 1857–1858.* Edinburgh: Blackwood.

Greeley, A. M. 1989. *Religious Change in America.* Cambridge, Mass.: Harvard University Press.

——. 1995. "The Persistence of Religion." *Cross Currents* 45:24–41.

Gregory VII. 1990. *The Correspondence of Pope Gregory VII: Selected Letters from the Registrum.* Translated and edited by Ephraim Emerton. New York: Columbia University Press.

——. 2002. *The Register of Pope Gregory VII: An English Translation.* Translated by H. E. J. Cowdrey. Oxford: Oxford University Press.

Grendler, Paul F. 2002. *The Universities of the Italian Renaissance.* Baltimore: Johns Hopkins University Press.

Gunny, Ahmad. 1978. "Montesquieu's View of Islam in the *Lettres persane.*" In Haydn Mason, ed., *Studies on Voltaire and the Eighteenth Century,* 174:151–166. Oxford: Voltaire Foundation.

Gutas, Dimitri. 1988. *Avicenna and the Aristotelian Tradition.* Leiden: Brill.

——. 1998. *Greek Thought, Arabic Culture: The Graeco-Arabic Translation Movement in Baghdad and Early Abbasid Society.* London: Routledge.

Gutting, Gary. 2005. "Foucault and the History of Madness." In *The Cambridge Companion to Foucault,* 2d ed., 49–73. Cambridge: Cambridge University Press.

Habermas, Jürgen. 1981. "Modernity Versus Postmodernity." *New German Critique* 22:3–14.

——. 1986. "Taking Aim at the Heart of the Present." In David Couzens Hoy, ed., *Foucault: A Critical Reader,* 103–108. Oxford: Blackwell.

Hackett, Jeremiah M. 1988. "Averroes and Roger Bacon on the Harmony of Religion and Philosophy." In Ruth Link-Salinger, Jeremiah Hackett, Michael S. Hyman, R. James Long, and Charles Manekin, eds., *A Straight Path: Studies in Medieval Philosophy and Culture: Essays in Honor of Arthur Hyman,* 98–112. Washington, D.C.: Catholic University of America Press.

——. 2002. "Adelard of Bath and Roger Bacon: Early English Natural Philosophers and Scientists." *Endeavour* 26, no. 2:70–74.

Hacking, Ian. 1986. "The Archaeology of Michel Foucault." In David Couzens Hoy, ed., *Foucault: A Critical Reader,* 27–40. Oxford: Blackwell.

Hallaq, Wael B. 1990. "The Use and Abuse of Evidence: The Question of Provincial and Roman Influences on Early Islamic Law." *Journal of the American Oriental Society* 110, no. 1:79–91.

——. 2002–2003. "The Quest for Origins or Doctrine? Islamic Legal Studies as Colonialist Discourse." *UCLA Journal of Islamic and Near Eastern Law* 2, no. 1:1–31.

——. Forthcoming. "On Orientalism, Self-Consciousness, and History." *Islamic Law and Society* 3–4.

Halliday, M. A. K. 1978. *Language as Social Semiotic: The Social Interpretation of Language and Meaning.* Baltimore: University Park Press.

——. 1994. *An Introduction to Functional Grammar.* 2d ed. London: Arnold.

Hankins, James. 1995. "Renaissance Crusaders: Humanist Crusade Literature in the Age of Mehmed II." *Dumbarton Oaks Papers* 49:111–207.

Hartner, Willy. 1969. "Nasir al-Din Tusi's Lunar Theory." *Physis* 11:287–304.

——. 1973. "Copernicus, the Man, the Work, and Its History." *Proceedings of the American Philosophical Society* 117, no. 3:413–422.

——. 1975. "The Islamic Astronomical Background to Nicholas Copernicus." *Studia Copernicana* 13:7–16.

Hartung, F. E. 1970. "Problems of the Sociology of Knowledge." In James E. Curtis and John W. Petras, eds., *Sociology of Knowledge: A Reader*, 686–703. London: Duckworth.

Harvey, John H. 1972. *The Medieval Architect.* London: Wayland.

——. 1986. "Geometry and Gothic Design." *Transactions of the Ancient Monuments Society* 30:43–56.

Hashmi, Sohail H. 1996. "Interpreting the Islamic Ethics of War and Peace." In Terry Nardin, ed., *The Ethics of War and Peace: Religious and Secular Perspectives*, 146–166. Princeton, N.J.: Princeton University Press.

Haskins, Charles Homer. 1915. "The Reception of Arabic Science in England." *English Historical Review* 30:56–69.

——. 1921a. "The 'De arte venandi cum avibus' of the Emperor Frederick II." *English Historical Review* 36:334–355.

——. 1921b. "Michael Scot and Frederick II." *Isis* 4, no. 2:250–275.

——. 1922. "Some Early Treatises on Falconry." *Romanic Review* 13:18–27.

——. 1927. *Studies in the History of Medieval Science.* Cambridge, Mass.: Harvard University Press.

——. 1928. "The 'Alchemy' Ascribed to Michael Scot." *Isis* 10, no. 2:350–359.

——. 1957. *The Rise of Universities.* Ithaca, N.Y.: Cornell University Press.

Al-Hassan, Ahmad Y. 1996. "Factors Behind the Decline of Islamic Science After the Sixteenth Century." In Sharifah Shifa Al-Attas, ed., *Islam and the Challenge of Modernity: Historical and Contemporary Contexts*, 351–389. Kuala Lumpur: International Institute of Islamic Thought and Civilisation.

Hasse, Dag Nikolaus. 2000. *Avicenna's "De anima" in the Latin West: The Formation of a Peripatetic Philosophy of the Soul, 1160–1300*. London: Warburg Institute.

Hassig, Debra. 1995. *Medieval Bestiaries: Text, Image, Ideology*. Cambridge: Cambridge University Press.

Hawkins, Gerald S., and David A. King. 1982. "On the Orientation of the Kaaba." *Journal for the History of Astronomy* 13:102–109.

Hay, Cynthia, ed. 1988. *Mathematics from Manuscript to Print, 1300–1600*. Oxford: Clarendon Press.

Healy, George R. 1999. "Translator's Introduction." In Montesquieu, *The Persian Letters*, translated and edited by George R. Healy, vii–xix. Cambridge: Hackett.

Heath, Thomas L. 1921. *A History of Greek Mathematics*. 2 vols. Oxford: Clarendon Press.

Heck, Paul L. 2004. "Jihad Revisited." *Journal of Religious Ethics* 32, no. 1:95–128.

Hegel, Georg W. F. 1861. *Lectures on the Philosophy of History*. Translated by J. Sibree. London: Bohn.

Herbert, Christopher. 2008. *War of No Pity: The Indian Mutiny and Victorian Trauma*. Princeton, N.J.: Princeton University Press.

Hill, Donald R. 1998. *Studies in Medieval Islamic Technology*. Aldershot, Eng.: Ashgate.

Hillenbrand, Carole. 1999. *The Crusades: Islamic Perspectives*. Chicago: Fitzroy Dearborn.

Hillenbrand, Robert. 1994. "The Ornament of the World: Medieval Cordoba as a Cultural Center." In Salma Khadra, ed., *The Legacy of Muslim Spain*, 112–135. Leiden: Brill.

Hodgson, Marshall G. S. 1974. *The Venture of Islam*. 3 vols. Chicago: University of Chicago Press.

Holmes, Oliver Wendell. 1894. *The Autocrat of the Breakfast Table*. Boston: Houghton Mifflin.

Hook, David, and Barry Taylor, eds. 1990. *Cultures in Contact in Medieval Spain: Historical and Literary Essays Presented to L. P. Harvey*. London: King's College.

Houben, Hubert. 2002. *Roger II of Sicily: A Ruler Between East and West*. Translated by Graham A. Lound and Diane Milburn. Cambridge: Cambridge University Press.

Hourani, A. H., and S. M. Stern, eds. 1970. *The Islamic City: A Colloquium*. Oxford: Cassirer.

Hourani, George F. 1967. "Introduction." In Averroes, *Averroes: On the Harmony of Religion and Philosophy*, translated and edited by George F. Hourani, 2–42. London: Luzac.

——. 1995. *Arab Seafaring in the Indian Ocean in Ancient and Early Medieval Times.* Princeton, N.J.: Princeton University Press.

Hoy, David Couzens. 1986. "Introduction." In David Couzens Hoy, ed., *Foucault: A Critical Reader*, 1–26. Oxford: Blackwell.

Høyrup, Jens. 1988. "Jordanus de Nemore, 13th-Century Mathematical Innovator: An Essay on Intellectual Context, Achievement, and Failure." *Archive for History of the Exact Sciences* 38, no. 4:307–363.

——. 1994. *In Measure, Number, and Weight: Studies in Mathematics and Culture.* Albany: State University of New York Press.

——. 1996. "The Formation of a Myth: Greek Mathematics—Our Mathematics." In Catherine Goldstein, Jeremy Gray, and Jim Ritter, eds., *L'Europe mathématique: Histoires, mythes, identités*, 103–119. Paris: Fondations de la maison des sciences de l'homme.

Huff, Toby. [1993] 2003. *The Rise of Early Modern Science: Islam, China, and the West.* New York: Cambridge University Press.

Hughes, Karen. 2005. Discussion with students at Dar al-Hekma College. September 27. Available at http://statelists.state.gov/scripts/wa.exe?A2=ind0510b& L=dossdo&P=515.

Huillard-Breholles, J. L. A. 1852–1861. *Historia diplomatica.* 7 vols. Paris: Plon Fratrres.

Huntington, Samuel P. 1993. "The Clash of Civilizations?" *Foreign Affairs* 72, no. 3:22–49.

——. 1996. *The Clash of Civilizations and the Remaking of the New World Order.* New York: Simon and Schuster.

Ibn Khaldun. 1967. *The Muqaddimah: An Introduction to History.* Translated and edited by Franz Rosenthal. Princeton, N.J.: Princeton University Press.

Ibn Munqidh, Usama. 2008. *The Book of Contemplation: Islam and the Crusades.* Translated by Paul M. Cobb. New York: Penguin.

Ibn al-Muthanna. 1967. *Ibn al-Muthanna's Commentary on the Astronomical Tables of al-Khwarizmi.* Translated and edited by Bernard R. Goldstein. New Haven, Conn.: Yale University Press.

Ibn al-Nadim. 1970. *The Fihrist of al-Nadim.* 2 vols. Translated and edited by Bayard Dodge. New York: Columbia University Press.

Ibn al-Qalanisi. 2002. *Damascus Chronicle of the Crusades.* Translated and edited by H. A. R. Gibb. Mineola, N.Y.: Dover.

Ifrah, Georges. 2000. *The Universal History of Numbers: From Prehistory to the Invention of the Computer.* Translated by David Bellos, Sophie Wood, and Ian Monk. New York: Wiley.

Iqbal, Muzaffar. 2002. *Islam and Science*. Burlington, Vt.: Ashgate.

Iraq Family Health Survey Study Group. 2008. "Violence Related Mortality in Iraq from 2002 to 2006." *New England Journal of Medicine* 358, no. 5:484–493.

Irwin, Jones. 2002. "Averroes' Reason: A Medieval Tale of Christianity and Islam." *The Philosopher* 90, no. 2. Available at http://www.the-philosopher.co.uk/averroes.htm.

Irwin, Robert. 2006. *Dangerous Knowledge: Orientalism and Its Discontents*. Woodstock, N.Y.: Overlook Press.

Isidore of Seville. 2006. *The Etymologies*. Translated and edited by Stephen A. Barney, W. J. Lewis, J. A. Beach, and Oliver Berghof. Cambridge: Cambridge University Press.

Issawi, Charles. 1982. *An Economic History of the Middle East and North Africa*. New York: Columbia University Press.

Al-Jabarti, Abd al-Rahman. 1993. *Al-Jabarti's Napoleon in Egypt*. Translated by Shmuel Moreh. Princeton, N.J.: Wiener.

Jackson, Richard. 2005. *Writing the War on Terrorism: Language, Politics, and Counter-Terrorism*. Manchester: Manchester University Press.

Jayyusi, Salma Khadra, ed. 1994. *The Legacy of Muslim Spain*. New York: Brill.

John of Damascus. 1972. *John of Damascus on Islam: The "Heresy of the Ismaelites."* Translated by Daniel J. Sahas. Leiden: Brill.

Johnson, Lawrence J. 1978. "The Linguistic Imperialism of Lorenzo Valla and the Renaissance Humanists." *Interpretation* 7, no. 3:29–49.

Kaegi, Walter Emil, Jr. 1969. "Initial Byzantine Reactions to the Arab Conquest." *Church History* 38:139–149.

Kaiser, Thomas. 2000. "The Evil Empire? The Debate on Turkish Despotism in Eighteenth-Century French Political Culture." *Journal of Modern History* 72, no. 1:6–34

Kamali, Mohammad Hashim. 1994. *Freedom of Expression in Islam*. Kuala Lumpur: Berita.

Kantorowicz, Ernst. 1931. *Frederick the Second: 1194-1250*. Translated by E. O. Lorimer. London: Constable.

Karl, Jonathan. 2005. "Karen of Arabia." *Weekly Standard*, October 10.

Kaul, Chandrika. 2003. *Reporting the Raj: The British Press and India, c. 1880-1922*. Manchester: Manchester University Press.

Kaye, John William. 1864–1880. *A History of the Sepoy War in India, 1857-1858*. 3 vols. London: Allen.

Kaye, John William, and G. B. Malleson. 1897–1898. *Kaye's and Malleson's History of the Indian Mutiny of 1857–1858.* 6 vols. London: Longmans, Green.

Kedar, Benjamin. 1984. *Crusade and Mission: European Approaches Toward the Muslims.* Princeton, N.J.: Princeton University Press.

Keddie, Nikki R., ed. 1972. *Scholars, Saints, and Sufis: Muslim Religious Institutions in the Middle East Since 1500.* Berkeley: University of California Press.

Kennedy, E. S., and Victor Roberts. 1959. "The Planetary Theory of Ibn al-Shatir." *Isis* 50, no. 3:227–235.

Kennedy, Hugh. 1996. *Muslim Spain and Portugal: A Political History of al-Andalus.* New York: Addison Wesley Longman.

——. 2004. *When Baghdad Ruled the Muslim World: The Rise and Fall of Islam's Greatest Dynasty.* New York: De Capo Press.

Keohane, Robert. 2003. *Power and Governance in a Partially Globalized World.* London: Routledge.

Khair, Tabish, Justin D. Edwards, Martin Leer, and Hanna Ziadeh, eds. 2005. *Other Routes: 1500 Years of African and Asian Travel Writing.* Bloomington: Indiana University Press.

Khatab, Sayed, and Gary D. Bouma. 2007. *Democracy in Islam.* New York: Routledge.

Al-Khwarizmi, Muhammad ibn Musa. 1986. *The Algebra of Mohammed ben Musa.* Translated and edited by Frederic Rosen. Hildesheim: Olms.

Kieckhefer, Richard. 1990. *Magic in the Middle Ages.* Cambridge: Cambridge University Press.

Kimble, George H. T. 1938. *Geography in the Middle Ages.* London: Methuen.

Kimerling, Jon. 2002. "Cartographic Methods for Determining the Qibla." *Journal of Geography* 101:20–26.

King, Charles. 1994. "Leonardo Fibonacci." In Frank J. Swetz, ed., *From Five Fingers to Infinity: A Journey Through the History of Mathematics,* 252–254. Chicago: Open Court.

King, David A. 1982. "The Sacred Direction in Islam: A Study of the Interaction of Religion and Science in the Middle Ages." *Journal for the History of Astronomy* 13:102–109.

——. 1983. *Al-Khwarizmi and New Trends in Mathematical Astronomy in the Ninth Century.* Occasional Papers on the Near East, no. 2. New York: Hagop Kevorkian Center for Near Eastern Studies, New York University.

——. 1987. *Islamic Astronomical Instruments.* London: Variorum.

——. 1993. *Astronomy in the Service of Islam.* Brookfield, Vt.: Variorum.

——. 2000. "Too Many Cooks . . . A Newly Rediscovered Account of the First Islamic Geodetic Measurements." *Suhayl: Journal for the History of the Exact and Natural Sciences in Islamic Civilisation* 1:207–241.

——. 2004. *In Synchrony with the Heavens: Studies in Astronomical Timekeeping and Instrumentation in Medieval Islamic Civilization.* Leiden: Brill.

King, David A., and Richard P. Lorch. 1987. "Qibla Charts, Qibla Maps, and Related Instruments." In J. B. Harley and David Woodward, eds., *The History of Cartography*, 2:189–205. Chicago: University of Chicago Press.

King, David A., and George Saliba, eds. 1987. *From Deferent to Equant.* New York: New York Academy of Sciences.

King, David A., and J. Samsó. 2001. "Astronomical Handbooks and Tables from the Islamic World (750–1900): An Interim Report." *Suhayl: Journal for the History of the Exact and Natural Sciences in Islamic Civilisation* 2:9–105.

Koebner, R. 1951. "Despot and Despotism: Vicissitudes of a Political Term." *Journal of the Warburg and Courtauld Institutes* 15:275–302.

Koestler, Arthur. 1989. *The Sleepwalkers: A History of Man's Changing Vision of the Universe.* London: Arkana.

Kopf, David. 1969. *British Orientalism and the Bengal Renaissance: The Dynamics of Indian Modernization, 1773–1835.* Berkeley: University of California Press.

Kramers, J. H. 1954. *Analecta Orientalia.* 2 vols. Leiden: Brill.

——. 1990. "Geography and Commerce." In M. J. L. Young, J. D. Latham, and R. B. Sergeant, eds., *Religion, Learning, and Science in the ʿAbbasid Period*, 79–107. Cambridge: Cambridge University Press.

Krey, August C., ed. 1921. *The First Crusades: The Accounts of Eyewitnesses and Participants.* Princeton, N.J.: Princeton University Press.

Kristeller, Paul Oskar. 1961. "Changing Views of the Intellectual History of the Renaissance Since Jacob Burkhardt." In Tinsely Helton, ed., *The Renaissance: A Reconsideration of the Theories and Interpretations of the Age*, 27–52. Madison: University of Wisconsin Press.

——. 1992. *Medieval Aspects of Renaissance Learning.* Translated by Edward P. Mahoney. New York: Columbia University Press.

Kristof, Nicholas. 2004. "Those Sexy Iranians." *New York Times*, May 8.

Kritzeck, James. 1956. "Peter the Venerable and the Toledan Collection." In Giles Constable and James Kritzeck, eds., *Petrus Venerabilis: Studies and Texts Commemorating the Eighth Centenary of His Death*, 176–201. Rome: Herder.

——. 1964. *Peter the Venerable and Islam.* Princeton, N.J.: Princeton University Press.

Kuhn, Thomas S. 1957. *The Copernican Revolution: Planetary Astronomy in the Development of Western Thought*. Cambridge, Mass.: Harvard University Press.

——. 1970. "Logic of Discovery or Psychology of Research." In Imre Lakatos and Alan Musgrave, eds., *Criticism and the Growth of Knowledge*, 1–23. Cambridge: Cambridge University Press.

——. 1996. *The Structure of Scientific Revolutions*. 3rd ed. Chicago: University of Chicago Press.

Kunitzsch, Paul. 1989. *The Arabs and the Stars: Texts and Traditions on the Fixed Stars, and Their Influence in Medieval Europe*. London: Variorum.

Lamartine, Alphonse de. 1877. *Voyage en Orient*. Paris: Calmann Lèvy.

Lancaster, John. 1997. "Egypt's Unveiled Industry; Sexy Lingerie a Hit in Muslim Land." *Washington Post*, April 24.

Lane, Edward William. 2003. *An Account of the Manners and Customs of the Modern Egyptians: The Definitive 1860 Edition*. Cairo: American University in Cairo Press.

Lane-Poole, Stanley. 1903. *Islam, a Prelection Delivered Before the University of Dublin*. Dublin: Hodges, Figgis.

Lapidus, Ira M. 2002. *A History of Islamic Societies*. New York: Cambridge University Press.

Lattis, James M. 1994. *Between Copernicus and Galileo: Christoph Clavius and the Collapse of Ptolemaic Cosmology*. Chicago: University of Chicago Press.

Law, John. 2004. *After Method: Mess in Social Science Research*. New York: Routledge.

Law, John, and Annemarie Mol, eds. 2002. *Complexities: Social Studies of Knowledge Practices*. Durham, N.C.: Duke University Press.

Leaman, Oliver. 1985. *An Introduction to Medieval Islamic Philosophy*. Cambridge: Cambridge University Press.

——. 1988. *Averroes and His Philosophy*. Oxford: Clarendon Press.

——. 1999. *A Brief Introduction to Islamic Philosophy*. Cambridge: Polity Press.

Leff, Gordon. 1968. *Paris and Oxford Universities in the Thirteenth and Fourteenth Centuries: An Institutional and Intellectual History*. New York: Wiley.

Le Goff, Jacques. 1980. *Time, Work, and Culture in the Middle Ages*. Translated by Arthur Goldhammer. Chicago: University of Chicago Press.

——. 1992. *History and Memory*. Translated by Steven Rendall and Elizabeth Claman. New York: Columbia University Press.

——. 1993. *Intellectuals in the Twelfth Century*. Translated by Teresa Lavender Fagan. Cambridge, Mass.: Blackwell.

Lemay, Richard Joseph. 1958. "The 'Introductorium in astronomiam' of Albumasar and the Reception of Aristotle's Natural Philosophy in the Twelfth Century." Ph.D. diss., Columbia University.

——. 1962. *Abu Mashar and Latin Aristotelianism in the 12th Century*. Beirut: American University of Beirut.

——. 1987. "The True Place of Astrology in Medieval Science and Philosophy: Towards a Definition." In Patrick Curry, ed., *Astrological Science and Society: Historical Essays*, 57–73. Woodbridge, Eng.: Boydell Press.

Le Strange, Guy. 1983. *Baghdad During the Abbasid Caliphate*. Westport, Conn.: Greenwood Press.

Lettinck, Paul. 1994. *Aristotle's Physics and Its Reception in the Arabic World*. Leiden: Brill.

Levey, Irving Maurice. 1947. "The Middle Commentary of Averroes on Aristotle's 'Meterologica.'" Ph.D. diss., Harvard University.

Levin, Daniel Z. 2002. "Which Way Is Jerusalem? Which Way Is Mecca? The Direction-Facing Problem in Religion and Geography." *Journal of Geography* 101:27–37.

Lewis, Bernard, ed. 1976. *Islam and the Arab World*. New York: Knopf.

——. 1988. *The Political Language of Islam*. Chicago: University of Chicago Press.

——. 1990. "The Roots of Muslim Rage: Why So Many Muslims Deeply Resent the West and Why Their Bitterness Will Not Be So Easily Mollified." *Atlantic Monthly*, September, 47–58.

——. 2001a. Interview, C-SPAN, December 30. Available at http://www.booknotes.org/Transcript/?ProgramID=1657.

——. 2001b. "Jihad vs. Crusade: A Historian's Guide to the New War." *Wall Street Journal*, September 27.

——. 2002. *What Went Wrong? Western Impact and Middle Eastern Response*. New York: Oxford University Press.

——. 2003. *The Crisis of Islam*. New York: Modern Library.

Lewis, Martin W., and Kären E. Wigen. 1997. *The Myth of Continents: A Critique of Metageography*. Berkeley: University of California Press.

Lindberg, David C., ed. 1978. *Science in the Middle Ages*. Chicago: University of Chicago Press.

——. 1992. *The Beginnings of Western Science: The European Scientific Tradition in Philosophical, Religious, and Institutional Context, 660 B.C. to A.D. 1450*. Chicago: University of Chicago Press.

Lindberg, David C., and Ronald L. Numbers, eds. 1986. *God and Nature: Historical Essays on the Encounter Between Christianity and Science*. Berkeley: University of California Press.

Llewellyn-Jones, Rosie. 2007. *The Great Uprising in India, 1857-58: Untold Stories, Indian and British*. Woodbridge, Eng.: Boydell Press.

Lowe, Lisa. 1990. "Rereadings in Orientalism: Oriental Inventions and Inventions of the Orient in Montesquieu's 'Lettres persanes.'" *Cultural Critique* 15:115–143.

Lu, Peter J., and Paul K. Steinhardt. 2007. "Decagonal and Quasi-Crystalline Tilings in Medieval Islamic Architecture." *Science* 315:1106–1110.

Lyons, Jonathan. 2009a. *The House of Wisdom: How the Arabs Transformed Western Civilization*. New York: Bloomsbury Press.

——. 2009b. "Islamic Medicine." *Lapham's Quarterly* 2, no. 4:189–194.

——. 2010. "Out of the Mouths of Babes: What the 'Danish Cartoons' Can Tell Us About the Multicultural Future." In David Wright-Neville and Anna Halafoff, eds., *Terrorism and Social Exclusion: Misplaced Risk–Common Security*, 136–154. Cheltenham, Eng.: Elgar.

Maalouf, Amin. 1984. *The Crusades Through Arab Eyes*. Translated by Jon Rothschild. New York: Schoken.

Mabro, Judy. 1991. "Introduction." In Judy Mabro, ed., *Veiled Half-Truths: Western Travellers' Perceptions of Middle Eastern Women*, 1–27. London: Tauris.

MacKay, Angus. 1977. *Spain in the Middle Ages: From Frontier to Empire, 1000-1500*. London: Macmillan.

Mackensen, Ruth S. 1932. "Four Great Libraries of Medieval Baghdad." *Library Quarterly* 2, no. 3:279–299.

MacLeod, Roy. 2000. "Nature and Empire: Science and the Colonial Enterprise." *Osiris*, 2d ser., 15:1–13.

Makdisi, George. 1981a. "Hanbalite Islam." In Merlin L. Swartz, trans. and ed., *Studies on Islam*, 216–274. New York: Oxford University Press.

——. 1981b. *The Rise of Colleges: Institutions of Learning in Islam and the West*. Edinburgh: Edinburgh University Press.

——. 1989. "Scholasticism and Humanism in Classical Islam and the Christian West." *Journal of the American Oriental Society* 109, no. 2:175–182.

——. 1990. *The Rise of Humanism in Classical Islam and the Christian West*. Edinburgh: Edinburgh University Press.

Malleson, G. B. 1857. *The Mutiny of the Bengal Army*. London: Bosworth and Harrison.

Mallette, Karla. 2005. *The Kingdom of Sicily, 1100-1250: A Literary History*. Philadelphia: University of Pennsylvania Press.

Mann, Nicholas. 1970. "Petrarch's Role as Moralist in Fifteenth-Century France." In A. H. T. Levi, ed., *Humanism in France*, 6–28. Manchester: University of Manchester Press.

Mannheim, Karl. 1936. *Ideology and Utopia*. Translated by Lewis Wirth and Edward Shills. New York: Harcourt Brace Jovanovich.

Marcus, Jacob. 1990. *The Jew in the Medieval World: A Sourcebook 315-1791*. Cincinnati: Hebrew Union College Press.

Marenbon, John. 1987. *Later Medieval Philosophy (1150-1350)*. London: Routledge & Kegan Paul.

Marks, James T. W. 1992. "Theory, Pragmatism, and Truth: Post-Modernism in the Context of Action." *Canadian Journal of Sociology/Cahiers canadiens de sociologie* 17, no. 2:161–173.

Mårtensson, Ulrika. 2007. "The Power of Subject: Weber, Foucault, and Islam." *Middle East Critique* 16, no. 2:97–136.

Martin, R. Montgomery. 1861. *The Mutiny of the Bengal Army*. London: London Printing and Publishing.

al-Masudi. 1989. *The Meadows of Gold*. Translated and edited by Paul Lunde and Caroline Stone. London: Kegan Paul.

Matin-Asgari, Afshin. 2004. "Islamic Studies and the Spirit of Max Weber: A Critique of Cultural Essentialism." *Middle East Critique* 13, no. 3:293–312.

McClenan, R. B. 1994. "Leonardo of Pisa and His 'Liber quadratorium.'" In Frank J. Swetz, ed., *From Five Fingers to Infinity: A Journey Through the History of Mathematics*, 255–260. Chicago: Open Court.

McCluskey, Stephen C. 1998. *Astronomies and Cultures in Early Medieval Europe*. New York: Cambridge University Press.

McKeon, Richard. 1973. "The Organization of Sciences and the Relations of Cultures in the 12th and 13th Centuries." In J. E. Murdoch and Edith Dudley Sylla, eds., *The Cultural Context of Medieval Learning*, 151–192. Dordrecht: Reidel.

McLaughlin, Mary M. 1955. "Paris Masters of the Thirteenth and Fourteenth Centuries and Ideas of Intellectual Freedom." *Church History* 24, no. 3:195–211.

Meehan, Denis. 1958. "Introduction." In Adamnan of Iona, *Adamnan's "De locis sanctis,"* translated and edited by Denis Meehan, 1–18. Dublin: Dublin Institute for Advanced Studies.

Melman, Billie. 1992. *Women's Orients: English Women and the Middle East, 1718-1918*. Ann Arbor: University of Michigan Press.

Menocal, María Rosa. 2002. *Ornament of the World: How Muslims, Jews, and Christians Created a Culture of Tolerance in Medieval Spain.* Boston: Little, Brown.

Mernissi, Fatima. 1987. *Beyond the Veil: Male-Female Dynamics in Modern Muslim Society.* Rev. ed. Bloomington: Indiana University Press.

Merton, Robert K. 1968. *Social Theory and Social Structure.* New York: Free Press.

——. 1970. *Science, Technology, and Society in Seventeenth-Century England.* New York: Harper & Row.

——. 1973. *The Sociology of Science: Theoretical and Empirical Investigations.* Chicago: University of Chicago Press.

Metcalfe, Charles T. 1898. *Two Native Narratives of the Mutiny in Delhi.* London: Archibald Constable.

Meyendorff, John. 1964. "Byzantine Views of Islam." *Dumbarton Oaks Papers* 18:113–132.

Miller, Robert. 1954. "An Aspect of Averroes' Influence on St. Albert." *Mediaeval Studies* 16:57–71.

Mills, C. Wright. 1940a. "Methodological Consequences of the Sociology of Knowledge." *American Journal of Sociology* 46, no. 3:316–330.

——. 1940b. "Situated Actions and Vocabularies of Motives." *American Sociological Review* 5:904–913.

——. 1956. *The Power Elite.* New York: Oxford University Press.

——. 1959. *The Sociological Imagination.* New York: Oxford University Press.

Minzesheimer, Bob. 2002. "War on Terrorism Boosts Bernard Lewis and Company." *USA Today,* January 24.

Mitchell, Timothy. 1991. *Colonising Egypt.* Berkeley: University of California Press.

Montagu, Lady Mary Wortley. 1893. *The Letters and Works of Lady Mary Wortley Montagu.* London: Swan Sonnenschein.

Montesquieu. 1864. *Ésprit des lois.* Paris: Librairie de Didot Frères.

——. 1875. *Œuvres complètes de Montesquieu: Lettres persanes.* Paris: Garnier Frères.

——. 1977. *The Political Theory of Montesquieu.* Translated and edited by Melvin Richter. Cambridge: Cambridge University Press.

——. 1999. *The Persian Letters.* Translated and edited by George R. Healy. Cambridge: Hackett.

Moore, Robert I. 1987. *Formation of a Persecuting Society: Power and Deviance in Western Europe, 950–1250.* Oxford: Blackwell.

Moran, Bruce T. 2005. *Distilling Knowledge: Alchemy, Chemistry, and the Scientific Revolution.* Cambridge, Mass.: Harvard University Press.

Morewedge, Parviz, ed. 1992. *Neoplatonism and Islamic Thought*. Albany: State University of New York Press.

Mottahedeh, Roy. 1996. "The Clash of Civilizations: An Islamicist's Critique." *Harvard Middle Eastern and Islamic Review* 2:1–26.

Mottahedeh, Roy, and Ridwan al-Sayyid. 2001. "The Idea of *Jihad* in Islam Before the Crusades." In Angeliki E. Laiou and Roy Mottahedeh, eds., *The Crusades from the Perspectives of Byzantium and the Muslim World*, 23–29. Washington, D.C.: Dumbarton Oaks.

Mudimbe, V. Y. 1988. *The Invention of Africa: Gnosis, Philosophy, and the Order of Knowledge*. Bloomington: Indiana University Press.

Muir, William. 1858–1861. *The Life of Mahomet*. 4 vols. London: Smith, Elder.

——. 1883. *The Rise and Decline of Islam*. London: Religious Tract Society.

——. 1892. *The Caliphate: Its Rise, Decline, and Fall: From Original Sources*. 2d ed. London: Religious Tract Society.

——. 1896. *The Coran: Its Composition and Teaching, and the Testimony It Bears to the Holy Scriptures*. London: Society for Promoting Christian Knowledge.

——. 1902. *Records of the Intelligence Department of the Government of the North-West Provinces of India During the Mutiny of 1857*. 2 vols. Edinburgh: Clark.

Mukherjee, Rudrangshu. 2002. *Awadh in Revolt, 1857–1858: A Study of Popular Resistance*. London: Anthem.

Müller, Frederick Max. 1892. *Address Delivered to the Opening of the Ninth International Congress of Orientalists*. Oxford: Oxford University Press.

Mumford, Lewis. 1963. *Technics and Civilization*. New York: Harcourt, Brace & World.

Munro, Dana C., ed. 1895. *Translations and Reprints from the Original Sources of European History*. Philadelphia: University of Pennsylvania.

Al-Muqaddasi. 1994. *The Best Divisions for Knowledge of the Regions*. Translated by Basil Anthony Collins. Reading, Eng.: Garnet.

Nadvi, Syed Sulaiman. 1966. *The Arab Navigation*. Translated by Syed Sabahuddin Abdu Rahman. Lahore, Pakistan: Sh. Muhammad Ashraf.

Nagy-Zekmi, Silvia, ed. 2006. *Paradoxical Citizenship: Edward Said*. Lanham, Md.: Lexington Books.

al-Najdi, Ahmad bin Majid. 1971. *Arab Navigation in the Indian Ocean Before the Coming of the Portuguese*. Translated and edited by G. G. Tibbetts. London: Royal Asiatic Society of Great Britain and Ireland.

Nasr, Seyyed Hossein. 1979. "Islamic Alchemy and the Birth of Chemistry." *Journal for the History of Arabic Science* 3, no. 1:40–45.

——. 1981. *Knowledge and the Sacred*. Edinburgh : Edinburgh University Press.

——. 1983. *Science and Civilization in Islam*. Lahore, Pakistan: Suhail Academy.

Nasr, Seyyed Hossein, and Oliver Leaman, eds. 1996. *History of Islamic Philosophy*. New York: Routledge.

Needham, Joseph. 1969. *The Grand Titration: Science and Society in East and West*. Toronto: University of Toronto Press.

Netton, Ian Richard. 1990. "The Mysteries of Islam." In G. S. Rousseau and Roy Porter, eds., *Exoticism in the Enlightenment*, 23–45. Manchester: Manchester University Press.

Neugebauer, Otto. 1975. *A History of Ancient Mathematical Astronomy*. 3 vols. Berlin: Springer.

Newman, William R. 1989. "Technology and Alchemical Debate in the Late Middle Ages." *Isis* 80, no. 3:424–445.

——. 2006. *Atoms and Alchemy*. Chicago: University of Chicago Press.

Newman, William R., and Anthony Grafton, eds. 2001. *Secrets of Nature: Astrology and Alchemy in Early Modern Europe*. Cambridge, Mass.: MIT Press.

North, J. D. 1989. *Stars, Minds, and Fate: Essays in Ancient and Medieval Cosmology*. London: Hambledon Press.

Ochoa, John. 2006. "Said's Foucault, or the Places of the Critic." In Silvia Nagy-Zekmi, ed., *Paradoxical Citizenship: Edward Said*, 49–56. Lanham, Md.: Lexington Books.

O'Farrell, Clare. 1989. *Foucault: Historian or Philosopher?* London: Macmillan.

——. 2005. *Michel Foucault*. London: Sage.

O'Leary, DeLacy. 1948. *How Greek Science Passed to the Arabs*. London: Routledge & Kegan Paul.

Oliver, Kelly. 2007. *Women as Weapons of War: Iraq, Sex, and the Media*. New York: Columbia University Press.

Owen, Roger. 2002. *The Middle East in the World Economy, 1800-1914*. London: Tauris.

Parekh, Bhiku. 2006. *Rethinking Multiculturalism: Cultural Diversity and Political Theory*. New York: Palgrave.

Park, Hyungji. 2000. " 'The Story of Our Lives': The Moonstone and the Indian Mutiny in *All Year Round*." In David Finkelstein and Douglas M. Peters, eds., *Negotiating India in the Nineteenth-Century Media*, 84–109. New York: St. Martin's Press.

Parsons, Talcott. 1965. "Introduction." In Max Weber, *The Sociology of Religion*, translated by Ephraim Fischoff, xx–xxi. London: Methuen.

——. 1977. *The Evolution of Societies*. Englewood Cliffs, N.J.: Prentice Hall.

Paxton, Nancy. 1999. *Writing Under the Raj: Gender, Race, and Rape in the British Colonial Imagination, 1830–1947.* New Brunswick, N.J.: Rutgers University Press.

Pedersen, Johannes. 1984. *The Arabic Book.* Translated by Geoffrey French. Princeton, N.J.: Princeton University Press.

Pedersen, Olaf. 1997. *The First Universities: Studium Generale and the Origins of University Education in Europe.* Translated by Richard North. Cambridge: Cambridge University Press.

Peters, Francis E. 1968. *Aristotle and the Arabs.* New York: New York University Press.

Peters, Laura. 2000. " 'Double-Dyed Traitors and Infernal Villains': *Illustrated London News, Household Words,* Charles Dickens, and the Indian Rebellion." In David Finkelstein and Douglas M. Peters, eds., *Negotiating India in the Nineteenth-Century Media,* 110–134. New York: St. Martin's Press.

Peters, Rudolph. 1996. *Jihad in Classical and Modern Islam.* Princeton, N.J.: Wiener.

Petrarch, Francesco. 1924. *The Life of Solitude (De vita solitaria).* Translated and edited by Jacob Zeitlin. Urbana: University of Illinois Press, 1924.

——. 1992. *Letters of Old Age (Rerum senilium libri).* 2 vols. Translated by Aldo S. Bernard, Saul Levin, and Reta A. Bernard. Baltimore: Johns Hopkins University Press.

——. 1996. *The Canzoniere, or Rerum vulgarium fragmenta.* Translated and edited by Mark Musa. Bloomington: Indiana University Press.

Petrus Alfonsi. 2006. *Dialogue Against the Jews.* Translated and edited by Irven M. Resnick. Washington, D.C.: Catholic University of America Press.

Pew Forum on Religious and Public Life. 2004. "Religion and Politics: Contention and Consensus, Part IV." Available at http://pewforum.org/docs/?DocID=30.

——. 2007. "Public Expresses Mixed Views on Islam, Mormonism." Available at http://pewforum.org/assets/files/religionviews07.pdf.

——. 2008. "Unfavorable Views of Jews and Muslims on the Increase in Europe." Available at http://pewglobal.org/reports/display.php?ReportID=262.

——. 2009. "Views of Religious Similarities and Differences." Available at http://pewforum.org/newassets/images/reports/summer09/survey0909.pdf.

——. 2010. "Public Remains Conflicted over Islam." Available at http://pewforum.org/uploadedFiles/Topics/Religious_Affiliation/Muslim/Islam-mosque-full-report.pdf.

Phillips, Jonathan. 1996. *Defenders of the Holy Land: Relations Between the Latin East and the West, 1119–1187.* Oxford: Clarendon Press.

——, ed. 1997. *The First Crusade: Origins and Impact.* Manchester: Manchester University Press.

Pickthall, Marmaduke. 1930. *The Meaning of the Glorious Koran: An Explanatory Translation*. London: Knopf.

Pines, Shlomo. 1963. "What Was Original in Arabic Science?" In A. C. Crombie, ed., *Scientific Change*, 181–205. New York: Basic Books.

——. 1986. *Studies in Arabic Versions of Greek Texts and in Medieval Science*. Jerusalem: Magnes Press, Hebrew University.

Pope, Alexander. 1956. *The Correspondence of Alexander Pope*. Edited by George Sherburn. Oxford: Clarendon Press.

Porter, Roy. 1990. "The Exotic as Erotic: Captain Cook at Tahiti." In G. S. Rousseau and Roy Porter, eds., *Exoticism in the Enlightenment*, 117–144. Manchester: Manchester University Press.

Potter, Simon J., ed. 2004. *Newspapers and Empire in Ireland and Britain: Reporting the British Empire, c. 1857–1921*. Dublin: Four Courts Press.

Poynting, Scott, and Victoria Mason. 2006. " 'Tolerance, Freedom, Justice, and Peace'? Britain, Australia and Anti-Muslim Racism Since 11th September 2001." *Journal of Intercultural Studies* 27, no. 4:365–392.

Poynting, Scott, and Greg Noble. 2004. *Living with Racism: The Experience and Reporting by Arab and Muslim Australians of Discrimination, Abuse, and Violence Since 11 September 2001*. Report to the Human Rights and Equal Opportunity Commission, April. Available at http://www.humanrights.gov.au/racial_discrimination/isma/research/index.html.

Program on International Policy Attitudes. 2005. "The American Public on the Islamic World." June 7. Available at http://www.worldpublicopinion.org/pipa/articles/views_on_countriesregions_bt/92.php?lb=btvoc&pnt=92&nid=&id=.

Pucci, Suzanne Rodin. 1990. "The Discreet Charms of the Exotic: Fictions of the Harem in 18th-Century France." In G. S. Rousseau and Roy Porter, eds., *Exoticism in the Enlightenment*, 145–174. Manchester: Manchester University Press.

Pym, Anthony. 2000. *Negotiating the Frontier: Translators and Intercultures in Hispanic History*. Manchester: St. Jerome.

Qutb, Sayyid. 1981. *Milestones*. Translated by S. Badrul Hasan. Karachi, Pakistan: International Islamic Publishers.

Ragep, Jamil F. 1987. "The Two Versions of the Tusi Couple." In David A. King and George Saliba, eds., *From Deferent to Equant*, 329–356. New York: New York Academy of Sciences.

Ramzy, Rasha I. 2006. "Historiography as a Means of Power: 'Otherization' and Imperialism Through the Writings of Edward Said." In Silvia Nagy-Zekmi, ed., *Paradoxical Citizenship: Edward Said*, 85–93. Lanham, Md.: Lexington Books.

Rashed, Roshdi. 1989. "Problems of the Transmission of Greek Scientific Thought into Arabic: Examples from Mathematics and Optics." *History of Science* 27:199–209.

——. 1994. *The Development of Arabic Mathematics: Between Arithmetic and Algebra.* Translated by A. F. W. Armstrong. Dordrecht: Kluwer.

Rashid, Ahmed. 2007. *Taliban: Islam, Oil, and the New Great Game in Central Asia.* London: Tauris.

Reid, Donald M. 1996. "Cromer and the Classics: Imperialism, Nationalism, and the Greco-Roman Past in Modern Egypt." *Middle Eastern Studies* 32, no. 1:1–29.

Renan, Ernest. 1858. *Histoire générale et système comparé des langues sémitiques.* Paris: Lévy Frères.

——. 1883. *L'Islamisme et la science: Conférence fait a la Sorbonne le 23 Mars 1883.* Paris: Calmann Lévy.

——. 1890. *L'Avenir de la science.* Paris: Calmann Lévy.

Resnick, Irven M. 2006. "Introduction." In Petrus Alfonsi, *Dialogue Against the Jews,* translated and edited by Irven M. Resnick, 3–38. Washington, D.C.: Catholic University of America Press.

Reuter, Christoph. 2004. *My Life as a Weapon: A Modern History of Suicide Bombing.* Translated by Helena Ragg-Kirkby. Princeton, N.J.: Princeton University Press.

Reynolds, Dwight. 2006. "*The Thousand and One Nights*: A History of the Text and Its Reception." In Roger Allen and D. S. Richards, eds., *The Cambridge History of Arabic Literature*, vol. 6, Arabic *Literature in the Post-Classical Period*, 270–290. Cambridge: Cambridge University Press.

Richter, Melvin. 1977. "Introduction." In Montesquieu, *The Political Theory of Montesquieu*, edited and translated by Melvin Richter, 1–110. Cambridge: Cambridge University Press.

Ricoeur, Paul. 1965. *History and Truth.* Translated by Charles A. Kelbley. Evanston, Ill.: Northwestern University Press.

——. 1984. *The Reality of the Historical Past.* Milwaukee: Marquette University Press.

Riley-Smith, Jonathan. 1986. *The First Crusade and the Idea of Crusading.* Philadelphia: University of Pennsylvania Press.

Robert the Monk. 2005. *Robert the Monk's History of the First Crusade: Historia Iherosolimitana.* Translated by Carol Sweetenham. Burlington, Vt.: Ashgate.

Roberts, Frederick Sleigh. 1897. *Forty-one Years in India: From Subaltern to Commander-in-Chief.* London: Bentley.

Robertson, Pat. 2002. Interview. *Fox News*, September 18. Available at http://www .nexis.com/research/home?_key=1062968365&_session=29c328aa-e176-11d7-8224-

c0a8645eaa77.1.3240421165.340768.%20.0.0&_state=&wchp=dGLbVlbzSkBW&_
md5=c0439b2ce26b18336df821a8b9f562e1.

Robertson, Roland, and Frank J. Lechner. 1985. "Modernization, Globalization, and the Problem of Culture in World Systems Theory." *Theory, Culture & Society* 2, no. 3:103–118.

Robinson, Benedict S. 2007. *Islam and Early Modern English Literature: The Politics of Romance from Spencer to Milton.* New York: Palgrave Macmillan.

Rodinson, Maxime. 1987. *Europe and the Mystique of Islam.* Translated by Roger Veinus. Seattle: University of Washington Press.

——. 2007. *Islam and Capitalism.* Translated by Bryan Pearce. London: Saqi Books.

Rorty, Richard. 1986. "Foucault and Epistemology." In David Couzens Hoy, ed., *Foucault: A Critical Reader,* 41–39. Oxford: Blackwell.

Rose, Paul Lawrence. 1973. "Humanist Culture and Renaissance Mathematics: The Italian Libraries of the Quattrocento." *Studies in the Renaissance* 20:46–105.

——. 1975. *The Italian Renaissance of Mathematics: Studies on Humanists and Mathematicians from Petrarch to Galileo.* Geneva: Librairie Droz.

Rosemann, Phillip W. 1999. *Understanding Scholastic Thought with Foucault.* London: Macmillan.

Rosenthal, Franz. 2007. *Knowledge Triumphant: The Concept of Knowledge in Medieval Islam.* Leiden: Brill.

Rubenstein, Richard E. 2003. *Aristotle's Children: How Christians, Muslims, and Jews Rediscovered Ancient Wisdom and Illuminated the Dark Ages.* Orlando, Fla.: Harcourt.

Runciman, Steven. 1951–1954. *A History of the Crusades.* 3 vols. Cambridge: Cambridge University Press.

——. 1960. *The Families of the Outremer: The Feudal Nobility of the Crusader Kingdom of Jerusalem, 1099–1291.* London: Athlone Press.

——. 2005. *The First Crusade.* New York: Cambridge University Press.

Russell, William Howard. 1860. *My Diary in India.* 2 vols. New York: Harper.

Ryan, Francis Rita. 1970. "Introduction." In Fulcher of Chartres, *A History of the Expedition to Jerusalem, 1095–1127,* translated by Frances Rita Ryan, 3–56. Knoxville: University of Tennessee Press.

Sabra, A. I. 1978. "An Eleventh Century Refutation of Ptolemy's Planetary Theory." *Studia Copernicana* 16:117–131.

——. 1979. "Ibn al-Haytham's Treatise: 'Solutions of the Difficulties Concerning the Movement of *Iltifaf.'" Journal for the History of Arabic Science* 3:388–422.

——. 1984. "The Andalusian Revolt Against Ptolemaic Astronomy: Averroes and al-Bitruj." In Everett Mendelsohn, ed., *Transformation and Tradition in the*

Sciences: Essays in Honor of I. Bernard Cohen, 133–154. London: Cambridge University Press.

——. 1987. "The Appropriation and Subsequent Naturalization of Greek Science in Medieval Islam: A Preliminary Statement." *History of Science* 25:223–243.

Sachs, Susan. 2002. "Baptist Pastor Attacks Islam, Inciting Cries of Intolerance." *New York Times*, June 15.

Saeed, Abdullah. 2006. *Interpreting the Qur'an: Towards a Contemporary Approach.* London: Routledge.

Sahas, Daniel J. 1972. "The Tradition of the Text." In John of Damascus, *John of Damascus on Islam: The "Heresy of the Ismaelite,"* translated and edited by Daniel J. Sahas, 51–98. Leiden: Brill.

Said, Edward W. 1986. "Foucault and the Imagination of Power." In David Couzens Hoy, ed., *Foucault: A Critical Reader*, 149–155. Oxford: Blackwell.

——. 1994a. *Culture and Imperialism.* New York: Vintage.

——. 1994b. "An Ethics of Language: Review of Michel Foucault's *Archaeology of Knowledge* and *The Discourse on Language.*" In Barry Smart, ed., *Michel Foucault: Critical Assessments*, 2:69–123. New York: Routledge.

——. 1997. *Covering Islam: How the Media and the Experts Determine How We See the Rest of the World.* New York: Vintage, 1997.

——. 2002. "Impossible Histories: Why the Many Islams Cannot Be Simplified." *Harper's*, July, 69–74.

——. [1978] 2003. *Orientalism.* 25th anniversary ed. New York: Vintage.

Saliba, George. 1985. "The Function of Mechanical Devices in Medieval Islamic Society." In Pamela O. Long, ed., *Science and Technology in Medieval Society*, 141–151. New York: New York Academy of Sciences.

——. 1999a. *Rethinking the Roots of Modern Science: Arabic Scientific Manuscripts in European Libraries.* Washington, D.C.: Center for Contemporary Arabic Studies, Georgetown University.

——. 1999b. "Seeking the Origins of Modern Science." *Royal Institute for Inter-Faith Studies* 1, no. 2. Available at http://www.riifs.org/review_articles/review_v1no2_sliba.htm.

——. 2002. "Greek Astronomy and the Medieval Arabic Tradition." *American Scientist* 90, no. 4:360–367.

——. 2007. *Islamic Science and the Making of the European Renaissance.* Cambridge, Mass.: MIT Press.

Sarton, George. 1927–1948. *Introduction to the History of Science.* 3 vols. Baltimore: Williams & Wilkins.

Saunders, J. J. 1963. "The Problem of Islamic Decadence." *Cahiers d'histoire mondiale* 7, no. 3:701–720.

Savage-Smith, Emilie. 1988. "Gleanings from an Arabist's Workshop: Current Trends in the Study of Medieval Islamic Science and Medicine." *Isis* 79, no. 2:246–272.

Sayili, Aydin. 1960. *The Observatory in Islam.* Ankara: Turk Tarih Kurumu Basimevi.

Sayyid-Marsot, Afaf Lutfi. 1969. *Egypt and Cromer: A Study in Anglo-Egyptian Relations.* New York: Praeger.

——. 1995. *Women and Men in Late Eighteenth-Century Egypt.* Austin: University of Texas Press.

Schacht, Joseph. 1957. "Ibn al-Nafis, Severtus, and Colombo." *Al-Andalus* 22:317–336.

Schaub, Uta Liebmann. 1989. "Foucault's Oriental Subtext." *Proceedings of the Modern Language Association* 104, no. 3:306–316.

Schelting, Alexander von. 1936. Review of *Ideologie und utopie*, by Karl Mannheim. *American Sociological Review* 1, no. 4:664–674.

Schwoebel, Robert H. 1965. "Coexistence, Conversion, and the Crusade Against the Turks." *Studies in the Renaissance* 12:164–187.

Septimus, Bernard. 1981. "Petrus Alfonsi on the Cult at Mecca." *Speculum* 56, no. 3:517–533.

Sezgin, Fuat. 2005. *Mathematical Geography and Cartography in Islam and Their Continuation in the Occident.* Frankfurt am Main: Institute for the History of Arabic-Islamic Science.

Shanley, Mary Lyndon, and Peter G. Stillman. 1982. "Political and Marital Despotism: Montesquieu's *Persian Letters*." In Jean Bethke Elshtain, ed., *The Family in Political Thought*, 66–79. Amherst: University of Massachusetts Press.

Sharawi, Huda. 1987. *Harem Years: The Memoirs of an Egyptian Feminist, 1879-1924.* Translated by Margot Badran. New York: Feminist Press.

Sharpe, Jenny. 1993. *Allegories of Empire: The Figure of Woman in the Colonial Text.* Minneapolis: University of Minnesota Press.

Shatzmiller, Maya, ed. 1993. *Crusaders and Muslims in Twelfth-Century Syria.* Leiden: Brill.

Sheer, Robert. 2002. "What's God Got to Do with It?" *Nation*, Web edition, February 26. Available at http://www.thenation.com/doc/20020311/20020225.

Shumway, David R. 1993. *Michel Foucault.* Charlottesville: University Press of Virginia.

Silverstein, Theodore. 1948. "Daniel of Morley, English Cosmologist and Student of Arabic Science." *Mediaeval Studies* 10:179–196.

Simonds, A. P. 1978. *Karl Mannheim's Sociology of Knowledge*. Oxford: Clarendon Press.

Singer, Charles. 1960. *A Short History of Scientific Ideas to 1900*. Oxford: Clarendon Press.

Sivin, Nathan. 1984. "Why the Scientific Revolution Did Not Take Place in China— or Didn't It?" In Everett Mendelsohn, ed., *Transformation and Tradition in the Sciences*, 531–554. Cambridge: Cambridge University Press.

Smith, Jane I., and Yvonne J. Haddad. 1975. "Women in the Afterlife: The Islamic View as Seen from Qurʾan and Tradition." *Journal of the American Academy of Religion* 34, no. 1:39–50.

Sontag, Susan. 2001. "The Talk of the Town." *New Yorker*, September 24.

Southern, Richard W. 1962. *Western Views of Islam in the Middle Ages*. Cambridge, Mass.: Harvard University Press.

——. 1970. *Medieval Humanism*. New York: Harper & Row.

Spear, Percival. 1980. *Twilight of the Mughuls: Studies in Late Mughul Delhi*. New York: Oxford University Press.

Spenser, Edmund. 1977. *The Faerie Queene*. Edited by A. C. Hamilton. London: Longman.

Spielvogel, Jackson J. 2007. *Western Civilization: A Brief History*. 2d ed. Belmont, Calif.: Wadsworth.

Spivak, Gayatri Chakravorty. 1988. "Can the Subaltern Speak?" In Cary Nelson and Lawrence Grossberg, eds., *Marxism and the Interpretation of Culture*, 271–313. Urbana: University of Illinois Press.

Sprinzak, Ehud. 1987. "From Messianic Pioneering to Vigilante Terrorism: The Case of the Gush Emunim Underground." *Journal of Strategic Studies* 10, no. 4:194–216.

Stark, Rodney. 1999. "Secularization, R. I. P." *Sociology of Religion* 60, no. 3:249–273.

Stark, Rodney, and William Sims Bainbridge. 1985. *The Future of Religion: Secularization, Revival, and Cult Formation*. Berkeley: University of California Press.

Stauth, Georg. 1991. "Revolution in Spiritless Times: An Essay on Michel Foucault's Enquiries into the Iranian Revolution." *International Sociology* 6, no. 3:259–280.

Stokes, Eric. 1978. *The Peasant and the Raj: Studies in Agrarian Society and Peasant Rebellion in Colonial India*. Cambridge: Cambridge University Press.

——. 1986. *The Peasant Armed: The Indian Revolt of 1857*. Oxford: Clarendon Press.

Streusand, Douglas. 1997. "What Does Jihad Mean?" *Middle East Quarterly* 4, no. 3:9–17.

Sutton, Philip W., and Stephen Vertigans. 2005. *Resurgent Islam: A Sociological Approach*. Cambridge: Polity Press.

Swatos, William H., Jr., and Kevin J. Christiano. 1999. "Secularization Theory: The Course of a Concept." *Sociology of Religion* 60, no. 3:209–228.

Sweetenham, Carol. 2005a. "Robert and the *Gesta Francorum*." In Robert the Monk, *Robert the Monk's History of the First Crusade: Historia Iherosolimitana*, translated and edited by Carol Sweetenham, 12–27. Burlington, Vt.: Ashgate.

——. 2005b. "The Textual History of the *Historia Iherosolimitana*." In Robert the Monk, *Robert the Monk's History of the First Crusade: Historia Iherosolimitana*, translated and edited by Carol Sweetenham, 1–11. Burlington, Vt.: Ashgate.

Sweezy, Paul M. 1953. *The Present as History*. New York: Monthly Review Press.

Swertz, Frank J. 1987. *Capitalism and Arithmetic: The New Mathematics of the 15th Century*. La Salle, Ill.: Open Court.

Swidler, Ann, and Jorge Arditi. 1994. "The New Sociology of Knowledge." *Annual Review of Sociology* 20:305–329.

Taylor, Charles. 1985. *Philosophy and the Human Sciences*. Vol. 2. Cambridge: Cambridge University Press.

——. 2007. *A Secular Age*. Cambridge, Mass.: Belknap Press of Harvard University Press.

Taylor, P. J. O. 1996. "Judex." In P. J. O. Taylor, ed., *A Companion to the "Indian Mutiny" of 1857*, 174. Delhi: Oxford University Press.

——. 1997. *What Really Happened During the Mutiny: A Day-by-Day Account of the Major Events of 1857–1859 in India*. New York: Oxford University Press.

Tester, S. J. 1987. *A History of Western Astrology*. Woodbridge, Eng.: Boydell Press.

Thijssen, J. M. M. H. 1998. *Censure and Heresy at the University of Paris*. Philadelphia: University of Pennsylvania Press.

Thomas, David, ed. 2003. *Christians at the Heart of Islamic Rule*. Leiden: Brill.

Thomas, Scott M. 2005. *The Global Resurgence of Religion and the Transformation of International Relations: The Struggle for the Soul of the Twenty-First Century*. New York: Palgrave Macmillan.

Thomas Aquinas. 1964a. *De aeternitate mundi*. In *St. Thomas Aquinas, Siger of Brabant, St. Bonaventure, On the Eternity of the World*, translated by Cyril Vollert, Lottie H. Kendzierski, and Paul M. Byrne, 19–25. Milwaukee: Marquette University Press.

——. 1964b. "*Summa theologiae*: Part I, Question XLVI, Articles 1 and 2." In *St. Thomas Aquinas, Siger of Brabant, St. Bonaventure, On the Eternity of the World*, translated by Cyril Vollert, Lottie H. Kendzierski, and Paul M. Byrne, 59–68. Milwaukee: Marquette University Press.

Thompson, James. W. 1929. "Introduction of Arabic Science into Lorraine in the Tenth Century." *Isis* 12, no. 2:187–199.

Thorndike, Lynn, 1923–1958. *History of Magic and Experimental Science*. 8 vols. New York, Macmillan.

——. 1955. "The True Place of Astrology in the History of Science." *Isis* 46, no. 3:273–278.

——. 1963. *Science and Thought in the Fifteenth Century*. New York: Hafner.

——. 1965. *Michael Scot*. London: Nelson.

——. 1967. *The Place of Magic in the Intellectual History of Europe*. New York: AMS Press.

——. 1975. *University Records and Life in the Middle Ages*. New York: Norton.

"Those Who Don't Share Our Values, Won't Integrate." 2006. *The Age*, September 11.

Tibi, Basam. 1996. "War and Peace in Islam." In Terry Nardin, ed., *The Ethics of War and Peace: Religious and Secular Perspectives*, 128–146. Princeton, N.J.: Princeton University Press.

Tignor, Robert L. 1966. *Modernization and British Colonial Rule in Egypt, 1882-1914*. Princeton, N.J.: Princeton University Press.

Tirman, John. 2010. "Immigration and Insecurity: Post-9/11 Fear in the United States." In David Wright-Neville and Anna Halafoff, eds., *Terrorism and Social Exclusion: Misplaced Risk-Common Security*, 16–29. Cheltenham, Eng.: Elgar.

Tolan, John V. 1998. "Peter the Venerable on the 'Diabolical Heresy of the Saracens.'" In Alberto Ferreiro, ed., *The Devil, Heresy, and Witchcraft in the Middle Ages: Essays in Honor of Jeffrey B. Russell*, 345–367. Leiden: Brill.

——, ed. 2000. *Medieval Christian Perceptions of Islam*. New York: Routledge.

——. 2002. *Saracens: Islam in the Medieval European Imagination*. New York: Columbia University Press.

——. 2008. *Sons of Ishmael: Muslims Through European Eyes in the Middle Ages*. Gainesville: University Press of Florida.

Tolmacheva, Marina. 1995. "The Medieval Arab Geographers and the Beginnings of Modern Orientalism." *International Journal of Middle East Studies* 27, no. 2:141–156.

Toomer, G. J. 1996. *Eastern Wisdom and Learning: The Study of Arabic in Seventeenth-Century England*. Oxford: Clarendon Press.

Torrell, Jean-Pierre. 1996. *Saint Thomas Aquinas: The Person and His Work*. Translated by Robert Royal. Washington, D.C.: Catholic University of America Press.

Trinkhaus, Charles. 1995. *In Our Likeness and Image: Humanity and Divinity in Italian Humanist Thought*. 2 vols. Notre Dame, Ind.: Notre Dame University Press.

Tucker, Judith E. 1986. *Women in Nineteenth-Century Egypt*. Cairo: American University in Cairo Press.

Turner, Bryan S. 1972. "Understanding Islam." *Middle East International* 12:19–21.

——. 1974. *Weber and Islam: A Critical Study*. London: Routledge & Kegan Paul.

——. 2000. "Liberal Citizenship and Cosmopolitan Virtue." In Andrew Vandenberg, ed., *Citizenship and Democracy in a Global Era*, 18–32. New York: St. Martin's Press.

——. 2001. "On the Concept of Axial Space." *Journal of Social Archaeology* 1, no. 1:62–74.

——. 2003. "Introduction: Islam and Islamic Studies." In Bryan S. Turner, ed., *Islam: Critical Concepts in Sociology*, 1:1–41. London: Routledge.

Tyan, E. 1991. "Djihad." In *Encyclopedia of Islam*, 2:538–540. Leiden: Brill.

Tyerman, Christopher. 1998. *The Invention of the Crusades*. Toronto: University of Toronto Press.

——. 2006. *God's War: A New History of the Crusades*. Cambridge, Mass.: Harvard University Press.

U.K. House of Commons. 1859. *Parliamentary Papers*. Vol. 18 (February 3–April 19).

Urvoy, Dominique. 1991. *Ibn Rushd (Averroes)*. Translated by Olivia Stewart. London: Routledge.

Valensi, Lucette. 1993. *The Birth of the Despot: Venice and the Sublime Porte*. Translated by Arthur Denner. Ithaca, N.Y.: Cornell University Press.

Van Cleve, Thomas Curtis. 1972. *The Emperor Frederick II of Hohenstaufen: Immutator Mundi*. Oxford: Clarendon Press.

Van Dijk, Teun A. 1985. *Handbook of Discourse Analysis*. London: Academic Press.

——. 1998a. "Discourse as Interaction in Society." In Teun A. van Dijk, ed., *Discourse as Social Interaction*, 1–37. London: Sage.

——. 1998b. *Ideology: A Multidisciplinary Approach*. London: Sage.

Van Steenberghen, Fernand. 1955. *Aristotle in the West: The Origins of Latin Aristotelianism*. Translated by Leonard Johnston. Louvain, Belgium: Nauwelaerts.

——. 1978. *Thomas Aquinas and Radical Aristotelianism*. Washington, D.C.: Catholic University of America Press.

Vartanian, Aram. 1969. "Eroticism and Politics in the *Lettres persanes*." *Romanic Review* 60:23–33.

Vaughan, Dorothy M. 1954. *Europe and the Turk: A Pattern of Alliances, 1350-1700.* Liverpool: Liverpool University Press.

Venturi, Franco. 1963. "Oriental Despotism." *Journal of the History of Ideas* 24, no. 1:133–142.

Veyne, Paul. 1984. *Writing History: Essay on Epistemology.* Manchester: Manchester University Press.

Vico, Giambattista. 1968. *The New Science of Giambattista Vico.* 3d ed. Translated by Thomas Goddard Bergin and Max Harold Fisch. Ithaca, N.Y.: Cornell University Press.

Viner, Katherine. 2002. "Feminism as Imperialism." *Guardian*, September 21.

Voll, John. 1994. *Islam: Continuity and Change in the Modern World.* Syracuse, N.Y.: Syracuse University Press.

——. 2004. "Islamic Renewal and the 'Failure of the West.'" In Prasenjit Duara, ed., *Decolonization: Perspectives from Now and Then*, 199–217. London: Routledge.

Von Drehle, David. 2002. "Debate over Iraq Focuses on Outcome." *Washington Post*, October 7.

Von Grunenbaum, Gustave. 1961. *Medieval Islam.* Chicago: University of Chicago Press.

Waldman, Peter. 2004. "A Historian's Take on Islam Steers U.S. in Terrorism Fight." *Wall Street Journal*, February 4.

Wallace-Hadrill, J. M. 1962. *Bede's Europe: The Jarrow Lecture.* Newcastle upon Tyne: Bealls.

——. 1988. *Bede's "Ecclesiastical History of the English People": A Historical Commentary.* Oxford: Clarendon Press.

Walter the Chancellor. 1999. *Walter the Chancellor's "The Antiochene Wars": A Translation and Commentary.* Translated and edited by Thomas S. Asbridge and Susan B. Edington. Brookfield, Vt.: Ashgate.

Walzer, Michael. 1986. "The Politics of Michel Foucault." In David Couzens Hoy, ed., *Michel Foucault: A Critical Reader*, 51–68. Oxford: Blackwell.

Walzer, Richard. 1945–1946. "Arabic Transmission of Greek Thought to Medieval Europe." *Bulletin of the John Rylands Library* 29:160–183.

——. 1962. *Greek into Arabic: Essays on Islamic Philosophy.* Cambridge, Mass.: Harvard University Press.

Waters, Malcolm. 1998. *Globalization.* London: Routledge.

Watson, Andrew M. 1983. *Agricultural Innovation in the Early Islamic World: The Diffusion of Crops and Farming Techniques, 700-1100.* Cambridge: Cambridge University Press.

Watt, W. Montgomery. 1956. *Muhammad at Medina*. London: Oxford University Press.

——. 1972. *The Influence of Islam on Medieval Europe*. Edinburgh: Edinburgh University Press.

——. 1985. *Islamic Philosophy and Theology*. Edinburgh: Edinburgh University Press.

——. 1990. *Early Islam*. Edinburgh: Edinburgh University Press.

Weber, Eugene. 1999. *Apocalypses: Prophecies, Cults, and Millennial Beliefs Through the Ages*. Cambridge, Mass.: Harvard University Press.

Weber, Max. 1947. *The Theory of Social and Economic Organization*. Translated and edited by Talcott Parsons. New York: Free Press.

——. 1958. *From Max Weber: Essays in Sociology*. Translated and edited by H. H. Gerth and C. Wright Mills. New York: Oxford University Press.

——. 1965. *The Sociology of Religion*. Translated by Ephraim Fischoff. London: Methuen.

——. 2002. *The Protestant Ethic and the Spirit of Capitalism*. Translated and edited by Peter Baehr and Gordon C. Wells. London: Penguin.

Weisheipl, J. A. 1983. "The Date and Context of Aquinas' *De aeternitate mundi*." In Lloyd P. Gerson, ed., *Graceful Reason: Essays in Ancient and Medieval Philosophy Presented to Joseph Owens*, 239–271. Toronto: Pontifical Institute of Mediaeval Studies.

Weissinger, Herbert. 1945. "The Renaissance Theory of the Reaction Against the Middle Ages as a Cause of the Renaissance." *Speculum* 20, no. 4:461–467.

White, Hayden. 1973. *Metahistory: The Historical Imagination in Nineteenth-Century Europe*. Baltimore: Johns Hopkins University Press.

——. 1978. *Topics of Discourse: Essays in Cultural Criticism*. Baltimore: Johns Hopkins University Press.

——. 1987. *The Content of the Form: Narrative Discourse and Historical Representation*. Baltimore: Johns Hopkins University Press.

Wicker, Brian, ed. 2006. *Witness to Faith? Martyrdom in Christianity and Islam*. Burlington, Vt.: Ashgate.

Wiet, Gaston. 1971. *Baghdad: Metropolis of the Abbasid Caliphate*. Translated by Seymour Feiler. Norman: University of Oklahoma Press.

Wilford, John Noble. 2007. "In Medieval Architecture, Signs of Advanced Math." *New York Times*, February 27.

Wilke, Richard. 2007. "Karen Hughes' Uphill Battle: Foreign Policy, Not Public Diplomacy, Mostly Determines How the World Views America." Pew

Global Attitudes Project, November 1. Available at http://pewresearch.org/pubs/627/karen-hughes.

William of Malmesbury. 1815. *History of the Kings of England*. Translated by John Sharpe. London: Longman, Hurst, Rees, Orme, and Brown.

Williams, John. 1993. "Purpose and Imagery in the Apocalypse Commentary of Beatus of Liébana." In Richard K. Emmerson and Bernard McGinn, eds., *The Apocalypse in the Middle Ages*, 217–233. Ithaca, N.Y.: Cornell University Press.

Wissink, J. B. M. 1990. *The Eternity of the World in the Thought of Thomas Aquinas and His Contemporaries*. Leiden: Brill.

Wodak, Ruth, ed. 1989. *Language, Power, and Ideology: Studies in Political Discourse*. Philadelphia: Benjamins.

Wolf, Kenneth Baxter. 1985. "Christian Martyrs in Muslim Spain: Eulogius of Cordoba and the Making of a Martyrs' Movement." Ph.D. diss., Stanford University.

——. 1986. "The Earliest Spanish Christian Views of Islam." *Church History* 55, no. 3:281–293.

——. 1990a. "An Andalusian Chronicler and the Muslims." In Kenneth Baxter Wolf, trans., *Conquerors and Chroniclers of Medieval Spain*, 24–42. Liverpool: Liverpool University Press.

——, trans. 1990b. *The Chronicle of 754*. In *Conquerors and Chroniclers of Medieval Spain*, 111–160. Liverpool: Liverpool University Press.

Wolff, Larry. 1994. *Inventing Eastern Europe: The Map of Civilization on the Mind of the Enlightenment*. Stanford, Calif.: Stanford University Press.

Wolfson, Harry Austryn. 1976. *The Philosophy of the Kalam*. Cambridge, Mass.: Harvard University Press.

Wuthnow, Robert. [2003] 2004. "Presidential Address: The Challenge of Diversity." *Journal for the Scientific Study of Religion* 43, no. 2:159–170.

Young, M. J. L., J. D. Latham, and R. B. Sergeant, eds. 1990. *Religion, Learning, and Science in the ʿAbbasid Period*. Cambridge: Cambridge University Press.

INDEX